BIBLE RECORDS OF SUFFOLK AND NANSEMOND COUNTY, VIRGINIA

Together with Other Statistical Data

Collected and Edited by
FILLMORE NORFLEET

CLEARFIELD

Reprinted for
Clearfield Company, Inc. by
Genealogical Publishing Co., Inc.
Baltimore, Maryland
1996, 2001

International Standard Book Number: 0-8063-4622-1

Made in the United States of America

Bible Records of Suffolk and
Nansemond County, Virginia,
Together With Other Statistical
Data.

Collected and Edited by

Fillmore Norfleet.

2

PREFACE.

Nansemond County's official records have been totally destroyed by three successive fires: (1) in April 1734 at the time the repository of official documents, the house of Christopher Jackson, the county clerk, was consumed; (2) on May 13, 1779, when the clerk's office along with almost the entire town of Suffolk was destroyed by a detachment of British infantry; and (3) on February 7, 1866, the fire being of unexplained origin. This total destruction of the past has presented an almost insurmountable problem to historians and genealogists, professional or otherwise, who have sought to throw more light on the people who lived in and the events that have taken place within the confines of one of the oldest counties in Virginia. Except for the Reverend Joseph Brown Dunn's admirable little volume, The History of Nansemond County, Virginia (1907), no authenticated history of the county or of its principal town has ever been written.

The population of Nansemond County resembles a palimpsest, each generation maintaining a dim impression of the preceding three or four and little if no knowledge at all of those generations which lived on the same land in the span of years from 1800 back to 1642, the year the county was first called "Nansimum." To capture the past from primary sources, one must go outside the county's borders, to the Virginia State Library, to the records of surrounding Virginia counties, Isle of Wight, Southhampton, Norfolk, to Gates County, in North Carolina, and to the National Archives, in all of which stray bits of information applicable to Nansemond may be gathered in land patents, wills, deeds, settlements of estates, military documents, and similar public records.

Today, after a little more than three hundred years, those pioneers who pushed their boats past the marshy banks of the Nansemond River and up its numerous meandering creeks, to a few hundred acres of sandy soil, royally granted, remain names only, buried in the cryptic caligraphy of Colonial Land Patent Books and Commonwealth Grants available in the Virginia State Library (hereinafter referred to as VSL). Fortunately the first five patent books (covering the years (1623-1666) have been transcribed and abstracted in Nell Marion Nugent's Cavaliers and Pioneers (Richmond, 1934). A goodly number of the patentees' names have survived, however, transmitted from one generation to another by rugged stock. These names, as redolent of the county as cattails and cypress trees, are intrinsically English: Jordan, Stallings, Duke, Lassiter, Brothers, Sumner, Norfleet, Odom, Beamon, Brinkley, Gwin, Baker, Knight, Lawrence, Spivey, Parker, Speight, King, Riddick, Copeland, Webb, Milteer, Godwin, and Powell, to name but a few. These landowners, transplanted Englishmen or their sons, who survived the first fifty years of the county's existence are listed in the Quit Rent Rolls of 1704, (Va. Mag. Vol. 29, p. 402) together with the number of acres comprising their plantations. Covering this period from the ecclesiastical side is a portion of an old vestry book of Chuckatuck Parish (photocopy in VSL) containing the proceedings from 1702 to 1709.

One other group of people of this time preserved its identity for the future--the Quakers. Settling on the banks of Chuckatuck Creek, they built their meeting-house and dutifully recorded, with complete disregard of orthography, births, marriages, and deaths in The Chuckatuck Record (The Lower Virginia Monthly Meeting Minutes and Register, 1647-1756). There is a human touch to these records that makes them far more interesting than the sterotyped and prosaic land patents with their metes and bounds, perishable landmarks, and appended lists of phonetically spelled "headrights, " male and female, few of whom have ever been identified.

From mid-eighteenth century to the Revolution, little more information is available than that contained in the continuous flow of patents, except for the chronological material that appears in two manuscripts of prime historical importance: The Vestry Book of the Upper Parish (1743-1793), and The Vestry Book of Suffolk (or Lower) Parish (1749-1856), the original of the latter being in the Clerk's Office of the Circuit Court in Suffolk. Both of these documents are a bewildering maze of unrelated names that seem to have little connection with anything but time, land, and ecclesiastical custom. The vestry met with businesslike regularity, financial charity was dispensed, tobacco and money were earmarked to pay parish debts, and the relentless annual processioning was recorded, processioner and processioned having gathered at the boundry lines of continguous plantations, ascertained the correct bounds by a long walk, and dispersed like mythical figures. The Vestry Book of the Upper Parish, Nansemond County, Virginia, 1743-1793, has been edited by Wilmer L. Hall, who contributed a highly informative "Introduction" on the formation of the parish, its ministers, and its churches and chapels.

As for literate Colonial travelers eyeing the county, Colonel William Byrd II seems the first. On his way to survey the dividing line in 1728, he found an "hospitable roof" at "Mr. Andrew Mead's, who lives upon Nansemond River" (actually "Mt. Pleasant" on what subsequently became known as Pitchkettle Creek), and "an abundance of primitive hospitality" at "Mr. Godwin's on the south branch of Nansemond river. ' George Washington on his way to o the Dismal Swamp in October 1763 picked his way down White Marsh Road, viewing with practical eye the soil that composed the plantations of, so far as is known, unrelated Riddicks: Willis, Henry, and John.

Of the Revolutionary period in Nansemond County little is known beyond the somewhat vivid description of the burning of Suffolk in 1779 by the British that occurs in Henry Howe's Historical Collections of Virginia (Charleston, 1849, pp. 26-31), an account duplicated, more or less, in other histories of the Colony. The Public Claim Papers (VSL) reveal an endless list of people seeking reimbursement for services rendered or food sold the Revolutionary army. The countless military records (Military Land Bounty Warrants and Rejected Claims in VSL, and the Revolutionary War Certificates in the National Archives) of the county's soldiers are available but, to be fruitful, they demand tenacious research and luck if one is to identify a soldier who is a mere name with a military rank. There exist no authortative lists of

Nansemond soldiers; in fact, the number of the county's militiamen is unknown (supposedly about eight hundred) and only a few of the militiamen themselves, except for the officers, have been properly identified. From the Nansemond County Petitions to the General Assembly of Virginia (VSL), one may get a glimpse of what condition some of the property of the shattered Established Church was in, read a plea for reimbursement for horses and pistols that had been impressed by a struggling army, a wife's supplication for the use of slaves and land of her husband's confiscated estate, or a Tory's plea for a reprieve from the hangman's noose.

A picture of Suffolk and its activity, from the time it was established in 1742 "at Constance's warehouse" and the adjacent fifty acres of land that belonged to Jethro Sumner to the burning of the town by the British in 1779, can be only a fleeting one. It was a likely spot for a town, this curl of the river, where even before 1742 "great numbers of people" had settled close to the public warehouse located "at the widow Constance." Houses went up with wooden chimneys, "hogs and goats" wandered "at large," and fairs were allowed until all, either dangerous or objectionable, were prohibited by special statutes.

The year 1748 was a notable one. The trustees of Suffolk (Lemuel Riddick, William Baker, William Wright, Edward Wright, John Gregory, Mills Riddick, and Edward Norfleet) delivered to Lemuel Riddick a deed for land (a lot or lots, of course, and at L13 an acre) in the town, and the vestry ordered built "at the end of Suffolk Town" (on Back, or today's Church, Street) "a handsome brick Church," granting Lemuel Riddick permission to build a private gallery "in one of the Crosses," and a similar privilege to David Meade "on the Oposite Wing." Lemuel Riddick's land, on which he was legally obligated to build within two years after the purchase, must have been that "adjoining the public wharf," at which point, in 1751, a ferry was establish "cross Nansemond river to Samuel Jordan's land." Daniel Pugh, who had undertaken the building of the church, had completed the structure by July 26, 1753, at which time "John Watson & Alexander Cairnes," (undoubtedly residents of the town), were granted "Leave to Build a Pew in the South end of the Parish Galere." On September 7, 1755, "John Hall, late of the Town of Suffolk, merchant but now of the Virginia Ridgment (sic) of Foot under the Command of Col. George Washington" appointed "James Coupland, merchant of Suffolk" his "lawful attorney." Lemuel Riddick was definitely a resident of the "Town of Suffolk" in 1757. Exactly a decade later there were four more identifiable citizens: Lemuel Riddick's second wife, Esther Robins (whose first husband had been Theophilus Pugh) whom he married May 5, 1761; John Jones and his wife Philishia, a daughter of Col. Daniel Pugh; and John Driver, an ambitious young merchant (subsequently the husband of Col. Daniel Pugh's granddaughter), who advertised for sale in The Virginia Gazette (May 7th) "a new ship...burthen about 350 hogsheads of tobacco...lying at Suffolk wharf."

For weary travelers there were inns, probably two kept simultaneously by a changing series of proprietors. Edmund Belson Wright must have directed one from 1761 through 1768, and Thomas Brickle another for the brief space of 1769, since the vestry of the Upper Parish, of which neither was a member, met at the "houses" of these men. From 1770 to 1774 Samuel Swann, an innkeeper, not only provided a place for the vestry to meet but revealed what went on in his place of business by offering a billiard table for sale in November 1772 that could be seen by applying to him "in Suffolk." In the same year, 1772, William Dixon, who kept "a Tavern in the Town of Suffolk," complained openly in the December 3d issue of The Virginia Gazette about the Reverend Patrick Lunan (rector of Suffolk Parish since 1760), who had been a guest for four consecutive days, "treating everybody who would condescend to drink with him," and then refusing to pay his bill. On March 21, 1775, the vestry held a meeting "at Mr. Thomas Langstons," an innkeeper not long for life, since he died in Suffolk on April 21, 1778, "a truly benevolent man, . . . a kind husband, a tender father."

When the Revolution began in 1775, Messrs. (Samuel) Donaldson and (John) Hamilton, Tories, were "merchants in the Town of Suffolk"; Mrs. Ann Pollock, on her way from Philadelphia to Edenton, stayed at an undescribed tavern until rescued by "Mr. Donaldson" who took her "to his house," a courtesy the townspeople usually accorded important visitors; and on April 1st, John Driver advertised for sale "at the Courthouse in Suffolk... European Good's, belonging to the Estate of Mr. David Meade, deceased." Two Suffolkians of equal importance likewise died that year: Lemuel Riddick and his wife Esther. With war clouds overhead, the eleven members of the Committee of Safety, with Col. Willis Riddick, chairman, gathered on November 22nd at the house of one John Aspray (Ashby?) "in Suffolk" to hold one of its many meetings.

In 1776 the State troops, quartered in the town, did considerable damage not only to the courthouse and poorhouse, but to a number of private houses belonging, severally, to thirteen-year-old Lemuel, "the infant son of Colonel Leml Riddick," Wills Cowper, John Nirney (sic), John Adams, Samuel Cohoon, William Webb, Charles Anderson, Luke Sumner, Samuel Fletcher, and Gibson & Company. Being a quartermaster's depot Suffolk necessarily had its constant allotment of soldiers, some of whom died. On February 11, 1777, William Whitfield, sexton of the the Suffolk church, was paid for "burying several Soldiers," in the church's graveyard, no doubt.

Ebenezer Hazard, "surveyor" of a collapsed postal system, on an inspection trip from Philadelphia to Edenton in 1777, entered Suffolk June 11th over a "very narrow ' bridge, saw the small brick courthouse, "lodged at Langston's," an ordinary he considered "a tolerable house," and had two disagreeable encounters with an "Episcopalian Clergyman of the name of Lunan" who was 'excessively drunk... and swore very much. " The Reverend Mr. Lunan's infamous conduct had been a cause celebre since 1767 and the vestry, unable legally to rid the parish of the objectionable clergyman, had just hired him to resign his charge.

Then, for almost two years, everything was peaceful, when suddenly, early in May, 1779, a British fleet arrived in Hampton Roads, landed troops, and took the fort at Portsmouth. On May 11th a detachment "of the King's troops, " under Colonel Garth, headed for Suffolk where there were "considerable magazines... (intended for the rebel army). ' Alerted, the poorly equipped Nansemond militia under Col. Willis Riddick assembled in Suffolk, then proceeded down the Norfolk road and encamped in a large field in front of Capt. James Murdaugh's house. There they remained in ignorance of what was marching towards them, since Josiah Riddick, Thomas Granbery, and Thomas Brickle, previously sent ahead to reconnoitre "at some distance from the town, " had been captured. The militia seemed to lack everything, including organization. Captain Richard Davis and a Captain King, who had 'repaired" to a tavern to spend the night were surprised by "a party of Hessians. " Davis was killed, but King escaped and gave the alarm. Since Col. Willis Riddick 'had retired to his own house ' (more than a considerable distance away), the command fell upon Colonel Edward Riddick, who marched the militia back to Suffolk, reaching the town before dawn. Two officers dispatched to ascertain the size of the advancing enemy, returned with news that there were about six hundred infantrymen. A call to arms was made but only about a hundred militiamen responded; the others had fled, following the terrified townspeople. Among those who remained and became prisoners were two clergymen, Thomas Davis and Henry John Burgess.

Then, on May 13th, 1779, the holocaust took place. Arriving in Suffolk, the British soldiers "broke up the bridge, " burned two vessels belonging to Mr. Cowper, ' and then so thoroughly set everything on fire, they "left only three dwelling houses standing in the town, " wrote John Driver. The survival of these three buildings was remarkable. Besides setting fire to the houses, the soldiers stove in the heads of barrels of tar, pitch, rum, and turpentine lying on the wharf thus releasing highly inflammable liquids that floated over the brackish water making the river seem on fire. The extensive marsh beyond soon became a sheet of fire, and in the conflagration of flames licking up from houses, river, and marsh came, at intervals, explosions of gunpowder in the magazines.

Then, learning that "a thousand barrels of pork, and a considerable quantity of beef" had been removed for safety from Suffolk to the plantation of Col. Willis Riddick on the White Marsh Road, the British troops went out to the 'residence" of the colonel commandant of the Nansemond County militia and "set fire to his dwelling, barn, and outhouses, in which the said public property was stored, and destroyed not only the public property and the buildings, but his furniture, corn, bacon, etc." Colonel Riddick lived but two years more, dying in 1781, without ever having been reimbursed by the State for his patriotism or loss. Not until April 17, 1834 was restitution made to the heirs of Willis Riddick by the Committee on Revolutionary Claims.

Rebuilding in everything started almost immediately. By June 22, 1779, John Driver, now married to Elizabeth Reid and living near "Suffolk," had for sale "A sloop, burthen 60 hogsheads, completely fitted for sea," and by September 22, he had "agreed with John Giles to build another House where the store formerly stood, but not so large." The phoenix was beginning to rise out of its own ashes, so that by 1785, because of the "rapid increase of building in the Town of Suffolk" and "the inability of mechanics and tradesmen to purchase Lotts of great value," the "inhabitants of the Town"petitioned the General Assembly to add to the town sixteen acres (to be laid off in lots) owned by John Granbery, who, incidentally, headed the list of petitioners.

About this time one John Ferdinand Dalziel Smyth, a sharp-eyed and acrimonious Englishman, on a tour of the Eastern seaboard (A Tour of the United States of America, 2 Vols., London, 1784; Vol. 2, p. 103) lingered in Suffolk just long enough to observe that it contained "about an hundred houses" and carried "on a pretty brisk trade."

"Suffolk," he continued, "stands on a soil so very sandy, that in every step in the street the sand comes above your ancles, which renders it extremely disagreeable; to remedy this inconvenience in some small degree, near their doors they have emptied barrils of tar or pitch, which spreads wide, the sand incorporating it, and forming a hard solid consistence, some kind of an apology for pavement, and thereby renders walking much more tolerable.

The houses in Suffolk are low, being generally not more than one story high, which is indeed the ground story only; the River Nansemond is navigable at and above the town, but there is a wooden bridge here, and only small vessels can come up even to Suffolk.

The trade of the place consists chiefly of turpentine, tar, pitch, tobacco, and pork which is killed, salted, and barrelled up here, also lumber, Indian corn, and some wheat.

We tarried only one day in Suffolk."

Despite Mr. Smyth's uninspiring comments, time brought changes. Solomon's Lodge, A. F. & A. M., chartered in October 1790, first met the following November 6st at the house of Dempsey Copeland on the First

Cross (Milner) street, those present being, Stephen C. Graham, Benjamin
Bartlett, Joseph Hay, Elisha Copeland, Jr., John Miles, Thomas Adams,
and Benjamin Street of the Norfolk Lodge. Within the next two years Dempsey
and Elisha Copeland became more absorbed in the town's affairs: their sister,
Elizabeth, married (1791) Robert Jordan, a Quaker, destined to become Suffolk
leading merchant in a store directly across from the Courthouse, and, although
a Quaker family, they were signers of a petition (1792) to the General Assembly
requesting authority to be granted to the vestry of the Upper Parish to raise
money by lottery for the purpose of rebuilding "the Episcopal Church in the
Town of Suffolk," it having been "in the late war between Great Britain and
America so torn to pieces and mutilated that it (had) become quite unfit for
use." In 1797, Elisha Copeland was granted a license to keep a tavern,
doubtless in Suffolk.

After the turn of the century, Suffolk expanded, spreading from the
river "up" the main street to a gentle hill, and beyond to the South Quay
Road, until 1837 when another fire that started in William Arnold's cabinet
shop at the corner of Main and the Second Cross (Mahan) Street destroyed
almost the whole lower part of the town. Nearly everything that had been
built since 1779, about one hundred and thirty houses including The Rising
Sun Tavern and Castle Inn, lay in smoldering ruins. Only one edifice
escaped: the clerk's office, a "fire proof" building whose foundation was
begun November 18, 1830.

From the Revolution on more information is available. With nearly
all the land taken up, the Commonwealth Grants, as patents were called
after 1779, diminished to a mere trickle, but in 1782 the Land Taxes (VSL)
began, pinning land owners down to definite districts. Almost simultaneously
began the Nansemond County Court Fee Books (VSL) containing names of
administrators and executors of wills, guardians, a few marriage entries, and,
of course, references to innumerable law suits brought by a very litigious people
But the human side is non-existant unless one is fortunate in locating his goal
in some personal letter or marginal notation in the letters and documents
contained in the two large repositories of Nansemondiana: the Webb-Prentis
Papers (1770-1808, ca. 10,000 items; see Bibliography), and the John
Richardson Kilby Papers (1755-1919, 33,262 items; see Bibliography). These
two collections of manuscripts represent the lifetime accumulation of business
and other papers of two prominent Suffolk lawyers, Joseph Prentis, II (1785-
1851), who was born in Williamsburg, and John Richardson Kilby (1819-1878),
a judge of the County Court of Nansemond, who was originally from Hanover
County.

There being no deeds or wills to consult before 1866, the year the clerk's
office fire consumed all records on file since 1799, no families, except in a
few instances, can trace their lineage farther back than the Revolution, and
many contemporary inhabitants of Suffolk and the county, whose ancestors
patented land in Nansemond County as early as 1637, when the county received
the name of Upper County of New Norfolk, are unable to go back beyond the
third generation.

Bible records, repititious, frequently illiterate, and excessively dull, have their role in the creation of a proper history. Homespun and accurate, these records of the three principal events in a man's life were laboriously set down on now yellowed pages, and handed down from one generation to the next, preserved by some member of the family proud, even if his family attained no local importance, at least of its indomitable continuity.

The Bible records in this volume, most of which were transcribed by the compiler, are fragments of history created by the people of Nansemond, a county whose natives have had much to offer in three centuries of living, but, like the Elizabethans, never found time to write down their observations on what was going on around them.

Fillmore Norfleet.

New Year's Day, 1962.

10

Contents.

Bible Records.

EDWARD ALLEN BIBLE.

(On page 913, at 'The End of the New Testament, " is a boxed provenance,
the underlined words being printed):

This book was purchased, / June, Anno Domini, 1803, /
By Edward Allen, price, Eight Dollars.

(On verso of page 591, containing "The End of the Prophets, " is the):
Family Record.

Mary Ann Allen daughter of / Archd & Mary Allen was born on / the 14th
day of July 1825, and / died 18 Sept. 1826.

Mary wife of Archd Allen was / delivered of a still-born male / infant
on Friday morning 6th / July 1827.

Edwd Tho. Allen son of Archd and / Mary Allen was born on the 27th / July
1828 and was baptised in / the Methodist Episcopal Church / by the Revd
Allen R. Bernard on the / 19th of April 1829.

Elizabeth Reid Allen daughter of / Archibald and Mary Allen was born /
20th Feby. 1831, and was baptised on the / 26th June 1831, by Revd Tho.
Crowder.

Archibald Allen son of Archd and / Mary Allen was born on the 5th of /
June 1833, and was baptised on the / 29th day of September / 1833 in the /
M. E. Church by Revd Thos. Crowder.

William Henry son of Archd & / Mary Allen was born on the 3d / day of
December 1835 & was bapti- / sed on the ___ day of ___ 1836 by Revd
Allen R. Bernard.

Mary Swepson daughter of Archd / & Mary Allen was born 4th October /
1837 and was baptised at home / 25th December 1837 by the Revd / Allen
R. Bernard.

Lucy Frances daughter of / Archd & Mary Allen was / born on the 20th day
of / January 1841, and baptised / in the Methodist Episcopal / Church by
Rev. Allen R. Ber- / nard on the ___ day June 1841.

Edward Archibald son of / Archd & Mary Allen was born / on the 3d October
1843 and was / baptised by Revd R. B. Hope on / the 20th July 1845, in M.
E. Church.

Robert Riddick, son of Archd / and Mary Allen was born / on the 18th
December 1845, / and was baptised ___ day of July / 1846, by Revd A. R.
Bernard. / Died Suffolk, Va., November / 15, 1920.

12

(Page one of a second);

Family Record.

Marriages.

Edward Allen & Elizabeth (Reid) his / wife was Married October 10th 1782.

Edward Allen & Maria (Calvert), his wife, / was married November 15th 1806.

Archibald Allen and / Mary (Swepson) his wife were married / July 22d 1824.

Henry J. Allen & Hannah / his wife was married 28th Oct. / 1813.

Page 2)   Births.

Edward Allen was born 23d June 1753.

Elizabeth (Reid), his wife, was born / 31st January 1759.

Edward Allen, Son of Edwd / & Eliza was born 26th August, 1783.

Henry Jno Allen, Son of Edwd & Eliza was born 24th ____1784.

Peggy Allen, Daughter of Edwd / & Eliza was born 23d April 1786.

William Allen, Son of Edwd & Eliza was born 6th November 1787.

Daniel Allen, Son of Edwd & Eliza was born 25th January 1790.

Mary Ann Allen, Daughter / of Edwd & Eliza was born 24th April / 1791.

Nathaniel Allen, Son of Edwd & / Eliza was born 7th March 1793.

Archibald Allen, Son (of) Edwd & / Eliza was born 17th September 1795.

Edwd and Eliza had a son born on / the 18th of August 1797 at midnight, / & on the 6th of Sept. following he died / at midnight ... lived 19 days.

Cornelius Edwd Allen son of / Edwd & Maria, was born 10th / of Sept. 1807.

Edwd & Maria had a son born on / the 12th of Sept. 1809, & on the 17th of the same / month he died ... lived only 5 days.

Thomas William Gilbert Allen, son of / Edw<u>d</u> & Maria, was born 29th of July / 1810.

Eliza Frances Tabb Allen, Daughter / of Edw<u>d</u> & Maria, was born 24th Sept. 1812 / & died Sunday night 28 March 18<u>1</u>3.

Mary Ann Allen daughter / of Archibald Allen & / Mary Allen was born 14th / day of July 1825 (Thursday / half past one o'clock P. M.).

Mary Allen wife of Arch<u>d</u> Allen / was delivered of a still-born male / infant on Friday morning 6th day / of July 1827.

Edward Thomas Allen son of / Archibald & Mary Allen was born / on Sunday 27th July 1828 - 4 o'clock / P. M. and was baptised in the / Methodist Episcopal Church (by / pouring) on the 19th Apl. 1829 / by the Rev<u>d</u> Allen R. Bernard.

Elizabeth Reid Allen daughter of / Arch<u>d</u> and Mary was born on Sunday / morning 1/2 past 4 o'clock - 20th Feby. / 1831 - and was baptised on the 26 June 1831 / by the Rev<u>d</u> Thomas Crowder.

(Page 3)   Births.

Hannah Allen wife of Henry J. Allen was born 12th Nov. 1791.

Mary Allen wife of / Archibald Allen was / born 16th February, 1810.

Archibald Allen son of Arch<u>d</u> & Mary was born 5th June 1833 & / was baptised on the ___ day of / ___ by Rev<u>d</u> Thos. Crowder.

William Henry son of Archi-/bald & Mary Allen was born on / the 3d day of December 1835, / & was baptised on the ___ day of ___ / 1836 by Rev<u>d</u> Allen R. / Bernard in the M. E. Church / Suffolk.

Deaths.

Peggy Allen, Daughter of Edw<u>d</u> & Eliz<u>a</u> died 4th October 1786.

Daniel Allen, Son of Edw<u>d</u> & Eliz<u>a</u> / died 30th August 1790.

Edward Allen, the first born Son of / Edw<u>d</u> & Eliz<u>a</u> died 15th September 1800, / in Norfolk, with yellow fever.

Elizabeth Allen wife of Edw<u>d</u> Allen / died in Hampton, the 1st day of / September 1804.

Eliza Frances Tabb Allen, Daughter of / Edw<u>d</u> & Maria, died Sunday night / 28th March 1813.

Nathaniel Allen, Son of Edw<u>d</u> / & Eliza<u> </u>died 4th Dec<u>r</u> 1813, at 4 o'clock/ in the morning.

(From this entry on the page has been torn off.)

(Page 4)   Deaths.

Henry John Allen son of / Edward and Eliza<u> </u>died in the / City of Washington where he had / gone for the benefit of his declining health on the 2d day / of August 1821. Aged 35 years / 11 months 9 days.

Mary Ann Allen daughter / of Archibald & Mary departed / this life Monday the 18th day / September 1826. Aged 1 year 2 / months & 4 days.

Edward Thomas Allen son of / Archibald & Mary Allen died / on Thursday 29th day of August / 1833. Aged 5 years 1 mo. 2 days.

Elizabeth Reid Allen daughter / of Arch<u>d</u> & Mary Allen died on the / 22nd of September 1833. Aged 2 yrs. / 7 mos. 2 days.

William Henry Allen son of Arch<u>d</u> / and Mary Allen, died on the ...

(The rest of this page has been torn off.)

John Reid Driver, the first / & only child of my wife Eliza<u> </u>/ by her first marriage to Captain Jn<u>o</u> / Driver, was born 25 July 1774 & died the ____ day of August 1793.

Archibald Allen, Son of / Edward and Eliza<u> </u>died on the 28th of February 1846, / aged 50 years, 5 months, 11 days.

(Additional items on loose sheets of paper:)

1. Mary Allen, relict of Archibald / Allen, departed this life 19th June 1860.

2. (A list of slaves beginning:)
   Record of Nancy's childrens ages:

3. Edward Allen was born on the 23d day of June 1753 and died 15th day of January 1816.

   Maria W. (Calvert) Allen was born 21st Nov. 1774 and died 26th day of May 1803.

Col. Robert Moore Riddick (died) 4 Dec. 1804.

Mary his wife (died) 12 Dec. 1805.

(On the spine: Holy Bible, of which the bibliographical page is torn out.
On page 591, after "The End of the Prophets" is printed: "Joseph Charles,
Printer, / Philadelphia." Between "The End of the Apocrypha," page 776.
and "The New Testament" is printed: "Mathew Cary, No. 118, Market
Street, Philadelphia, October 27, 1802." The Bible, owned by Mrs. Robert
Henning Webb, was transcribed in 1962.
Note: Edward Allen (1753-1815; son of William Allen of Elizabeth City
Co., Va., and Mary Tabb, his wife), lived at "Rose Hill," on Nansemond
River, just east of Suffolk. He joined the 4th Virginia Regiment, C.L.,
in March, 1776, became ensign in Sept. 1776, 2nd Lieutenant, Jan. 12,
1777, 1st lieutenant, Oct. 4, 1777, and resigned Dec. 1, 1779, having
served more than three years as an officer of the Continental Line.)

****

ALLMAND (NOTES)

Aaron Allmand, son of James & Christian Allmand, was born in Gloucester
Co., Va., on Sept. 14th 1727 - was married to Susannah Frith July 16,
1752, & to Ann Harrison Sept. 1, 1756, & died May 10, 1792. Susannah's
two children died in infancy.

Ann Harrison, second wife, was born April 3, 1738 and died Sept. 14,
1807.

Harrison, first son of Aaron & Ann Allmand, was born August 8, 1757 and
died April 16, 1822.

Mildred, first daughter, was born March 23, 1759, was married to Capt.
Thomas Roberts, of Nansemond Co., & died sometime in 1818.

William, Alma & Sally Allmand died in childhood.

Harrison Allmand was married to Louisa Keele (widow of Isaiah Keele), on
Dec. 1, 1785. She was the daughter of John & Sarah Driver, & was born Feb.
10, 1763 - died May 8, 1802.

Harrison & Louisa Allmand's children --
William, born Sept. 26 - died Nov. 1, 1790.
Harrison, born June 26, 1788 - died Sept. 27, 1810.
Albert, born May 13, 1793 - died April 21, 1831.
Alma, born Jan. 2, 1795 - died Jan. 23, 1795.
Caroline, born March 10, 1798 - died Jan. 27, 1799.
John Driver, born Aug. 7, 1799 - died April 30, 1851.
Louisa, born Sept. 5, 1801 - died June 7, 1802.

Mary Thomas Walker, second wife of Harrison Allmand, was born in
Suffolk, Va., May 15, 1785, was married July 10, 1803, died Nov. 5,
1811. She was the daughter of Thomas & Elizabeth Walker.

Augustus, son of Harrison & Mary Allmand, was born April 28, 1804-
died Sept. 16, 1804.

Emeline, was born Oct. 30, 1805 - married Mr. P. E. Tabb, of Gloucester
Co., Va. - died April 2, 1838.

Henry, born March 7, 1810 - died Jan. 20, 1843.

Robert, born Mar. 7, 1810 - died Feb. 11, 1835.

Lucy Campbell, third wife of Harrison Allmand. was born Feb. 10, 1776,
was married Dec. 15, 1812, & died Jan. 10, 1831.

Gilbert, son of Harrison & Lucy Allmand, was born April 28, 1814, died
Sept. 17, 1821.

Harrison Allmand died April 16, 1822.

Two of his sons married & have descendants living in Norfolk.

Albert Allmand married Margaret O'Grady, daughter of Capt. (?) O'Grady
of the Royal English Navy.

John Allmand married Mary Ann Parker, daughter of Copeland & Elizabeth
Sinclair Parker, formerly of Smithfield, Va. Copeland was a nephew   of
Col. Josiah Parker, an aide of Gen. Washington. Their home was at
Macclesfield, near Smithfield.

Elizabeth, daughter of John & Mary Allmand, married _____Archer.

(The notes, transcribed from a Bible record, were contributed by Miss
Caroline Archer.)

****

WALTER WOOD BALLARD BIBLE.

Walter Wood Ballard was born February 4, 1867, in Nansemond Co.,
and died July 20, 1936, in Suffolk, Va. He was the son of Robert M.
Ballard, Jr., and Virginia Louïsa Parker, his wife. On Feb. 19, 1880,
he married Annie Riddick Norfleet (1860-1948), and had issue: 1. Virginia
Norfleet Ballard (b. 1882).

A transcript of the entire Bible record will be found in Elisha
Norfleet, p. 6.

****

BOOTHE BIBLE.

Mary Griffin, daughter of Nathaniel Griffin and Elizabeth his wife,
was born Oct. 4th 1793.

Joseph Nathaniel Boothe, son of Joseph and Mollie E. Boothe, born
October 3d 1869.

Mary Boothe, daughter of Joseph and Mollie E. Boothe, born Feby. 23rd
1872.

Joseph Nathaniel Boothe, son of Joseph and Mollie E. Boothe, died
April 23rd 1873.

(The Holy Bible, American Bible Society, New York, 1852. Owned by Mrs.
James Vincent Knott Walker, nee Mary Boothe.)

BOOTHE (NOTES)

Josiah (sic) Boothe, the son of Nathaniel Boothe and Mary his wife, was
born April the 15th, A.D. 1832.

John Boothe, the son of Nathaniel Boothe and Mary his wife, was born
October 2nd A.D. 1834.

Mary Amanda Boothe, the daughter of Nathaniel Boothe & Mary his wife,
was born on the 8th day of May A.D. 1838.

(Notes inscribed on the flyleaf of Armistead's Lectures on American
Grammar, Norfolk, Va., 1823. Owned by Mrs. James Vincent Knott
Walker, nee Mary Boothe.)

****

ADMIRAL BRINKLEY BIBLE.

Admiral Brinkley, son of Jacob Brinkley (and Apsley Griffin, his wife), was born February 22nd, 1809.

Margaret Jane (1817-1853), daughter of Job Saunders, was born August 27th, 1817.

A(dmiral) Brinkley and Margaret Jane Saunders were married September 10th, 1835.

Admiral Brinkley died December 11th, 1849, at the age of 40 years, 9 months and 19 days.

Robert Beverly Brinkley, son of Admiral and Margaret Jane Brinkley, was born Jan. 27th, 1836. (Died May 25, 1864.)

John Randolph Brinkley, son of Admiral and Margaret Jane Brinkley, was born Octo. 22nd, 1837. (Died 1884; m. March 21, 1861, Mary Eliza Roundtree)

Hugh (Griffin) Brinkley, son of Admiral and Margaret Jane Brinkley, was born August 15th, 1840. (Died 1869; m. June 19, 1867, Catherine Susan Daughtrey, and had issue: 1. Hugh Griffin Brinkley, Jr., 1868-1918, and 2. Mary Catherine Brinkley, born Oct. 25, 1869, m. 1898, Charles Reuben Welton)

Mary E(liza) Brinkley, daughter of Admiral and Margaret Jane Brinkley, was born January 3rd, 1839. (Died April 13, 1877; m. Feb. 26, 1868, Joseph Booth)

Cornelia Brinkley, daughter of Admiral and Margaret Jane Brinkley, was born May 16th, 1842. (Died Sept. 24, 1881; m. Feb. 21, 1867, Daniel Brothers.)

Margaret Ann Brinkley, daughter of Admiral and Margaret Jane Brinkley, was born November 23rd, 1846. (Died June 6, 1880; m. March 7, 1866, Keely Harrison, of Norfolk).

Admiral Brinkley, son of Admiral and Margaret Jane Brinkley, was born March 8th, 1850. (Married 3 times: 1, 1871, Frances Fern Daughtrey; 2. 1876, Laura O. Warren; 3. in 1907, Annie Land.)

(The owner of the Bible is unknown).

****

JACKSON BRINKLEY BIBLE.

Jackson Brinkley, son of John Brinkley and Sarah Barr (his first wife), was born Feb. 8, 1810.

Martha Amanda Brinkley, daughter of David Parker and Jeannette Carter Parker his wife was born May 5th 1811.

Andrew Jackson, son of Jackson and Amanda Brinkley, was born Dec. 5, 1832.

Mary Louisa, daughter of Jackson and Amanda Brinkley was born Dec. 18, 1833. (m. Richard H. Rodgers).

Sarah Jane, daughter of Jackson and Amanda Brinkley, was born Dec. 3, 1835. (m. _____ Warrington).

Dawson Lafayette, son of Jackson and Amanda Brinkley, was born Jan. 15, 1838.

Martha Eliza Brown Brinkley, daughter of Jackson and Amanda Brinkley, was born Sept. 7, 1839.

Thomas Samuel Brinkley, son of Jackson and Amanda Brinkley, was born April 26, 1842.

Lazarus Parke, son of Jackson and Amanda Brinkley, was born June 17, 1844.

---   ---

Louisa J. Brinkley, daughter of John Brinkley and Christian Skinner, his wife, was born Oct. 5th, 1813. (m. Frank Eppes).

Joel Holloman Brinkley, son of Jackson and Amanda, was born July 8, 1847. (m. 2/18/74 Mary Alice Darden).

Robert Frank Rogers, son of Richard H. and Mary Louisa Rogers, was born June 14, 1854.

Caroline Virgilia Brinkley, daughter of Jackson and Amanda, was born May 17th, 1856.

Louisa J. Eppes, daughter of John Brinkley and Christian Skinner, and wife of Francis Eppes, died Dec. 15, 1832, at the age of 19. (Their daugher was Josephine Eppes, who married a Norfleet. Her granddaughter is Louise Gayle Bentley, of Selma, Ala.)

Jackson Brinkley, son of John Brinkley and Sarah Barr Brinkley, died
June 6, 1869. (He had been a member of Cypress Chapel Christian Church
36 years, and led the singing for many years. He represented the church in
the annual conferences many years. Aged 59 years.)

Martha Amanda Brinkley, wife of Jackson Brinkley, died suddenly in the
morning of May 11, 1885, in the 75th year of her age.

Louisa J. Brinkley, daughter of John Brinkley and Christian Skinner, was
born Oct. 5, 1813. She married Francis Eppes, and died Dec. 15, 1832.
Francis Eppes and Louisa J. Brinkley Eppes had a daughter Josephine. (I
do not have the dates of Josephine's birth, but about 1830 or 1831). I am
told that she married a Norfleet and lived in the far South, probably
Alabama. Louisa J. Brinkley was a half-sister of my grandfather Jackson
Brinkley; his mother was Sarah Barr.

Hamlin Eppes, brother of Francis Eppes, married the widow of John
Brinkley, Christian Skinner Brinkley.

L. Parke Brinkley enlisted in Barham's Company 24th Va. Cavalry at
Franklin, May 1863, and served until Appomattox.

Jackson Brinkley and Martha Amanda Parker were married March 7, 1832.

Richard Henry Rogers and Mary Louisa Brinkley were married Dec. 16,1852.

Philip Syng Physic Corbin and Martha Eliza Brown Brinkley were married
Feb. 16, 1860.

Lazarus Parke Brinkley and Sallie E. Rogers were married Feb. 23rd, 1870.

Joel Holloman Brinkley and Mary Alice Darden were married Feb. 18, 1874.

Lelia L. Rogers, daughter of Richard H. Rogers and Mary Louisa Brinkley,
his wife, was born April 27, 1867.

Luther Carroll Corbin, son of Dr. P.S.P. Corbin and Martha E. Brown
Brinkley, his wife, was born Jan. 22, 1861, and died 1924.

C. E. Byrd and Lelia L. Rogers were married Feb. 25, 1886.

Marion Xerxes Corbin, son of Dr. P.S.P. Corbin and wife and May Thirza
Williams were married Nov. 12, 1896. (Issue: Gawin Lane Corbin; Marion T.
Corbin; Elizabeth Tayloe Corbin.)

Gawinae Corbin, daughter of P. S. P. Corbin and Martha Eliza Brown Corbin, b. ___, married J. William Sowers.

James Jacob Norfleet, brother of Seth Norfleet, married Josephine Eppes.

(The Bible was formerly owned by Miss Julia Amanda Brinkley, who added the notes.)

****

JOHN PRESTON BROTHERS BIBLE.

John Preston Brothers, the son of Edward and Peggy Ann Brothers, was born March 4, 1854, in Nansemond Co., and died Oct. 25, 1903, in Norfolk Co. On Nov. 27, 1879, he married Sarah Katherine Norfleet (1858-1941), and had issue: 1. Minnie Olivia (1880-1900); 2. Sarah Lucille (b. 1883); 3. Ethel Preston (b. 1886); and 4. Sarah Katherine (1888-1960).

A transcript of the entire Bible record will be found in Elisha Norfleet, p. 7.

****

BROWNE BIBLE.

(Inscribed on flyleaf): Catherine Browne Bible.

Marriages.

Edward Browne son of Samuel and / Mary Browne was married to / Ann Knott daughter of Elvinton / and Mary Knott September the / 6th 1787.

Edward Browne son of Samuel / and Mary Browne was married / to Catherine B. Bruce daughter of / William and Mary Bruce / May the third 1804.

Married in Smithfield on the / first day of September 1814 / by the Revd Jacob Keeling / Doctr Elvinton K. Browne / son of Edward and Ann Knott / Browne to Ann Marlow / Shepherd daughter of Thomas and Mary Shepherd.

Married on Thursday / the 20th of November / 1828 at Dr Samuel / Brownes Mr. John H. / Blamire of Richmond / to Miss Mary Ann Browne of Nansemond / daughter of Edward / and Catharine B. / Browne.

Married at Colonel Sumners in / North Carolina by ___ on the / 11th November 1812 Doctor Samuel / Browne to Eliza Minton / daughter of Mills Minton Senr.

Married in Portsmouth December (torn) / Joseph B. McGuire son of James (torn) / to Catharine Bruce daughter of Edward & Catharine Bruce.

Births.

Samuel Browne son of Edward / and Ann Browne was born / December 1st 1788.

Elvinton Knott Browne son of / Edward and Ann Browne was / born October the 25th 1791.

Anthony Browne son of Edward / and Ann Browne was born / January the 7th 1795.

Edward W. Browne and Charles / J. Browne sons of Edward / and Ann Browne was born / October 5th 1797.

John Anthony Browne son of / Edward and Ann Browne was / born the 28th October 1799.

Mary Ann Browne daughter / of Edward and Ann Browne / was born May the 4th 1802.

Mary Ann Browne daughter / of Edward and Catherine Browne / was born May the 12th 1805.

William B. Browne son of / Edward and Catharine Browne / was born September the 20th 1807.

Lucretia F. Browne daughter / of Edward and Catharine Browne / was born September the 3rd 1810. (Note: Lucretia, grandmother of Laura McGuire Dawson, m. Blamire, and died in 1843).

George W. Browne, son of / Edward and Catharine Browne / was born April the 8th 1811.

Edward Browne son of / Edward & Catharine Browne / was born April the 6th 1815.

Ann Knott Browne, daughter / of Elvinton and Ann M. / Browne was born September the 13th 1815.

Adaline S. Browne daughter of / Evlinton and Ann M. Browne / was born the 13th day of February / 1817.

Malvina Ann Browne / daughter of Elvinton K. and / Ann M. Browne was born / on the 17th of October 1819.

Mary Eliza E. Browne daughter / of Elvinton K. and Ann M. / Browne was born on the / 15 day of July 1823.

Mary A___ Bruce daughter of / Jos Bruce and Ann his wife was / born May 6, 1807.

James M. Bruce son of Jos Bruce / and Ann his wife was born Nov. (illegible).

Deaths.

Anthony Browne son of Edward / and Ann Browne departed / this life September the 13th 1796.

Charles J. Browne son of Edward / and Ann Browne departed / this life October the 12th 1797.

John Anthony Browne son of / Edward and Ann Browne / departed this life October / the 20th 1800.

Mary Ann Browne, daughter / of Edward and Ann Browne / departed this life May the 9th 1802.

Edward W. Browne son of / Edward and Ann Browne / departed this life July the / 18th 1809.

Ann Browne wife of Edward / Browne departed this life / July the 12th 1803.

John Hudnal departed / this life November the / 11th 1803.

William B. Browne son / of Edward and Catharine / Browne departed this life November / the first 1813.

Doctor Samuel Browne / son of Edward and / Ann Knott Browne / departed this life on / Sunday 1/2 past 9 o'clock / A. M. on the 4 day of / January 1829.

Elizabeth Browne wife of Doctor / Samuel Browne Junr departed this / life Saturday September 14th 1822.

William John Browne son of / Samuel and Elizabeth his wife / departed this life Sunday morning the / 20th of October 1822.

Martha Browne daughter of / Samuel and Elizabeth Browne de/parted this life the 5th September 1814.

Mills Minton Browne son of Sam/uel and Elizabeth Browne, departed / this life (torn) morning the 25th of / October 18 (torn).

(In a different handwriting):

Edward G. Blamire / departed this life in Portsmouth on April the 29th, 1868.

Edward Browne son of / Edward & Catharine Browne / departed this life on the / 29th day of August 1815.

Ann Knott Browne daughter of / Edward and Ann M. Browne / departed this life on Sunday the / 17th September 1815.

Edward Browne son of Samuel / and Mary Browne departed this / life on Tuesday evening 30 minutes past 9 P. M. the 29 day of December / 1818. Aged 50 years.

Mary Eliza Elvinton / Browne daughter of Dr / Elvinton Knott and Ann / Mallory Browne departed / this life on Friday the 6th / day of October 1826.

Malvina Ann Browne / daughter of Dr Elvinton / Knott and Ann Mallory / Browne, departed this life / on Wednesday the 28th of / August 1827.

Catherine Browne wife of / Edward Browne departed this / life in Nansemond County Sept. / 14th 1832.

John H. Blamire departed / this life in Richmond April / 3rd 1831.

Mary Ann E. Blamire / departed this life in Portsmouth / Sept. 1834.

Births.

Ann Eliza Browne, was born August / the 16th 1813, daughter of Doctor Samuel / Browne and Elizabeth his wife.

Martha Browne, daughter of Samuel / and Elizabeth Browne was born August / the 26th 1814.

Mills Minton Browne son of Samuel / and Elizabeth his wife, was born Nov- / ember the 28th 1816.

James Browne son of Samuel / and Elizabeth Browne was born March the / 5th 1818.

Edward Browne son of Samuel and / Elizabeth Browne was born November the / 21st 1820.

William John Browne son of Samuel / and Elizabeth Browne was born September / 14th 1822.

Elvinton Knott Blamire, son of / Jno and Mary Ann E. Blamire / was born the 4th of Octo / 1829 in the County of Nansemond.

After the Death of his Father (John H. Blamire) his name was changed to John Elvington by which name he was Baptized.

Marriages.

Married on Wednesday Evening / February 5th 1834 in Portsmouth / E. T. Blamire, to Lucretia F. Browne, Daughter of Edward & / Catherine Browne of Nansemond.

Catherine Bruce Blamire / Daughter of E. T. & L. F. Blamire / was born February 10th 1835.

James Edward, son of Lucretia / and E. T. Blamire was born / January 9th 1837.

James Edward son of Lucretia / F. and E. T. Blamire Departed / this life January 21st 1837. "Of such is the Kingdom of Heaven. !'

James Alexander, Son of / Lucretia F. & E. T. Blamire / was born February 22, 1838.

Edward Bruce, son of / Lucretia F. & (torn) / was born (torn)

H. (torn) of / E. T. & L. (torn) / was born the ___ day, / of June 1843.

Lucretia F. Blamire / wife of E. T. Blamire / departed this life Nov. / 10th 1843 aged 33. "Let me die the death of the Righteous and let my last end be like hers. " Amen! and amen! B.

George Washington Browne Died in / Suffolk January the 24th / A. D. 1854 - & was buried at Mintonsville.

(On a sheet pinned to the last page of the record):

Edward Bruce son of / Lucretia & E. T. Blamire / departed this life Oct. 10th '96.

Catherine Bruce daughter of Lucretia & E. T. Blamire / departed this life April 7th '98.

(Bible. Printed by Hopkins and Seymour / For Robert McDermut, and sold at his Book - Store, No. (torn) April, 1806, New York. Formerly owned by Mrs. Harry Dawson, nee Laura McGuire, and copied in July 1946.)

****

JAMES SÁMUEL BROWNE BIBLE.

Marriages

James S., son of Dr. Samuel Browne, and Mary F., daughter of James G. Green, Esq., were married Nov. 14th, 1839.

Births.

James Samuel, son of Dr. Samuel Browne and Elizabeth, his wife, was born at Knotts Neck Plantation, Mar. 5th, 1818.

Mary Frances, daughter of James G. Green and Ann T. R. (Hancock), his wife, was born at Rosedale, Nov. 18, 1822.

Born at Oakland Farm, Nansemond County, Va. (and dressed for the grave) Nov. 26, 1840, Son of James S. Browne and Mary Frances, his wife.

Fanny Green Minton, daughter of James S. Browne and Mary Frances, his wife, was born in Suffolk, Va., Jan. 7, 1845.

Ann Eliza Hancock, daughter of James S. Browne and Mary Frances, his wife, was born in Suffolk, Va., Jan. 1, 1847.

Octavia Knott, daughter of James S. Browne, and Mary Frances, his wife, was born in Suffolk, Va., on the afternoon of the 15th day of August, A. D., 1852.

Mary George, daughter of James S. Browne, and Mary Frances, his wife, was born in Suffolk, Va., on the afternoon of the 24th day of Feb. A. D., 1854.

Jamesetta, daughter of James S. Browne, and Mary Frances, his wife, was born at Suffolk, Va., on the morning of Oct. the 9th, at 2 o'clock, A. D., 1856.

Deaths.

Died at her father's residence at Suffolk, Va., of scarlet fever, Dec. 29, 1850, Ann Eliza Hancock, daughter of James S. & Mary F. Browne, buried the 1st day of Jan. 1851. The birthday of her 4th year. Even from the grave she hath powers to charm! Time may partly assuage the deep, pungent and overwhelmin grief her death inflicted; but eternity can only heal the wounded hearts of her devoted parents.

Died just before sunrise, on the 17th day of Feb. 1858, my dear, faithful, affectionate and devoted wife Mary Frances Browne. She passed from the scenes of earth to an inheritance with saints immortal in Heaven. She had a good heart and an amiable and affectionate disposition. Eternity alone can now bind up and heal my crushed and bleeding heart.

Octavia Knott, my daughter, died at her Father's residence, of diphtheria, June 29, 1861.

Jamesetta, my youngest child, died of the same disease July 10, 1861.

Mary George, my third dau. died of the same disease about midnight of July 18, 1861.

Fanny Green Minton Browne, daughter of Dr. James Samuel Browne, and Mary Frances, his wife, was born Jan. 7, 1845. She married Col. James Binford. Their children died in infancy.

(Bible owned by Mrs. Henry Alvin Rawles, nee Virginia Browne Riddick.)

****

Causey Bible.

Mary Colvin born in Scotland 28th Sept. 1813, married Aug. 1836 to William Causey born Kent Co., Maryland, May 12, 1815.

Charles Henry Causey, the son of Wm. Causey & Mary his wife, was born the 14th day of July 1837. (Born in New Castle, Del.)

Wm. Norris Causey, son of William Causey and Mary his wife, was born May 12, 1839. (Born in New Castle, Del.)

James Colvin Causey, son of William Causey & Mary his wife, was born on the 24th of September in the year of our Lord, 1841. (Born at 'Montross,' Hampton, Va.)

(The Bible, published in 1823, is owned by Mrs. Marion Kelly Kendrick, nee Mary Douglas Causey.)

****

CHARLES HENRY CAUSEY BIBLE.
Marriages.

Charles Henry Causey & Martha Josephine Prentis were married on the 26th day of September, 1864.

28

George Lloyd Barton and Marianna Prentis Causey were married on the 20th day of October 1890.

Dr. John Edwin Phillips and Eliza Wrenn Causey were married the 11th day of December 1894.

James Campbell Causey and Marguerite Whitfield Crump were married on the 27th day of December 1900.

Martha Josephine Causey and Thos. Spindle Miller were married December 30th 1902.

Deaths.

Margaret Webb Causey died May 27, 1889, aged 13 years, 2 mos., 14 days.

Charles Henry Causey died Aug. 27, 1890, Aged 53 years, 1 mo., 13 days.

Eliza Wrenn Causey Phillips died April 10th, 1905, aged 34 years, 1 mo., 3 days.

Charles Henry Causey, Jr., died on Feb. 13, 1924, aged 55 years, 2 mos. 28

Martha Josephine Prentis Causey died Feb. 9, 1909.

Births.

William Bowdoin Causey was born 24th June 1865.

Marianna Prentis Causey was born 19th Aug. 1866.

Charles Henry Causey was born Nov. 16, 1868.

Eliza Wrenn Causey was born March 7, 1871.

Peter P. Causey was born Nov. 16, 1872.

James Campbell Causey was born July 23, 1874.

Margaret W. Causey was born March 13, 1877.

Martha Josephine Causey was born March 2, 1878.

(The Bible was formerly owned by Mrs. George Lloyd Barton, nee Marianna Prentis Causey.)

****

CHARLTON BIBLE.

Elizabeth Stone who married Jasper Charlton was born April 12th 1773 - Died December 28, 1822.

Elizabeth Ellener Stone Charlton her daughter was born February 4th 1792. - Died December, 1828.

Francis David Charlton her son was born January 18th 1794 - Died February 28th 1844.

Ann Elizabeth Woolford her Daughter was born March 21st 1812 -

Elizabeth Stone widow of Jasper Charlton married Dr. Arthur Woolford, of Maryland, June 4th 1797.

Elizabeth Ellener Stone Charlton married Col. Joseph Holladay, of Nansemond County, Virginia.

Francis David Charlton married Mary Ann Flynn, of Suffolk, Virginia, September 2nd 1817.

Ann Elizabeth Woolford married James Harvey March 20, 1827.

(The transcription was made by Mrs. Robert Henley Pretlow, nee Katharine Beverly Holladay. For a partial genealogy, see Suffolk, pp. 90-91.)

****

(Inscribed on flyleaf):

JOHN COWPER COHOON BIBLE.

Marriages.

Wm J. Cohoon and Emily E. Flynn was married in St. Paul's Church, Suffolk, by the Revd Aristidas Smith on the 19th day of October 1853.

Married 30th November 1859 at the late residence of the brides father William J. C. Cohoon to Sallie L. Beamon.

John C. Cohoon, Jr., was married June 1st 1813 to Louisa Everit.

Frances W. C. Cohoon was married July 31st 1821 to Francis B. Gamble Lieut of the U. S. Navy. (Note: from New Jersey).

30

Births.

Louisa Everitte Nov. 28th 1792.

John C. Cohoon, Jr., born Dec. 26, 1789.

Frances W. C. Cohoon born Dec. 10th 1798.

Samuel E. Cohoon born Dec. 20, 1800.

Philip A. R. C. Cohoon born 28th of April 1805 or 1806.

John C. Cohoon born Dec̲r 26th 1789.

Frances W. C. Cohoon born December 10th 1798.

Sam̲l E. Cohoon born Dec̲r 24th 1800.

Philip A. R. C. Cohoon born April 28th 1806.

Wm̲J. Cohoon son of John C. Cohoon & Louisa his wife was born on the 6th day June 1829 - at Cedar Vale -

Emily E. Flynn daughter of O. R. & Emily J. Flynn was born on the 4th day June 1833.

Emily Louisa daughter of W. J. & Emily E. Cohoon was born on the 3rd day of August 1854, 50 past 10 P.M. Thursday at Cedar Vale.

Births.

Willis Everitt son of Wm̲.J. & Sallie L. Cohoon was born in Suffolk on the 10th day of September 1860 at 5 o'clock A. M.

Annie Beamon Cohoon daughter of W. J. & S. L. Cohoon was born in the Town of Murfreesboro N. Carolina on the 17th day of January 1863 at 6 o'clock P. M.

Claude Cowper Cohoon son of W. J. & S. L. Cohoon was born in Suffolk on the 8th day of March 1866.

Sallie Coquese daughter of W. J. & S. L. Cohoon was born in Suffolk on the 8th day of July 1868.

Paul Tosh Cohoon son of W. J. & S. L. Cohoon was born in Suffolk on the 13th day of July 1870.

Richard Samuel son of W. J. & S. L. Cohoon was born in Suffolk on the 4th day of September 1876.

(The following are pages extracted from an older Bible and inserted):

31

Deaths.

Genl Jno C. Cohoon Departed this life on Friday the 17th October 1823 about 2 o'clock in the afternoon in the 58th or 9th year of his age, he was married the 8th December 1786 & lived 36 years 10 months & 7 days after marriage.

Mrs Ann Cohoon wife of John C. Cohoon Senr departed this life on Monday night the 7th of July 1823 about 4 o'clock in the Morning, in the 56th year of her age. She was married 8th December 1786, & lived 36 years 7 months after her marriage.

Mrs. Frances W. C. Muren daughter of the late Genl John C. Cohoon decd departed this life at the residence of Mrs. Margaret Read in the County of Northampton on the Eastern Shore of Virginia on Monday the 12th day of February 1838, at 4 after five o'clock P. M.

Departed this life in Suffolk at the residence of her father Capt. Owen R. Flynn, on Saturday the 31st day of May 1856, 50 minutes after 12 o'clock A. M. Mrs. Emily E. wife of William J. R. Cohoon aged 22 years 11 months and 27 days, her death was such as to leave not a shadow of doubt upon the minds of her sorrowing friends that their loss was her eternal gain...

Sallie Coquese the daughter of W. J. and S. L. Cohoon departed this life on the 6 day of August 1869 in Suffolk.

Deaths.

Departed this life at his residence on Nansemond River on Saturday the 22d day of August 1863, 50 minutes past one o'clock Capt. John C. Cohoon Aged 73 years 7 months and 26 days, he died as he had lived honored and beloved by all and his family had every assurance that there . . . .

Departed this life in the City of Baltimore on the 8th day of March 1883 our precious daughter Annie B. Cohoon aged 20.

Births.

John Cowper Cohoon, Junr was born at Blue Hill Mills December 26, 1789.

Louisa Everitt was born 28th day of November 1792 (at Everetts Bridge).

Deaths.

Thomas, Alexander, John, Cowper, Abraham Cohoon Departed this life on Tuesday the 28 day of June 1853 at 1/2 before 4 o'clock in the afternoon, aged 27 years 5 months,17 days 10 hours & 57 minutes,beloved by all who knew him.

Deaths.

Departed this life at his residence on Nancymond river on Saturday the 22d day of August 1863, 50 minutes past one o'clock, Capt. John C. Cohoon, aged 73 years, 7 months, and 26 days ...

John, Willis, Everitt, Cowper Cohoon son of John & Louiza Cohoon departed this life on Sunday the 20th day of September 1818 - 34 past 6 o'clock P.M. aged 4 years 4 months - 24 days 13 hours & 13 minutes.

Margaret, Ann, Cowper, Cohoon Daughter of Jno. C. and Louisa Cohoon Departed this life on Saturday the 5th day of October 1822 3 o'clock A.M. aged 5 years 9 months 25 days 8 hours and 26 minutes.

Alexander Wilkinson departed this life on Thursday the 7th day of November 1816 in Latitude 29o on his passage home from Martinico where he took the yellow fever & lingered 8 days he was son of Willis & Martha Wilkinson.

John, Samuel, Edward, Wright, Willis, Everett, Cowper Cohoon son of Jno. C. & Louiza Cohoon Departed this life on Friday the 18th day of March 1825 - at 11 o'clock P.M. aged 5 years 2 months 8 days 6 hours & 16 minutes.

Louisa Cohoon Departed this life on Friday the 3rd day of October 1834 at 40 past 6 o'clock A.M. aged 3 months 10 days & 11 hours.

Louiza Everitt Margaret Ann John Cowper Cohoon daughter of John C. & Louisa Cohoon departed this life on Saturday the 26th day of August 1837 at 26 past 4 o'clock P.M. aged 10 months 17 hours & 53 minutes.

Marriages.

John C. Cohoon Junr and Louiza Everitt were married on Tuesday the first day of June in the year of our Lord one thousand eight hundred and Thirteen (1813) in the Town of Suffolk at the residence of Mrs: Ann Poole.

Births.

John, Willis, Everitt, Cowper Cohoon son of John C. & Louiza Cohoon was born on Wednesday the 27th day of April 1814 - 47 after 5 o'clock in the morning (at Vaughans Old Place).

Margaret, Ann, Cowper Cohoon Daughter of Jno. C. & Louiza Cohoon was born on Monday the 9 day of December 1816 - 45 after 4 o'clock in the afternoon at Somerset.

John, Samuel, Edward, Wright, Willis, Everitt, Cowper Cohoon son of Jno.
C. & Louiza Cohoon was born at Cedar Vale on the 10 day of January 1820 - 16
after 3 o'clock on Monday morning.

Willis, Everitt, John, Cowper Cohoon their Son was born on Saturday the 4th
day of January 1823 - 30 after 10 o'clock in the Evening (at Cedar Vale).

Thomas, Alexander, John, Cowper, Abraham Cohoon son of Jno. C. & Louisa
Cohoon was born on Wednesday morning 5 o'clock January 11th 1826 (at Cedar
Vale).

William, John, Phillip, Cowper Cohoon son of John C. & Louiza Cohoon
was born on Saturday morning the 6th day of June 1828 - 40 after 12 o'clock
(before day).

Louiza, Everitt, John, Cowper Cohoon daughter of Jno. C. & Louiza Cohoon
was born on Monday 23d day of June 1834, 44 after 5 o'clock P.M. (at Cedar
Vale).

Louiza, Everitt, Margaret, Ann, John, Cowper Cohoon Daughter of Jno. C.
& Louiza Cohoon was born on Tuesday 25 day of October 1836, 30 after 11
o'clock P.M. (at Cedar Vale).

(The Bible, Printed and Published by M. Carey, No. 121 Chestnut Street,
Philadelphia, 1815, was formerly owned by Paul Tosh Cohoon, Sr., and
transcribed Aug. 2, 1947. For a partial genealogy, see Suffolk, p. 91.)

****

BENJAMIN COPELAND BIBLE.

Family Record

Marriages

Benjamin Copeland, son of Elisha & Marian ("Meriam" in the Copeland-
Whitlock Bible) Copeland, was married to Sophia Jones, Daughter of Whitmel
& Dorcas Jones, the 16th of Feby. 1810.

Benjamin Copeland, Son as above, was married to Ann Jones, Daughter of
above and his 2nd wife, the 1st day of July 1821.

Oliver Perry Copeland, son of Benjamin and Sophia Copeland, was married to
Sarah Hill the _____ of April, 1839.

Winfield Scott Copeland, son as above, was married the 3rd of Decr 1840 to Catherine E. Randolph, Daughter of Bryan and Martha Randolph.

Virginia Ann Copeland, Daughter of Benjamin & Ann Copeland, was married to Thos C. Curtis Octr 1844.

Anna Jones Copeland, daughter of W. S. Copeland and C. E. Copeland, was married to Jos. P. Hall, Jr., March 11th 1880.

In Petersburg, Va. at the Residence of Miss S. E. Grigg, Mary Augustine Christian and Walter Scott Copeland, Oct. 13th 1885.

In Richmond, Va., Residence of her uncle, Wm. H. Scott, 102 E. Franklin St., Grace Beale Cunningham and Walter Scott Copeland, April 25, 1906.

In Petersburg, Va., at the residence of her uncle Judge Mullen, Mary Catherine Copeland married Lane Lacy - June 1908.

Mary Catherine Copeland married (as second husband) William Robertson in 1936.

Elizabeth Randolph Copeland, daughter of Walter Scott Copeland and Grace Beale Cunningham, his second wife, married Nov. 19, 1938, Robert Fillmore Norfleet at Charlottesvile, Va., the Rev. W. H. Laird officiating.

Randolph Scott Copeland married Detta Beverley Osburn, daughter of the Rev. Herbert S. Osburn and Fanny Beverley, of "Blandfield," his wife, Sept. 27, 1941, in Tappahannock, Va., the Rev. Mr. Osburn officiating.

Births

Benjamin Copeland, son of Elisha & Marian Copeland, was born July the 26th 1787.

Oliver Perry Copeland, son of Benjamin and Sophia Copeland, was born the 23rd of November, 1816.

Winfield Scott Copeland, son as above, was born Nov. 7th 1817.

Sophia Ann Copeland, daughter of Benjamin and Ann Copeland, was born April the 9th 1822.

Virginia Ann Copeland, daughter as above, was born Decr 6th, 1823.

Deborah Copeland, daughter as above, was born May the 16th, 1826.

Mary Elizabeth Porter Copeland, daughter as above, was born the 14th January, 1829.

Catherine E. Copeland, wife of W. S. Copeland, was born 23rd Sept., 1822.

Virginius Copeland, son of Winfield S. & Catherine E. Copeland, was born the 13th of Aug. 1841.

Sophia Randolph Copeland, daughter as above, was born the 15th of Aug. 1843.

Anna Jones Copeland, daughter as above, was born the 15th of May, 1845.

Pattie Randolph Copeland was born 23rd of Aug. 1848.

Elizabeth Copeland, daughter as above, was born July the 4th, 1851.

Walter Scott Copeland, son as above, was born March 14th 1856.

Catherine Randolph Hall, daughter of Jos. P. & Anna J. Hall, was born Jany. 11th 1882.

Mary Catherine Copeland, daughter of W. S. and Mary Christian Copeland (daughter of W. S. and Mary A. Christian) was born Dec. 21st 1886, at Danville, Va.

Elizabeth Randolph Copeland, daughter of W. S. and Grace Cunningham Copeland, was born May 3, 1908 at 7:45 o'clock in the morning at 2007 Grove Ave., Richmond, Va.

Randolph Scott Copeland, son as above, was born July 26, 1914, at Newport News, Va.

Robert Fillmore Norfleet, Jr., son of Robert Fillmore and Elizabeth Randolph Copeland Norfleet, was born February 9, 1940, in Richmond, Va.

Mary Abigail Fillmore Norfleet, daughter of Robert Fillmore Norfleet and Elizabeth Randolph Copeland, his wife, was born December 4, 1947, in Richmond, Va.

Deaths

Sophia Copeland, wife of Benjamin Copeland, died 23rd Sept. 1819.

Ann Copeland, 2nd wife of Benjamin Copeland, died 28th of Nov. 1832.

Sophia Ann Copeland, daughter of Benjamin & Ann Copeland, his 2nd wife, died the 24th of July 1824.

Deborah Copeland, daughter as above, died the ____ of Sept., 1831.

Mary Elizabeth Porter Copeland, daughter as above, died the ___ of June, 1832.

Benjamin Copeland, son of Elisha & Marian Copeland, died the 18 of Feby., 1837.

Sophia Randolph Copeland, daughter of Winfield and Catherine E. Copeland, died the 18th of March, 1844.

Virginia Ann Curtis, daughter of Benjamin & Ann Copeland, died the 4th of Jan. 1850.

Elizabeth Copeland, infant daughter of W. S. and Catherine Copeland, died Dec. 15, 1851.

Virginius Copeland, son of W. S. & Catherine E. Copeland, died Dec. 6th, 1863.
> He was mortally wounded in battle in Northern Va. after serving nearly 3 years and being many times engaged in battle.

Catherine E. Copeland, wife of W. S. Copeland, died July 15th, 1865.

W. S. Copeland, Sr., died on May 3rd 1879 (in Jackson, N. C.).

Pattie Randolph Copeland died in Suffolk, Va., Apl. 9th, 1887.

Catherine Randolph Hall died July 11th, 1882.

Entered into life eternal at Suffolk, Va., June 14, 1905, Anna J. Hall, beloved wife of Jos. P. Hall, Jr.
> "The strife is o'er, the battle is done
> The victory of life is won."

Walter Scott Copeland, son of W. S. and Catherine E. Randolph Copeland, died July 24, 1928, at Newport News, Va.

Baptisms

Virginius Copeland was baptized about the 1st of May, 1852 by Rev. Isaac M. Arnold.

Anna Jones Copeland was baptized about the 1st of May, 1852 by Rev. Isaac M. Arnold.

Pattie Randolph Copeland was baptized about the 1st May, 1852, by Rev. Isaac M. Arnold.

Elizabeth Copeland was baptized 10th Dec. 1851 by Rev. Frederick Fitzgerald.

Walter Scott Copeland was Baptized the 27th Feby. 1857 by Rev. W. H. Wheel-Wright.

Elizabeth Randolph Copeland was baptized Oct. 11, 1908 at St. James Episcopal Church (Richmond, Va.) by Rev. Wm. Meade Clarke after the morning service.

Randolph Scott Copeland was baptized in Spring of 1915 at 1803 Grove Ave., Richmond, by the Rev. John G. Scott.

Robert Fillmore Norfleet, Jr., was baptized on Dec. 15, 1940, at 106 North Plum St., Richmond, by the Rev. John Garlick Scott.

Mary Abigail Fillmore Norfleet was baptized on May 9, 1948, at St. Andrew's Chapel, Woodberry Forest, Virginia, by the Rev. John Garlick Scott, the Rev. Francis P. Burke, assisting.

Slaves in Winfield Scott Copeland Family

Luke
Rose
Emmeline - Children: Ida & Ellen
Charity (bt. 1845 aged 24) Children: Frances, Louis, Mary.
Louiza (born 1821) Children: John, Sarah, Leah, Emily, Nina.

(Bible owned by Randolph Scott Copeland).

****

ELISHA COPELAND - WHITLOCK BIBLE.

(Inscribed on flyleaf):

This Family Bible was imported by Alexander Cotten, a merchant near Winton, North Carolina, and was sold at his sale in the year 1763, for five pounds, purchased by Elisha Copeland and was used as a register of ages by him and after his death by his wife Meriam Copeland at their seat in Nansemond county near Suffolk, Va. She died in 1815, Elisha Everett bought it at $7.00 and I bought it of him in November 1821 and removed it from Nancemond to Richmond City.

Given under my hand this
First day of January 1823

William C. Whitlock

Witnessed: Richard H. Whitlock

Richard H. Whitlock bought it from W. C. Whitlock

The State Capitol gave way in the room of the Court of Appeals on account of a large assemblage of persons to hear the decision for mayor (Ellison and Cahoon being the candidates) on the 23rd day of April 1870, destroying the lives of about fifty persons, and disabling others for life -- one of the saddest affairs on record.

Freshet in James River.

1814 -- August -- the greatest freshet

1816 -- Greatest freshet since our rememberance

The Battle of Manassas was fought on the 21st of July 1861. The Confederates, led by the brave Generals Beauregard and Johnson, came off victoriously. In this battle the Yankees, all celebrated for the swiftness of their flight, and made much better use of their feet than their hands. Some of the Yankees, having a great desire to visit Richmond, were gratified and had the pleasure of taking up their residence in the Tobacco Factories and there let them rest.

The winter of 1823 and part of '24 was the mildest known in many years.

1860 -- December 24th -- arrived in Richmond -- David Jordan.

South Carolina seceded from the United States in November 1860 and immediate afterward was followed by the Gulf States. On April 17th, 1861, Virginia seced and all the border states -- then war began: On April 19th, 1861, Saturday night the Federals left the Navy Yard at Portsmouth, Virginia, after setting fire to th yard and destroying all the property that they could. I was a spectator to the fi and will never forget that night -- as it is long to be remembered by those who witnessed it.

Florence G. Jordan.

The Battle of Bethel was fought the 10th of June, 1861, in which Robert H. Whitlock was engaged and the Confederates came off victoriously.

Robert H. Whitlock, son of Richard H. Whitlock and Jane Copeland, was wounded through the body the 24th day of June 1864 at Brandy Station, Charles City County, Virginia. He was thought to be mortally wounded and was confined to his bed 45 days, but having the best medical aid that could be procured, together with good nursing from the family, he was restored, although we think his health will be impaired in consequence. This was a truly remarkable cure.

The Old Burnside Fleet has had many hard wishes put on her by the Confederates.

September 2, 1775 -- Great Gust
August 11, 1777 - Gust
August 2, 1795 -- Gust
September 4, 1815 -- A Gust
April 11, 1815 -- Great Wind, rain and hale -- the hardest wind ever known

Benjamin Copeland, son of Elisha and Meriam, was married to Sophia Jones on the 14th day of Feb. 1816.

Oliver P. Copeland, son of Benjamin and Sophia, was born Nov. 23, 1816.
Winfield S.Copeland, "   "   "   "   "   was born Nov. 7, 1817.

Zachariah Copeland, son of Henry and Darcas, was born Sept. 23, 1743.

Henry, son of Zachariah and Sarah Copeland, was born Feb. 1, 1770-died July 6, 1805.
Betty, daughter of "   "   "   "   , was born Aug. 25, 1771.
William, son   " "   "   "   "   , was born Feb. 22, 1773
Joseph,   "   " "   "   "   "   , was born Jan. 28, 1775
Benjamin, "   " "   "   "   "   , was born Dec. __, 1777
Joseph II, "   " "   "   "   "   , was born Mar. 23, 1780
Polly, daughter " "   "   "   "   , was born Feb. 23, 1790
Sarah,   "   " "   "   "   "   , was born (not given)

Elisha Everett and Mary Griffin were married Sept. 27, 1804

James Copeland and Orinia Ellyson were married Oct. 4, 1804

Zachariah Copeland, son of Demsey, was born Feb. 25, 1784

Robert W. Jordan, born Dec. 9, 1796

David Jordan, born Dec. 26, 1800

Children of Elisha and Meriam Copeland:

Dempsey	born Dec. 23, 1761
Elisha	born Oct. 18, 1763
Hezekiah	born July 23, 1765
Peninah	born Sept. 4, 1767 -- married June 4, 1788--died March 10, 1810

Elizabeth	born Feb. 17, 1769
Nancy	born Jan. 25, 1771
Lydiakiah	born Oct. 28, 1774
Lemuel Ezikias	born Sept. 11, 1776
Exum	born Aug. 24, 1778
Anthony	born June 2, 1781
William	born May 22, 1784
Benjamin	born July 26, 1787
Polly	born April 2, 1773

Elizabeth Jordan, wife of Robert Jordan, died Feb. 7, 1816 with the prevailing epidemic.

Peninah Copeland Whitlock died March 10, 1810

Charles Whitlock died Aug. 24, 1820 and was buried with his wife at William Savedge's Plantation called Bottoms Bridge on the Chickahomeny River in Henrico County Virginia where a moment has been erected to their memory by their children.

Children of Charles and Peninah Whitlock:

James Raglan	born Aug. 25, 1790
Ann	born Oct. 19, 1792 - died Oct. 3, 1793
Richard H.	born Dec. 19, 1797
Charles C.	born Feb. 1, 1799-died 1800
William C.	born Dec. 8, 1800
Charles Cicero	born July 5, 1804 - died Nov. 5, 1805
Eliza Ann	born Oct. 7, 1805 - died May 25, 1806

The marriages of Elisha and Meriam Copeland's children:

Dempsey	married Oct. 3, 1782
Elisha	married Sept. 11, 1784
Peninah	married June 4, 1788
Elizabeth	married Oct. 27, 1792
Nancy	married Sept. 25, 1801

Porter children:

Sarah	born Aug. 15, 1747
Elizabeth	born Jan. 5, 1749
Lidia	born Aug. 8, 1750
John	born Aug. 2, 1752

Joseph	born Jan. 1, 1754
Mary	born Mar. 1, 1755
Ann	born June 24, 1765
Peninah	born Sept. 28, 1757
Benjamin	born Mar 4, 1759
William	born Dec. 18, 1762

Joseph Porter, son of John and Mary Porter, born Dec. 1, 1781.

Children of William Cotten and his wife Ann:

Emma	born Nov. 30, 1763
Salley	born June 24, 1765
Samuel	born Jan. 15, 1768
Sellia	born April 24, 1769

William Everett	died Oct. 4, 1787
John Everett	died Dec. 28, 1795
Mary Everett	died Sept. 27, 1814

Archibald Copeland, son of Elisha and Bethsheba, born July 15, 1786 -- died Aug. 9, 1790.

Bethsheba Copeland died Dec. 5, 1788

Mary Ann Everett	born Aug. 18, 1805
Elisha Everett	born April 17, 1807 - died Dec. 14, 1808
Seth Everett	born Jan. 14, 1809
John Everett	born Sept. 29, 1810

Louisa Copeland died Oct. 2, 1799

Elisha Copeland died Oct. 7, 1807

Robert Jordan died in Suffolk, Virginia Jan. 14, 1824

David and Zehpa Jones' children:

Nansey	born Feb. 17, 1771
Allen	born Dec. 21, 1772
David	born Feb. 18, 1775
Andrew	born May 18, 1777
Brittain	born Mar. 20, 1779
John	born Feb. 24, 1783

Children of Elisha and Louisa Copeland:

Elisa Ann	born Sept. 16, 1791 -- died Sept. 20, 1792
Josiah Porter	born May 2, 1793 -- died Oct. 21, 1793
Elisha	born June 13, 1795
Richard	died in infancy Oct. 16, 1798
Elewisa	born Feb. 18, 1799

Derren and Nancy Daughtrey's children:

Charles	born Oct. 9, 1802 -- died Aug. 10, 1805
Albert Gray	born Sept. 2, 1804
Mills	born Oct. 13, 1806

James Evans of Suffolk died Sept. 18, 1823
Fred Hall died in Suffolk Sept. 27, 1823

Children of Robert and Elizabeth Jordan:

William Robert	born April __, 1822
Richard David	born May __, 1824
Susanna Jordan	born Jan. 18, 1803-married to Dr. Crawley Finney Feb. 8, 1827

Evelina Maria Finney was born Nov. 18, 1827

Frances Whitlock died Oct. 20, 1824

Richard Whitlock was married to Jane Jordan, Dec. 1, 1825

David Jordan was married to Mary Eliza Grice Aug. 1, 1840

Florence Grice Jordan, Daughter of David and Mary Eliza, was born Dec. 4, 1841

Florence Grice Jordan married William S. Bogart of Savannah, Oct. 5, 1859

William Robert Jordan married Mary Louisa Tanner March 22, 1845

James Raglan Whitlock married Eliza Ann Swepson April 14, 1814

Elizabeth Whitlock, daughter of Richard H. and Jane Jordan Whitlock, married George D. Harwood in 1847.

Ellen, daughter of R. H. and Jane Whitlock was married to James W. Pedin on April 15, 1856.

Henry Copeland, son of William and Sarah, was born Jan. 22, 1764

William Copeland, son of William and Sarah, was born May 14, 1789

Samuel Ellyson was born July 11, 1784

Harriet Virginia Whitlock, the prettiest daughter of R. H. and J. C. Whitlock, returned from West Town School in Pennsylvania, about the 15th of October 1860, and has a perfect hatred for peach pie and all who like it.

(Bible owned by Frank Tyree Bates, Jr., of Richmond. For a partial genealogy of the Copeland, Jordan, and Whitlock families, see Suffolk, pp. 78-102.)

****

HENRY COPELAND BIBLE.

Marriages

Henry Copeland son of William Copeland and Sarah his wife, and Sarah Smith, daughter of Arthur Smith and Ann his wife, were married the 29th day of November, 1792.

Thos. B. Riddick, son of Robb Riddick and Mary his wife and Sarah S. Copeland daughter of Henry Copeland and Sarah his wife were married the 23rd day of April, 1840.

Dempsey Odom son of John W. Odom and Mary his wife and Pattie L. B. Riddick daughter of Thos. B. Riddick and Sarah S., his wife, were married the 29th day of Dec. 1870.

Births

Henry Copeland, son of William and Sarah Copeland, his wife, was born the 22nd day of January 1763.

Sarah Copeland, daughter of Arthur Smith and Ann, his wife, was born the 15th day of Jan. 1773.

Ann Copeland, daughter of Henry Copeland and Sarah, his wife, was born the 25th day of Oct. 1793.

Elizabeth Copeland, daughter of Henry Copeland and Sarah, his wife, was born the 21st day of Feb. 1795.

Martha Copeland, daughter of Henry Copeland and Sarah, his wife, was born the 5th day of Nov. 1796.

William Copeland, son of Henry Copeland and Sarah, his wife, was born on the 13th day of Nov. 1798.

Margaret Copeland, daughter of Henry Copeland and Sarah, his wife, was born the 7th day of May, 1800.

Mary Copeland, daughter of Henry Copeland and Sarah, his wife, was born the 1st day of April, 1802.

Sarah Copeland, daughter of Henry Copeland and Sarah, his wife, was born the 23rd day of Oct. 1803.

Penninah Copeland, daughter of Henry Copeland and Sarah, his wife, was born the 1st day of Dec. 1805.

Louisa Copeland, daughter of Henry Copeland and Sarah, his wife, was born the 9th day of January, 1808.

Susan S. Copeland, daughter of Henry Copeland and Sarah, his wife, was born the 21st day of March, 1811.

Anna Maria Copeland, daughter of Henry Copeland and Sarah, his wife, was born the 16th day of Nov. 1813.

Mary Henretta Copeland, daughter of Henry Copeland and Sarah, his wife, was born the 26th day of Feby. 1817.

William A. Riddick, son of Thos. B. Riddick and Sarah, his wife, was born the 14th day of June, 1841.

Mary S. Riddick, daughter of Thos. B. Riddick and Sarah, his wife, was born the 1st day of Feb. 1843.

M. L. B. (Pattie) Riddick, daughter of Thos. B. Riddick and Sarah, his wife, was born the 18th day of Nov. 1845.

Jas. R. Riddick, son of Thos. B. Riddick and Sarah, his wife, was born the 28th day of Feb. 1848.

Deaths

Mary Copeland, daughter of Henry Copeland and Sarah, his wife, departed this life the 12th day of April 1815.

William Copeland, son of Henry Copeland and Sarah, his wife, departed this life the 27th of March, 1816.

Sarah Copeland, wife of Henry Copeland, departed this life the 2nd day of June, 1817.

Anna Maria Copeland, daughter of Henry Copeland and Sarah his wife, departed this life the 7th day of Oct. 1820.

William P. Jamerson, husband of Margaret Copeland, departed this life the 23rd day of April, 1821.

Henry Copeland, son of Wm. Copeland and Sarah his wife, departed this life the 25th day of Sept. 1823.

Sarah S. Riddick, wife of Thos. B. Riddick, died July 18th, 1860, aged 58 years.

(Bible Published and Sold by Edmund Cushing in the Year of 1828, Lunenburg, Mass. Formerly owned by Mrs. Sarah S. Copeland Riddick.
    Note. Dempsey Odom and Martha L. Borland (Pattie)Riddick, his wife, had issue: 1. Mary Shepard Odom, m. Surry Parker. 2. Patty Borland Odom, m., as 2nd wife, Surry Parker. 3. John Robert Odom, m. Mamie Beavers. 4. Elizabeth Brownley Odom, m. Henry Holmes Hunter, M.D.)

****

THOMAS COPELAND'S ACCOUNT BOOK
Extracts.

p. 8)
Emma Copeland daughter of Thomas and Mary Copeland was born 11th mo. 16th between 8 & 9 o'clock in the morning 1822.

p. 11)
1824, __ mo. 28th between 10 & 11 o'clock A.M., Ann Shepherd departed this life.

p. 12)
1st day, about 8 o'clock A.M. 11th mo. 28th 1824, Leonora Copeland daughter of Tho & Mary Copeland was born.

p. 15)
1825, 6th mo. Whitty Jones deceased.

p. 16)
1825, 12th mo. 24th, Priscilla Copeland deceased.

p. 16)
12th mo. 21st, Jesse Hare, Senr died.

46

p. 25)
1826, 8th, 16. John Shepherd deceased & buried.

p. 38)
3rd mo. 12, E. Everett deceased.

p. 39)
1829, 4th mo. 16th, Jas. Hare Decd, 17th, buried.

p. 42)
1829, - 8, Job Holland deceased.

p. 46)
1829, 3 - 29. Betty Faulk married.

p. 53)
Jennet Copeland, Daughter of Tho. Copeland & Mary his wife was born 12th
mo. 10th 1820.

(Owner: Miss Doris Jones: Note. For Thomas Copeland and his family, see
These Twain (no date, Greensboro, N.C.), by W. E. McClenny, E. E. Holland
W. W. Staley, and J. O. Atkinson.)

****

SAMUEL CROSS (NOTES)

Samuel Cross (son of Hardy Cross) married March 26, 1816, Elizabeth
Copeland, born 21st Feb. 1795 - died Jan. 14, 1865.

Their issue

William H. Cross, born May 27th 1817 - died Dec. 15th 1865.

Sarah Ann Cross, born March 31st 1819 - died 1889, married Jesse Eason, of
Gates Co. No issue.

James Augustus Hardy Cross, born Jan. 25, 1821; married 6th March 1865
Alice Daughtrey, daughter of Charles & Rebecca Haynes Daughtrey. Their
issue: Elizabeth Daisy Cross, born Feb. 12, 1867, and Charles Cross, died
in infancy.

Mary Elizabeth Cross, born June 21, 1823 - died Aug. 30th 1835.

(Notes contributed by Mrs. Charles Reuben Welton, nee Mary Catherine
Brinkley.)

****

CRUMP - GODWIN BIBLE.

(Inscribed on flyleaf:)

Elizabeth Judith Crump 1843.

Family Record

Marriages

Geo. H. Crump and Elizabeth J. Rochelle were married October 1st 1840.

Geo. H. Crump and Lulie Finney were married October 28th 1868.

Births

Jno. C. Crump was born Jany. 22d 1788.

Geo. H. Crump was born March 7th 1816.

Elizabeth J., wife of Geo. H. Crump, was born Octr 1st 1821.

Lulie Wilson, first daughter of Geo. H. & Lulie F. Crump, was born 10th September 1869.

Georgia Crafford, second daughter of Geo. H. & Lulie F. Crump, was born 26th October 1871.

Lulie Finney, wife of Geo. H. Crump, Daughter of Crawley Finney, was born July 18th 1844.

Ann Everite, daughter of Etheldred Everite and Elizabeth his wife, was born January 16th 1791.

Marriages

Joseph H. Godwin and Jennet M. J. Godwin were married by the Revd Jacob Keeling, on Thursday the 18th day of Decmr 1824.

Births

Joseph H. Godwin, Son of John & Mary Godwin, was born the 19th day of December 1799.

Jennet M. J. Godwin, daughter of Allen G. Godwin & Susanna J. M. J. Godwin, was born on the 7th day of September 1808.

Susanna Holladay Godwin, Daughter of Jos. H. & Jennette McR. J. Godwin, was born April 6th 1828.

Bernadotte Godwin, son of Jos. H. & Jenet MR. J. Godwin, was born December 12, 1829.

Ann Cowper Godwin, Daughter of Jos. H. Godwin and Janet MR. J. Godwin, was born April 25, 1832.

Frances N. Whitfield, daughter of Henry . . . .

Margaret Ann Whitfield, daughter of Henry Holladay G. Whitfield, was born June 4, 1819.

Deaths

Joseph H. Godwin, son of John and Mary Godwin, died the 20 of November 1833.

Janette M. G. Godwin, wife of Jos. H. Godwin, died . . . . . .

Susanna Meador, daughter of Joseph H. and Janette Godwin, and wife of Jas. C. Meador, died the ___ Aug. 1889.

Bernadette Godwin, son of Joseph and Janet Godwin, died the 20 of July 1833.

Ann Cowper Godwin, daughter of Joseph H. and Janet McG. Godwin, died the 14th of January 1842.

John C. Crump departed this life Jany. 27th at 12 1/2 o'clk A. M. 1856.

Clement Rochelle departed this life 28th Octr 1844.

Ann, wife of Clement Rochelle, departed this life 8th of June 1843.

Elizabeth Judith - wife of Geo H. Crump - Daughter of Clement Rochelle - departed this life on the 8th of December 1866.

(The Holy Bible, H. & E. Phinney's Stereotype Edition, Published and sold by E. & E. Phinney, Sold also by I. Tiffany, Utica. Cooperstown, N. Y., 1843, Owner: Miss Lulie Crump. Transcribed: 1947.)

****

ALGERNON SIDNEY DARDEN BIBLE.

(Written on the flyleaf:)

This Holy Book was presented to / Algernon S. and Mary S.
Darden / on the day of their marriage. / By their affectionate Mother. / Mary Allen. Novr 27th 1855.

Family Record.

Algernon Sidney Darden / was born January 28th 1829.

Mary Swepson Allen was / born October 4th 1837.

Mary Allen daughter of / Algernon S. & Mary S. Darden / was born the
5th day of Nov- / ember 1856, at 20 minutes /after 2 o'clock A. M.

Annie Jordan daughter of / Algernon S. & Mary S. Darden / was born the
17th day of Aug-/ust 1858, at 10 minutes before / 3 o'clock P.M.

Mary Allen daughter / of Algernon S. & Mary S. / Darden was born the 8th /
day of September 1861, / at 20 minutes past 7 o'clock A. M.

Archd Allen son of / Algernon S. & Mary S. / Darden was born the 15th day
of November 1868, / at 15 minutes to 12 o'clock P. M.

Robert Henning Webb, son of Joseph / P. and Annie Webb, born the 21st /
day of February 1882.

Janet Whitehead Prentis daughter / of Robert R. and Mary Allen Prentis /
born the 28th day of October 1887.

Joseph Prentis Webb, son of Robert / H. and Blanche F. Webb, / born at the
University of Virginia, June / 3rd 1913.

Marriages

Algernon S. Darden and / Mary S. Allen were married / in the M. E. Church,
Suffolk, / on the 27th November 1855, / by Rev. A. R. Bernard.

Joseph Prentis Webb and Annie / Jordan Darden were married at / the
residence of the bride's father / Algernon S. Darden, Esq. on the / 27th
day of January 1881 by Rev. / James Murray, D. D.

Robert Riddick Prentis and Mary / Allen Darden were married at the / residence of the bride's father Algernon / S. Darden, Esq., 72 Main Street, Suffolk, / Va. on the 6th day of January 1887 by / Rev. James Murray, D.D.

Robert Henning Webb and Blanche / Farrington Miller married June 26th, 1912.

Deaths.

Mary Allen daughter of / Algernon S. & Mary S. Darden / died the 30th day of May 1857.

Archibald Allen, Son / of Algernon S. & Mary S. Darden, died the 22nd / day of March 1888.

Algernon Sidney Darden died / the 3d day of April 1893.

Joseph Prentis Webb died the / 27th day of December 1892.

Mary Allen Prentis died the / 27th day of June 1904.

Janet Whitehead Prentis died Au- / gust 20, 1888.

Mary Swepson Darden died the 16th day of October 1913.

(The Holy Bible, containing the Old and New Testaments, Together with the Apocrypha: &c. H. C. Peck & Theo. Bliss., Philadelphia, 1854. The Bible, owned by Mrs. Robert Henning Webb, was transcribed in 1962.)

****

ABRAM DAUGHTREY BIBLE.

Deaths

Abram Daughtrey departed this life Sept. 2, 1828.

Sarah Haynes departed this life June 14, 1825.

Abram Taylor Daughtrey departed this life Oct. 19, 1817.

Catharine Susan Daughtrey departed this life July 18, 1825.

George N. Daughtrey departed this life Feb. 14, 1847.

Martha S. Haynes departed this life Jany. 11th 1849.

Patrick Henry Haynes departed this life Nov. 24th 1845.

Charles A. Daughtrey departed thi s life 27th day of March 1852, aged 39 years & 6 Months.

Mary Ann E. Brownley departed this lfe on the 26th day of September 1857. Age 43 years.

George Thomas Haynes departed this life on the 4th day of August 1858, age nearly 17 years.

Elizabeth Haynes wife of John L. Haynes departed this life on the 2nd day of April 1860. Age 72 years.

P. H. Haynes departed this life December 18th 1865.

Births

Abram Daughtrey was born Aug. 16, 1788.

Elizabeth (Cross) Daughtrey wife of Abram Daughtrey was born March 4, 1788.

John L. Haynes second husband of Elizabeth Daughtrey was born Decem. 17, 1789.

George N. Daughtrey son of Abram and Elizabeth Daughtrey was born Nov. 29, 1810.

Charles A. Daughtrey son of Abram and Elizabeth Daughtrey was born Sept. 21, 1812.

Mary Ann E. Daughtrey daughter of Abram Daughtrey and Elizabeth Daughtrey was born July 13, 1814.

Abram T. Daughtrey son of Abram Daughtrey and Elizabeth Daughtrey was born Oct. 1, 1816.

Marmaduke F. Daughtrey son of Abram Daughtrey and Elizabeth Daughtrey was born Jan. 2, 1818.

Martha S. Daughtrey daughter of Abram Daughtrey and Elizabeth Daughtrey was born Oct. 30, 1819.

Patrick H. Daughtrey son of Abram Daughtrey and Elizabeth Daughtrey was born Jan. 11, 1823.

Catharine Susan Daughtrey daughter of Abram Daughtrey and Elizabeth Daughtrey was born Oct. 20, 1824.

52

Deaths

Departed this life / Sarah Elizabeth the daughter of Charles and Rebecca Daughtrey August 25, 1846.

Charles A. Daughtrey / Departed this life 27th day of March 1852 age 39 years & 6 months.

Births

Samuel Cross was born the 11 of March 1793.

Elizabeth Copeland was born the 21st of February 1795.

William H. Cross Born May the 27th 1817.

Sarah Ann Cross was Born March the 31st 1819.

James Augustus Hardy Cross was born January the 25th 1821.

Mary Elizabeth Cross was born January 21st 1823.

Deaths

William Charles Cross son of James A. Cross and Mary A. his wife departed this life Feb. 22nd 1871.

Births

Sarah Haynes, wife of John L. Haynes, was born Nov. 21, 1788.

Erasmus D. Haynes, son of John L. Haynes & Sarah Haynes, was born Feb. 14, 1815.

Rebecca Frances Haynes, daughter of John L. Haynes and Sarah Haynes, was born Feb. 1, 1824.

Mary Elizabeth Haynes, daughter of Erasmus and Martha Sarah was born August 23rd, 1841.

George Thomas Haynes, son of Erasmus & Martha Sarah, was born Dec. 2nd,

Patrick Henry Haynes, son of Erasmus & Martha Sarah, was born June 25, 184

53

Marriages

Abram Daughtrey and Elizabety Daughtrey was married Nov. 10, 1809.

John L. Haynes and Sarah Haynes his wife was married March 16, 1811.

John L. Haynes and Elizabeth Haynes his second wife was married Jan. 1, 1835.

Erasmus D. Haynes was married to Martha S(arah) Daughtrey Oct. 30th, 1840.

(The Bible is owned by Mrs. Charles Reuben Welton, nee Mary Catherine Brinkley, who contributed the following:

Abram Daughtrey (1788-1825) married in 1809, as first husband, Mary Elizabeth Cross (March 4, 1788-April 2, 1860; daughter of Hardy Cross; she married, 2nd Jan. 1, 1835, as 2nd wife, John L. Haynes).
Their issue
George N. Daughtrey (1810-1847), unmarried.

Charles A. Daughtrey (1812-1852), married 1842 Rebecca Haynes (daughter of John L. Haynes and Sarah Simmons, his first wife), and had issue: Mary Alice Daughtrey (b. April 2, 1845), married March 6, 1865, James Augustus Hardy Cross; Susan Catherine Daughtrey (1847-1920), married June 19, 1867, Hugh Griffin Brinkley, Jr.; Frances Fern Daughtrey (1850-1874), married 1874, Admiral Brinkley, Jr.

Mary Ann Daughtrey (1814-1857), married twice: (1) Lemuel Cleaves, and (2) John Brownely, of Warwick Co.

Abram Taylor Daughtrey (1816-1817).

Marmaduke Daughtrey (1818-1897), married twice, (1) Fannie Dicson, and (2) Elizabeth Hervey Moodey.

Martha Sarah Daughtrey (1819-1849), married Oct. 30, 1840, Erasmus Haynes.

Patrick Henry Daughtrey (1823-1865), lawyer.

Catherine Susan Daughtrey (1824-1825).

****

WILLIAM ELEY BIBLE.

Births

William Thomas Eley Son of William Eley & Lydia E., his wife, was born the 17th day of January in the year of our Lord 1838.

Virginia Priscilla Day Eley, daughter of William Eley & Lydia E., his wife, was born the 21st day of June, in the year of our Lord 1839.

Monimia Eley, Daughter of William Eley & Lydia, his wife, was born the 15th of October in the year of our Lord 1841.

Edith Wortley, Daughter of William & Lydia E. Eley, was born the 24th of February 1844.

Fanny Day, Daughter of William Eley & Lydia E., his wife, was born 15th of Oct. 1845.

Lizzy, Daughter of William Eley and Lydia E., his wife, was born 6th February 1847.

Eudora Lydia Ballard, daughter of William Eley and Lydia E., his wife, was born 9th of Octr 1848.

Josephine Florence Eley, Daughter of William Eley and Lydia E., his wife, was born 30th of May 1850.

William Francis, Son of William Eley and Lydia E., his wife, was born the 2nd day of December 1851.

William Walter Eley, son of William Eley & Lydia E., his wife, was born the 8th Day of May 1854.

Sarah Caroline Eley departed this life the 22nd day of August in the year of our Lord 1832 aged 15 years, 4 months, 10 days.

Lizzie Eley departed this life the 16th day of January

Year	Mo	Day
1857	1 .	16
1847	2	6
9	11	10

Lydia D. Eley Departed this life the 18th day of March 1857 -- Aged 39 years 2 mo. & 3 days.

William Eley, Sr., Departed this life the 14th day of November 1884, Aged 76 years, 5 mo., 27 days.

Dr. Wm Thos. Eley Departed this life in the City of Richmond on the 11th day of July 1862, from a wound received in defending the City on the 30th of June 1862, Aged 24 years 5 mo. & 24 days.

Fannie Day Hargrove departed this life the 8 day of December 1895 Age 50 years, 1 mo., 23 days.

Josephine F. Eley departed this life the 3rd day of July 1900, aged 50 years, 1 mo., 3 days.

E. Wortley Duke departed this life the 11th of October 1906, Age 62 years, 7 months, 14 days.

Marriages.

William Eley & Sarah Caroline Riddick was married in the year of our Lord 1831 May 31st.

William Eley and Lydia E. Day were married Oct. 18th 1836 - Lived together 20 years 5 mos.

Births.

Lydia Eley Day Daughter of Thos. R. Day & Edith his wife was born the 15th day of January in the year of our Lord 1818.

William Eley, son of William (Eley) & Betsey (Copeland) his wife was born in the year of our Lord 1808 May 17th.

Sarah Caroline Riddick, Daughter of John Riddick & Sarah his wife, was born April 12, in the year of our Lord 1817.

(Copied from leaves torn from the Bible of William Eley, of "Level Green," South Quay (Holland) Road. Formerly owned by Mrs. Claude Dennis, nee Erma Kilby. Transcribed: 1947.)

****

CRAWLEY FINNEY BIBLE.

Born in Amelia County Virgina the 17th day of January 1798 Crawley Finney son of John & Nancy Finney.

Births

Born in Suffolk, the 18th of November 1827 Evelina Maria, daughter of Crawley and Susannah Finney. Baptised by the Rev. Allen R. Bernard.

Born in Suffolk, the 27th of May 1830, Robert Jordan, son of Crawley & Susannah Finney. Baptised by the Rev. John French.

Born at Sharon, Nansemond County, February 6th 1832, Susan Wesley, daughter of C. & Susannah Finney.

Born in Suffolk, September the 7th 1833, Sarah Ann, daughter of C. & S. Finney. Baptised by Dr. Jo French.

Deaths.

Died Sept. 10th 1832 Susan Wesley, daughter of C. & S. Finney.

Died June 18th 1833 Robert Jordan, son of C. & S. Finney after an illness of nearly two years duration.

Died November 6th 1907, Wilbur John Kilby in the 58th year of his age. A kind and loving husband.

Died March (9), 1900, Eva M. Finney, daughter of Dr. Crawley Finney & his wife Susannah.

(Died) May 23rd 1915 Sarah Ann Finney daughter of Dr. Crawley Finney & his wife Susannah.

Died June 14th 1885, Martha Jordan Finney, daughter of Dr. Crawley Finney and Susannah his wife.

Died June 19th 1913 Fanny T. Finney, daughter of Dr. Crawley Finney and his wife Margaret Whitfield Finney.

Marriages.

Married on the 24th of June, 1841, Dr. Crawley Finney to Miss Fanny A. Whitfield, daughter of Henry Holladay Godwin Whitfield.

Married to Miss Margaret A. Whitfield on the 31st of December 1842, Dr. Crawley Finney (daughter of Henry Holladay Godwin Whitfield & sister of Fanny N. Whitfield).

Married in June, 1855, Dr. C. Finney & Rebecca Percival.

Family Record
Marriages.

Married on the Sixteenth of October 1817, by the Reverend M. M. Dance,
Crawley Finney son of John & Nancy Finney of Amelia County Virginia to
Miss Eliza Woodward second Daughter of Mr. James Woodward, Norfolk, Va.

Births

Born on the 12th of August 1818 Sarah Anne, daughter of Crawley & Eliza
Finney (recorded this 10th December 1818 in the Borough of Norfolk by C.
Finney). Baptised by Rev. M. M. Dance.

(Born) on the 19th of August 1820 in Norfolk Eliza Crawley daughter of
Crawley & Eliza Finney, Baptised by Dr. Jo French.

(Born) on the 28th of November 1823 Mary Mettauer, daughter of Crawley
& Eliza Finney & Baptised 25th Dec. 1823 by Dr. Jo French. Born also in Norfolk.

Born on the 10th of April 1841 Eliza Woodward daughter of Eliza & Drury
Phillips.

Born of the same parents on the 14th December 1842 Mary Drury Phillips.

Deaths.

Died - Wednesday morning 8th Septr 1824, Mrs. Eliza Finney (in the Town
of Suffolk, Va.) A husband who loved her whilst living, and who will ever
honour and cherish her memory with truth. She was an affectionate (illegible) wife,
a fond mother, a pure Christian.

Decd October 31st 182__ Mary Mettauer Finney. She was buried in the same
vault with her mother, in Norfolk.

Died Oct. 2nd 1832 Sarah Ann daughter of Crawley and Eliza Finney aged 14
years, 1 mo. & 20 days.

Died 26 of June 1842 Mrs. Drury Phillips and on the 18th of June Eliza W.
Phillips daughter of Drury & Eliza Phillips. Died on 27th of Sept. 1850 Mary
Drury Phillips.

Marriages

Married Thursday evening the 5th of February 1827 by the Rev. Robert Cox,
Crawley Finney, M.D., to Susanna daughter of Robert Jordan, deceased, all
of Suffolk, Virginia.

Died Sept. 26th 1913 Lulie F. Crump, daughter of Dr. Crawley Finney and Margaret Whitfield Finney.

Died May 23, 1915, Sarah Anne Finney.

Births.

Born in Isle of Wight the 24th May 183_ (torn: 6?) Martha Jordan, daughter of C. & S. Finney. Baptised by Dr. John French.

Born at Holladays Point, Nansemond County, the 4th April 1838, Jane Elizabeth daughter of C. & S. Finney.

Born on the 28th of Oct. 1840, Susannah Finney, daughter of Crawley & Susanna Finney.

Deaths.

Died in Nansemond County, Virginia, on the 4th of November 1840, Mrs. Susannah Finney in the 37th year of her age. Funeral preached by Rev. J. G. Whitfield from the 3rd Chapt. and 11 verse of 2nd Peter.

Died on the 24th of December 1840, Jane Elizabeth, daughter of Crawley & Susannah Finney.

Died on the 26th of Jan. 1841, Susannah Finney, daughter of Crawley & Susannah Finney.

Died on the 24th of August 1856, Dr. Crawley Finney in the 59th year of his age. Funeral service by Rev. W. McGee. "There remaineth therefore a rest unto the people of God."

Marriages.

Married on the 10th of Jan. 1839, Eliza C. Finney & Mr. Drury Phillips.

Married on the 28th of October 1868 Louisiana Finney to George H. Crump.

Married on the 23rd of January, 1889, Mary Drury Holladay Finney (daughter of Crawley & Margaret Finney (deceased), to Wilbur John Kilby, son of John R. Kilby.

Mary Drury Holladay Kilby, wife of Wilbur J. Kilby, died at 9:50 o'clock A. M. on December 19th 1917, at 305 Main St., Suffolk, age 67 years and one month.

Births.

Born in Nansemond County, Va., on the 18th of July 1844, Louisiana
Finney, daughter of Crawley and Margaret A. Finney.

Born in the same county and of the same parents Fanny Taylor on the
29th of January, 1848.

Born in Isle of Wight County, Virginia, of the same parents, Mary Drury
Holladay Finney on the 18th of November 1850.

Deaths.

Died on the 20th of December 1841, Fanny N., wife of Dr. C. Finney.

Died on the 24th September 1852, Mrs. Margaret A. Finney.

Died at the Suffolk Female Institute June 14th 1855, after a short illness,
Martha J. Finney.

(Died) On Friday March 9th 1900 at about 6:30 P.M., Evalina Maria
Finney entered into that rest that remains for the people of God.

Died at the home of her sister, Mrs. Wilbur J. Kilby, June 19, 1913,
Fannie T. Finney.

(The Bible, greatly worn, is owned by Miss Lulie Crump, Transcribed in
1946.)

****

ALLEN G. GODWIN BIBLE.

Allen G. Godwin was born the 30th March 1780.

Susanna Jennette McCray Jack Godwin was born the 6 of March 1789.

Allen and Susanna was married the 17th of June 1806.

Jennette McCray Jack Godwin daughter of Allen and Susanna, was born 7th
of September 1808.

Susanna Jennette McCray Jack Godwin departed this life 29th of November
1811. She fulfilled the duties of wife, and mother, with the utmost propriety
and was Sincerely Regretted by her husband and Friends.

Allen G. Godwin and Barbara Godwin was married the 6th of May 1813.

(This was evidently taken from a Bible, for part of the death record of one person is visible beneath the above item.)

Joseph H. Godwin and Jennette M. J. Godwin were married by the Rev. Jacob Keeling on Thursday the 18th of Dec. 1824.

The above parties were my mother's brother Joseph who married Aunt Jennette Godwin who was a daughter of Allen Godwin and 1st cousin to her husband.

Joseph H. Godwin was the son of John & Mary Holladay Godwin (my grandparents) and was born Dec. 19th 1799.

Jennette M. J. Godwin daughter of Allen G. Godwin & Susanna J. M. J. Godwin was born on the 7th of September 1808.

Susanna Holladay Godwin (cousin Sue) daughter of Jos. H. and Jennette M. J. Godwin was born April 6th 1828.

Bernadotte Godwin, son of Jos. H. and Janette Godwin was born Dec. 12th 1829.

Ann Cowper Godwin, daughter of Jos. H. and Janette M. J. Godwin was born April 26th 1832.

Jos. H. Godwin son of John and Mary Godwin died 20th of November 1833.

(This record has written on verso: "Acct. of A. G. Godwin's Births, Marriages &c." Owner: Miss Lulie Crump. Transcribed: August 1946.)

****

MILLS GODWIN BIBLE.

Marriages.

Joseph Holladay and Patience Godwin were married by the Reverend _____ on the ____ day of _____Anno Domini 17___

Mills Godwin and Sarah Blount were married by the Reverend Henry John Burgess on Tuesday the 8th day of February Anno Domino 1780.

Births

Joseph Holladay was born on the ___day of __in the year of our Lord 17___

Patience Godwin wife of the above Joseph Holladay was born on the ___ day of ____ in the year of our Lord 17___

Mills Godwin was born on the 2nd day of February in the year of our Lord 1760.

Sarah Blount wife of the above named Mills Godwin was born on the 13th day of October in the year of our Lord 1758.

Henry Blount Godwin their Son was born on the 9th day of December 1781.

They had a Daughter born that lived only six days.

Louise Caroline Godwin their third child, was born the 15th of April 1784.

Ann Gray Godwin their fourth child was born the 23d day of February 1786.

Thomas Henry Pitt Godwin their fifth child was Born on the 25th day of December 1788.

(Polyglott Bible with numerous additions from Sagster's Comprehensive Bible. Robinson, Pratt & Co., 63 Wall Street, New York, 1841. Owner: Miss Mary Edith Kelly. Transcribed: 1947.)

****

SAMUEL GODWIN RECORD.

Samuel Godwin born 20th day of May 1687/8.

My wife Mary Godwin, daughter of Col. James Jossey, was borne the first day of February 1696.

Samuel Godwin was married to Mary his wife the 19th day of June 1711, by Sam'l Wallis, Minister.

Samuel Godwin was borne on 29 day of March 1712, on Saturday.

Thomas Godwin was borne 1st day of Feb. 1714, on tuesday.

Mary Godwin was born on the 27th day of October 1717, on Fryday.

A son borne dead 22nd day of September 1720 on Thursday.

My dear & loveing wife Mary Godwin departed this life a Fryday morning about sunrize, itt being the 23 day of Sept. 1720.

I was married to Catherine my recent wife the 19th day of December 1721.

Martha Godwin borne 10th day of Oct. 1722, on Wednesday afternoon.

Elizabeth Godwin born on the 16th day of Feb. 1723, on Sunday night.

62

Christian Godwin borne on 23 of Sept. 1725, on thursday.

My daughter Christian Godwin departed this life Sunday morning, it being the 18th day of Septr 1726.

Joseph Godwin (was born) 18 Oct. 1729, Munday afternoon.

Richard Godwin (was born) 10 Nov. 1732, thursday.

Edmond Godwin (was born) 29 Oct. 1735, Wednesday morning.

Elizabeth Godwin (was born) 14 April, 1751, Sunday.

Samuel Godwin born 28 June 1759 on Thu. night about 10 o'clock.

Joseph G. (was born) 24 March 1762, Wednesday.

(A record of slaves follows in a different handwriting.)

(Transcribed from the Account Book of Samuel Godwin, now in the manuscript collection of the Huntington Library, San Marino, California.
    Note. "Militia Officers of Nansemond, 1680. /Captain James Jossey (Horse)."
John B. Boddie, Seventeen Century Isle of Wight County, Virginia, p. 168.)

****

JOSEPH PATTON HALL BIBLE.

Marriages.

Jos. P. Hall was married to Laura Ann Murdaugh by the Rev. Jacob Keeling on the 16h day of February 1837.

Jos. P. Hall married Jerusha Walke Murdaugh 12th day of May 1859 by the Rev. Allen R. Bernard.

Births.

First son still born on the 16th day of Dec. 1837, and was burried the next day.

First daughter Laura Patton Hall born on the 28th day of August at 5 o'clock A.M., 1839.

Second son Jos. John Hall was born on the 11th day of July, 1841, at 6 o'clock, A.M.

Third son Jos. P. Hall, Junior, was born on the 3rd day of January at 3 o'clock, A.M., 1843.

Fourth son John Murdaugh Hall was born on the 4th day of February, 1845.

Second daughter Ann Jordan Hall was born on the 28th day of Dec., 1847.

Third daughter Virginia Cooper Hall was born on the 19th of Sept., Friday at 10 o'clock, A. M., 1852.

Fourth daughter Emma Eugenia Hall was born on the 21st January, 1854.

Jos. P. Hall was born in Middletown, Conn., on the 4th of Nov. 1809, son of Wm. C. & Olivia C(ooper) Hall.

Virginia Hall Jordan was born on the 4th day of May, 1879, at one o'clock, A. M., and was baptized by the Rev. J(ames) B. Craighill in St. Paul's Church on the 11th Sunday after Trinity, August 24, 1879.

The first child of second marriage Edward Walke Hall was born on the 20th day of February, 1861, at 7 o'clock, P. M.

Catharine Randolph Hall, daughter of Jos. P. Hall, Jr. and Anna (Jones) Hall, born January 11th, 1882.

Deaths.

Second son Joseph John Hall departed this life on the 8th day of Sept. at 6 o'clock, P. M., 1841.

Laura Ann Hall, wife of Jos. P. Hall, departed this life on the 9th day of May, 1856.

Jos. P. Hall departed this life May 14 A. D. 1889 at dawn of day aged 79 years, 6 mos. and 10 days.

Marriages.

Louis Walton Jordan and Emma Eugenia Hall were married the 11th day of July, 1878, by the Rev. J. B. Craighill.

Joseph P. Hall, Jr. and Anna J(ones) Copeland were married in Jackson, N. C., March 11, 1880, by the Rev. Gilbert Higg.

(Bible, Stereotyped by James Conner, New York; Hartford & Son, 1843. Owned by Mrs. Harvey Milton Holland, nee Eloise Walton Jordan.)

****

64

AMOS HARRELL BIBLE.

Jesse E. Harrell and Annie Williamson married April 31, 1889.

Jesse E. Harrell, son of Amos Harrell and Cida his wife, was born Jan. 20, 1852.

Charley L. Harrell, son of Amos Harrell and Cida his wife, was born Dec. 6, 1854.

Junas T. Harrell, son of Amos & Cittia, was born Sept. 1, 1857.

William Charles Harrell, son of Amos and Kittie his wife, was born Dec. 2, 1866.

Amos Harrell, son of Jethro Harrell and Mary, his wife, was born May 10th, 1819.

Amos Harrell died Feb. 25, 1890.

Annie Harrell, wife of Jesse E. Harrell died Feb. 5, 1910.

Marguerite Harrell, daughter of Jesse E. Harrell and Annie Harrell, died Oct. 1, 1908.

Jesse E. Harrell, son of Amos & Kittie Harrell, died Dec. 4, 1925.

Christian Rabey, daughter of Abram Rabey and Nancey his wife, was born June 15, 1826.

Marguerite Harrell, daughter of Jesse E. Harrell and Annie his wife, was born Dec. 7, 1891.

Jesse Amos Harrell, son of Jesse E. Harrell and Annie his wife, was born Feb. 11, 1898.

Christian Harrell, wife of Amos Harrell, died July 30th, 1884.

(Owner: Jesse Amos Harrell. Transcribed: September 1942.)

****

REUBIN HARRELL:
A BOOK OF AGES.

(Page 1)
Rubin Harrell son of John Harrell and Mary Harrell was born February
the 3rd day in the year 1775.

(Page 2)
Elizabeth Warren Daughter of Jesse Warren and Drusilla his wife was
born May the 9th 1774.

Barsha Harrell daughter of Rubin Harrell and his wife Elizabeth was
born December 5th 1801.

Elvy Harrell Son of Rubin Harrell and Elizabeth his wife, born Sept.
8th 1809

(Page 3)
Peggy Harrell Daughter of Reubin Harrell and Elizabeth His wife was
born February 25th 1813

(Page 5)
My Negro Girl Jane was Born May 17th 1821.

(A manuscript booklet formerly owned by Francis Edward Parker).

****

THOMAS AND ISABEL HARRELL BIBLE.

(Inscribed on flyleaf:)   Thomas Harrell his book.
                                 Isabel Harrell her book.

John Harrell, Son of Thomas and Isabel his wife, was born the 4th day
of November, 1750.

Mary Harrell, Daughter of Thomas Harrell and Isabel his wife, was born
the 16th day of December, 1751.

Thomas Harrell, Son of Thomas Harrell and Isabel his wife, was born 21st
day of February, 1753.

Moses Harrell, Son of Thomas Harrell and Isabel his wife, was born the 27th
day of August, 1754.

Elizabeth Harrell, Daughter of Thomas Harrell and Isabel his wife, was born
the 17th day of March, 1756.

Isabel Harrell, Daughter of Thomas Harrell and Isabel his wife, was born
the 19th day of April, 1758.

Rebekah Harrell, Daughter of Thomas Harrell and Isabel his wife, was born the 30th day of September, 1761.

Peninnah Harrell, Daughter of Thomas Harrell and Isabel his wife, was born the 30th day of may, 1763.

Aaron Harrell, son of Thomas Harrell and Isabel his wife, was born the 14th day of January in the year 1766.

Mills Rogers.

Admiral Brinkley, The Son of Jacob Brinkley and Apsley his wife, was born February 22nd day in the year of Our Lord and Saviour 1810.

Charity Stallings, Daughter of Robert Stallings and Peninnah his wife, was born August 10th, 1807.

James Stallings, Son of Robert Stallings and Penninnah his wife, was born February 12th day, 1812.

Peninnah Stallings, Daughter of Robert Stallings and Peninnah, his wife, was born November 20, 1814.

Virginia and Robert Stallings, Daughter and Son and Twins of Robert Stallings and Peninnah his wife, was born February 15th, 1817.

Basheba Norfleet, Daughter of Elisha Norfleet and Martha his wife, was born October 19th, 1807.

Richard T. Rogers, son of James Rogers and Emily his wife, was born March 3rd, 1834.

Mills Rogers, son of James Rogers and Emily his wife, was born 10th June, 1836.

Sarah E. Rogers, Daughter of James Rogers and Emily his wife, was born January 10th, 1838.

Nancy Rogers, Daughter of James Rogers and Emily his wife, was born April 15th , 1839.

Robert U. I. Rogers, Son of James Rogers & Emily his wife, was born Nov. 1839.

James E. Rogers, son of James Rogers and Emily his wife, was born August 18, 1841.

James G. Rogers, son of James Rogers and Emily his wife, was born April 14, 1843.

The Baby was born Sept. 14th, 1844.

Mary F. Rogers, Daughter of James Rogers and Emily his wife, was born Oct. 19th, 1846.

Phillip L. Rogers, the son of James Rogers and ____ his wife, was born Feb. 21st, 1864.

(Bible Printed by Mark Baskett, Printer to the King's Most Excellent Majesty; and by the Assigns of Robert Baskett, London, MDCCLXIII. Former owner: Phillip L. Rogers. Transcribed by Wilbur E. MacClenny, Aug. 15, 1936.)

****

HATTON BIBLE.

John G. H. Hatton was married to Isabella Woodward on the 5th day of February 1835 by the Rev. W. A. Smith.

On the 26th of June 1850 John G. H. Hatton and Sarah Eliza Methaner were married in Petersburg by the Rev. D. J. Daggett.

Mary Hobday Hatton, second child, was born July 19, 1836.

The first child was born 14 Sept. 1835, premature, and died on the 15th, living about 24 hours.

Sarah Howard, their third child, was born the 17th January 1840.

John Frances, fourth child, was born the 13th Sept. 1842.

Julian - fifth child, was born 12th Sept. 1844.

James Goodrich - sixth child was born the 10th October 1846.

Mary Methaner, first child of John G. H. and Sarah E. Hatton, was born the 3rd June 1851.

Margaret Elizabeth - second child, was born Oct. 10, 1853.

68

Mary Hobday, the second child of John G. H. and Isabella Hatton, died 4th
March 1840 - age 3 years - 7 month - 12 days.

Julian, the fifth child, died the 16th July 1845.

Isabella, the wife of Jno. G. H. Hatton, died the 12th October 1842 in the
37th year of her age after a protracted illness of consumption.

(The Bible, found in a Negro church near Suffolk, is now owned by the
descendants of Mrs. William Edward Smith, nee Juliette Riddick Hatton.)

****

JOSEPH HOLLADAY BIBLE.

Joseph Holladay & Elizabeth Charlton were married February 20th 1812.

Colo Joseph Holladay was born the 10 of January 1787.

Elizabeth E. S. Charlton was born the 4th of February 1793.

Francis David Holladay was born June 8th 1817.

Emily Susan Pinner daughter of Dixon Pinner and Emily Pinner born 29th
Feb. 1817.

Alto Francis Holladay son of F. D. Holladay and Emily S. Pinner, his wife,
born 26th June 1844.

Katharine Beverly daughter of A. F. & J. B. Holladay born July 23, 1870.

Deaths

Died 20th of June 1855 Colo Joseph Holladay in the 66 year of his age.

Elizabeth E. S. Holladay died on the 19th of Oct. 1828.

Died on the 3rd day of July 1868 Francis D. Holladay aged 51.

Died the 27th day of October 1900 Emily Susan Holladay aged 83 years
8 mo., wife of Francis D. Holladay.

(The Holy Bible, Stereotyped by James Conner, New York. Robinson and
Franklin, Successors to Leasat, Lord and Co., 1839, Owned by Mrs. John
Copeland Holladay. For a partial genealogy, see Suffolk, p. 93.)

****

HOLLADAY NOTES.

John R. Copeland and Judith A. Hunter his wife were married on Oct. 11, 1836.

Alto Francis Holladay and Judity Beverly Hunter Copeland were married Feb. 16, 1866.

J. Ballentine Riddick and Mary Catharine Copeland were married June 10, 1879.

John Copeland and Mary Saunders were married Oct. 1810.

Edward Beverly Hunter, son of Edward Riddick Hunter and Catharine Hannah, his wife, was born April 3, 1817.

John R. Copeland, son of John Copeland and Mary, his wife, was born Nov. 11, 1811.

Judith Ann Hunter, wife of John R. Copeland and daughter of Edward R. Hunter and Catharine Hannah his wife, was born Feb. 13, 1819.

Mary Catharine Copeland, daughter of John R. Copeland and Judith Ann his wife, was born Feb. 25, 1840.

Judith Beverly Hunter Copeland, daughter of John R. Copeland and Judith Ann, his wife, was born Aug. 16, 1848.

Judith Susan Holladay, daughter of Alto F. Holladay and Judith Beverly Hunter, his wife, was born June 17, 1867.

The infant son of A. F. Holladay and Judith Beverly was born Sept. 10, 1868 and died Oct. 26, 1868.

Katharine Beverly Holladay was born July 23, 1870.

Alto Frank Holladay was born Oct. 19, 1873.

John Copeland Holladay was born July 30, 1875.

Joseph Edward Bridger Holladay was born March 18, 1880.

Beverly Mary Holladay was born May 30, 1891, and died June 23, 1892.

John Copeland died Jan. 29, 1861, aged 81.

Edward B. Hunter died Nov. 26, 1861, aged 76.

E. Beverly Hunter died July 3, 1873.

Mary Copeland mother of John R. Copeland died July 20, 1824.

Joseph Bridger Dorlon died Aug. 1863.

Judith Ann Copeland, wife of John R. Copeland, died June 18, 1880.

J. B. Riddick died Dec. 11, 1887.

John R. Copeland died Oct. 21, 1892, aged 82.

B. B. B. Hunter and Antoinette Stith were married Nov. 5, 1831.

Edward R. Hunter and Sallie Baker were married March 31, 1810.

Edward R. Hunter and Catherine H. Hodges were married June 16, 1816.

Edward R. Hunter and Ann P. Dorlon were married July 2, 1826.

Dr. Edward R. Hunter and Catharine M. Sinclair were married Feb. 25, 1830.

Benjamin Blake Baker Hunter was born Jan. 10, 1811, son of Edward R. Hunter and Sally Hunter.

William Dorlon Hodges was born Jan. 19, 1811.

Mary C. Copeland, daughter of John R. Copeland and Judith Ann, his wife, was born Feb. 25, 1840.

Judith Beverly Hunter, daughter of John R. Copeland and Judith Ann, was born Aug. 16, 1848.

(These Bible entries, copied in 1946, were transcribed by Mrs. Robert H. Pretlow, nee Katharine Beverly Holladay.)

****

AUGUSTUS H. HOLLAND BIBLE.

Augustus H. Holland, son of Job Holland & Patsy, was born Feb. 6, 1801.

William T. Holland, son of A. H. Holland & Anne, his wife, was born April 11, 1828.

Augustus H. Holland, son of the above named parents, was born Jan. 4, 1832.

Cathran Hanah Holland, daughter of the above named parents, was born June 24, 1834.

Zachary Holland, son of the same parents, was born Jan. 27, 1836. Died Feb. 6, 1908.

Augustus H. Holland, son of Job Holland, was married to Ann Winborn, 2d of August, 1825.

James M. C. Luke, son of Isaac V. Luke, was married to Catharine Hannah Holland, daughter of Augustus & Ann Holland, Dec. 16, 1852.

William T. Holland, son of Augustus Holland & Ann Holland, married Sarah Catharine Abra Cross, daughter of Abram & Eliza Cross.

The sons Augustus & Zachary never married. Augustus was killed in war.

(The Bible was owned in 1938 by Miss Novella V. Holland.)

****

LEMUEL CARR HOLLAND BIBLE.

Marriages

On the 25 of May 1836 by Rev. Jacob Keeling Dr Lemuel C. Holland to Miss Catharine B. Woodley.

On the 21 of Nov. 1855 by Rev. Robert D. Woodley Mr Jesse B. Brewer to Miss Elfrida C. Holland.

Dec. 13th 1888 by Rev. George Dana Boardman Annie W. Brewer to W. W. White.

March 10, 1865 by Rev. A. R. Bernard, Geo. W. Lewis to Mrs. Elfrida C. Brewer.

March 1866 by Rev. Mr. Wingfield, G. S. P. Holland to Miss Monimia Pinner.

Sept. 1879 by Rev. Mr. Martin, Mr. G. S. P. Holland to Miss Nettie Hall.

Births

Feb. 24, 1837 A. D. Elfrida Charlotte, daughter of Lemuel C. Holland & Catharine, his wife.

Granville S. P. Holland, son of Catharine & Lemuel, born Dec. 8th, 1838.

Harrison Woodley, son of Leml & Catharine B. Holland, Dec. 30, 1841.

The twin babes of L. C. Holland & Cathe on 5th of March 1843.

Robert Doyne Woodley Holland born Aug. 8, 1846, died Oct. 25, 1857 (son of Lemuel & Catharine Holland).

Born August 18th 1872 Mary Augusta, daughter of Geo. W. & Elfrida C. Lewis.

Oct. 16, 1856, Elfrida Alice Bruce Brewer, daughter of Jesse Brewer & Elfrida, his wife. (Died Dec. 16th, 1936).

Oct. 15, 1857
Sarah Brewer, daughter of Elfrida & Jesse B. Brewer.

Dec. 5, 1859
Annie Woodley, daughter of Elfrida C. & Jesse Bruce Brewer. (Annie Woodley Brewer White died May 13, 1930).

April 17th, 1866
George Holland, son of Geo. W. & Elfrida C. Lewis.

Oct. 19th, 1870
Catharine Seymour, daughter of Geo. W. & Elfrida C. Lewis.

Deaths
Oct. 25, 1857
Rev. Robert D. Woodley, S. J. departed this life at 6 1/2 o'clock P. M.

Little Sarah Brewer departed this life Oct. 15, 1857.

March 26th 1873
Mrs. Catharine B. Holland departed this life in the 59th year of her age, 9 1/2 in the evening.

August 23d 1880 little Lemuel, son of G. S. P. & Nettie Holland.

Elfrida C. Lewis died Oct. 13, 1925, 89th year.

Departed this life Catharine B. wife of Dr. L. C. Holland March 26th 1873, aged about 59.

Departed this life Dr. L. C. Holland Oct. 31st 1878, age 65.

April 11th 1883, George H. Lewis, age 17 - Taken sick March 30th.

Jan. 5th 1896, Col. Geo. W. Lewis, Quincy, Ill., age 69.

Miscellaneous

Born Nov. 6th 1874, Clifford Lewis, son of Geo. W. & Elfrida C. Lewis.

Born Oct. 28th 1867, Annie H. Holland, daughter of G. S. P. & Monimia Holland.

Born Sept. 24, 1881, Linwood Carr, son of G. S. P. Holland & Nettie, his wife.

Born Nov. 25th 1893, Fred B. White, died Dec.

Granville S. P. Holland, Jr., born Apr. 13, 1884.

Jesse B. White, daughter of Annie B. & W. H. White, born Aug. 6th 1890, died April 27th 1892.

W. Harrison White, born April 22nd 1899.

Clifford Lemuel Lewis, died Jan. 25th 1940, age 65.

Catherine Seymour Lewis Crowder died Oct. 2, 1945, at 9:45.

(Bible published by D. & J. Sadlier & Co., 164 Williams St., New York, 1853. Former owner: Dr. Linwood Carr Holland. Transcribed: 1947.)

****

HOWELL BIBLE.

Edward Howell, son of Edward Howell and Sarah his wife, was born the 28th day of April A.D. 1750.

Ann Howell, wife of Edward Howell, was born the 14th day of May A.D. 1768.

Peggy Howell, daugher of Edward Howell and Ann, his wife, was born the 9th day of July A. D. 1790.

Sarah Howell, daughter of Edward Howell and Ann, his wife, was born the 10th day of March A. D. 1792.

Dixon Howell, son of Edward Howell and Ann, his wife, was born the 18th day of June A. D. 1794.

Edward Howell, son of Edward Howell and Ann, his wife, was born the 5th day of June A. D. 1797.

Matilda Ann Howell, daughter of Edward Howell and Ann, his wife, was born the 19th day of September A. D. 1799.

Dempsey Howell, son of Edward Howell and Ann, his wife, was born the 13th day of June A. D. 1802.

John Howell, son of Edward Howell and Ann, his wife, was born the 14th day of September A. D. 1804.

Mildred Howell, daughter of Edward Howell and Ann, his wife, was born the 16th day of May A. D. 1807.

Deaths

Edward Howell departed this life August the 10th day at 3 o'clock in the afternoon in the year A. D. 1817.

Ann Howell departed this life on Thursday morning November 5th A. D. 1828.

	Born	Death
Joseph Freeman	Feb. 22, 1772	Oct. 23rd 1842.
Christine Rawles	Feb. 15, 1778	Oct. 3rd 1843.

Joseph Freeman & Christine Rawles were married Jan. 31st, 1799.

Polly Freeman	Dec. 29th, 1799	Sept. 12, 1842
Nanse Freeman	April 6th, 1806	Nov. 30th, 1885.
Patsey Freeman	Oct. 10th, 1808	Jan. 31st, 1888.
Harriett Freeman	July 10th, 1812	April 6th, 1889.

John Freeman, son of Joseph & Christine Freeman, was born Nov. 28th, 1801, and died November 1st, 1855.

(Transcribed by Wilbur E. MacClenny, and included, in part, in Lee Pretlow Holland's The Hollands and Their Kin, pp 30-31.)

****

EDWARD RIDDICK HUNTER BIBLE.

Marriages

Edward R. Hunter and Sally Baker his wife were married March the 31, 1810.

Edward R. Hunter and Catharine H. Dorlon (Hodges) his wife were married June 16, 1816.

Edward R. Hunter and Ann P. Dorlon his wife were married July 2nd, 1826.

Edward R. Hunter and Catharine M. Sinclair his wife were married on the 25th of February 1830.

John R. Copeland and Judith Ann Hunter his wife were married on the 11th of Oct. 1836.

Births

Edward Riddick Hunter was born the 4th of Nov. A. D. 1786.

Catharine H. Dorlon (Hodges) daughter of John Dorlon and Judith Bridger his wife was born ___.

Edward Beverly Hunter son of Edward R. Hunter and Catharine H. Hunter was born April 3rd 1817.

Judith Ann Hunter daughter of Edward R. Hunter and Catharine H. Hunter was born Feb. 13th 1819.

Judith Beverly Hunter Cope'and daughter of John R. Copeland and Judith Ann his wife was born the 16th of August 1848.

Ann P. Dorlon, daughter of John Dorlon and Judith Bridger was born ____.

Deaths

Sally Hunter, wife of Edward R. Hunter, departed this life 19th of January A. D. 1811.

Catharine Hannah, wife of Edward R. Hunter, departed this life December 2nd 1822.

Ann P. Hunter, wife of Edward R. Hunter, departed this life on the 23d of October 1825.

Catherine M. Hunter, wife of Edward R. Hunter, departed this life at 1/2 after 4 o'clock P. M. of Monday the 15th of August 1842.

Edward R. Hunter died the 26th November 1861, Aged 76 years. (Note: Dr. Edward R. Hunter married four times - two sisters and a first cousin. My great-grandmother was Catharine H. Dorlon (widow Hodges).)

Edward Riddick Hunter born Nov. 9, 1786.

Sally Baker Daughter of Ben. B. B. Hunter and Antoinette Hunter born Jan. 19, 1833. (Note: Benjamin Blake Baker Hunter, son of Edward H. Hunter, went to Texas; his wife nee Antoinette Stith.)

Catharine H(annah) Hodges, daughter of John Dorlon and Judith Bridger, born ___.

Edward Beverly Hunter, son of Edward R. Hunter & Catharine H. Hunter, was born April 3, 1817.

John Dorlon Hunter, son of Edward R. Hunter & Ann P(arker) Dorlon, born March 23, 1827.

Beverly Baker Hunter, son of Benjamin Blake Baker (Hunter) & Caroline his wife, born March 31, 1839.

Sally Hunter, wife of Edward R. Hunter, departed this life Jan. 19, 1811.

Catharine Hannah Hunter, wife of Edward R. Hunter, died Dec. 21, 1822.

Ann Parker Dorlon Hunter, wife of Edward R. Hunter, died Oct. 23, 1828.

John Dorlon Hunter, son of Edward R. Hunter & Ann P., died Nov.9, 1828.

Antoinette Hunter, wife of B. B. B. Hunter, died at Wythe Court House May 3, 1835.

William D. Hodges died Feb. 26, 1840 in the city of Richmond, Delegate in the State Legislature.

Catharine M. Hunter, wife of Edward R. Hunter, died Aug. 15, 1842.

(Bible printed at Cooperstown, N.Y., Sterotyped, printed and published by
H. & E. Phinney, 1831. Owner: Mrs. John Copeland Holladay.)

****

ISAAC HUNTER BIBLE.
Marriages

Isaac Hunter - son of Jacob & Sarah Hill Hunter was married to Sophia Riddick,
June 8, 1785.

Isaac Hunter - son of Jacob & Sarah Hill Hunter was married to Mary Gordon,
daughter of Jacob & Barsha Gordon, Dec. 22, 1796.

Isaac Hunter - son of Jacob & Sarah Hill Hunter was married to Mary Gordon,
daughter of Benjamin & Tamar Copeland Gordon, Oct. 7, 1804.

Mary Elizabeth McCampbell, born Riddick, and Orren Randolph Smith were
married June 10, 1863, in Granville Co., N. C., at the home of Capt. James
Beverly Hunter by Mr. Hodges, Rector of the Episcopal Church at Warrenton.
Witnesses: John Williams, Spotswood Burwell, A. B. Capehart and others.

Willis F. Riddick and Sarah Edna Adeline Hunter were married Dec. 2, 1829.

Willis F. Riddick and Sarah Ann Hunter were married Sept. 9, 1847.

Willis F. Riddick and Adeline Burr Currier were married Nov. 1866.

E. J. H. McCampbell and Mary Elizabeth Riddick were married Feb. 8, 1859.

Births

Jacob Hunter, first son of Isaac & Sophia, was born Oct. 12, 1786.
Edward R. Hunter   was born Aug. 29, 1788.
Isaac R. Hunter   was born Jan. 14, 1791
Sophia Hunter, first daughter of his second wife, was born Oct. 18, 1797.
Armisia Hunter   was born Feb. 1, 1799.
John Omega Hunter   was born Dec. 4, 1802.

Barsha Eliza, by his third wife, was born Aug. 3, 1807.

Jacob Benjamin Hunter   was born July 7, 1812.

Sarah Edna Adeline Hunter   was born July 27, 1814.

Mary Elizabeth Riddick was born April 6, 1831.

Emily Maria Riddick was born Sept. 20, 1848.

Elizabeth Ann Hunter, born Pugh, died March 11, 1887, at Yazoo City, Mississippi.

Isaac Hunter   was born Aug. 29, 1759.

Sophia Hunter   was born Nov. 3, 1768.

Mary Gordon of Jacob   was born Jan. 12, 1772.

Mary Hunter   was born April 13, 1783 (daughter of Benjamin Gordon and his wife Tamar born Copeland).

Sarah Ann Hunter   was born Nov. 28, 1830.

Deaths

Jacob Hunter, my father, died June 8, 1784.

Sarah, My mother, died Nov. 19, 1793.

Leah Parker died Jan. 8, 1806.

Sophia Hunter, my first wife, died Jan. 28, 1791.

Mary Hunter died Dec. 14, 1802.

Jacob Hunter died Oct. 30, 1810.

Barsha E. Hunter died Oct. 22, 1808.

Mary Hunter died Aug. 1, 1838; she was the mother of Sarah E. A. Hunter, wife of Willis F. Riddick.

Jacob Benjamin Hunter died Oct. 10, 1839.

Sarah E. A. Hunter died Dec. 10, 1843.

Willis F. Riddick died Feb. 28, 1871.

Isaac Hunter died Jan. 1816, son of Jacob Hunter & his wife Sarah.

John Omega Hunter, son of Jacob & Mary, died April 29, 1878, in Yazoo City, Miss.

Elizabeth Ann Hunter, born Pugh, died March 11, 1887, in Yazoo City, Miss.

Isaac Henry Hunter, son of John C. Hunter & his wife Elizabeth Ann, born Pugh, died Jan. 12, 1879.

Elizabeth, born Riddick, was born Feb. 14, 1772, married Micajah Riddick and was the mother of 3 sons and 8 daughters. She died on her birthday Feb. 14, 1836, and was buried in the burying ground at Middle Swamp next to her husband.

(Copied by Marshall W. Butt from Miss Jessica Randolph Smith's transcription of the Hunter Bible made in 1925).

****

JOHN STREETER HUNTER BIBLE.
(Excerpts)

Deaths

Nancy Barron Nixon daughter of Riddick Hunter & Nancy his wife departed this life at Elizh City, N. C., 8th June 1840.

John S(treeter) Hunter son of Riddick Hunter and Ann Hunter his wife died on the 11th Sept. 1865, 73 years 2 mos. 8 days.

Births

John S(treeter) Hunter son of Riddick Hunter & Ann his wife was born on the 3rd day of Sept. A.D. 1792.

Marriages

John S(treeter) Hunter, son of Riddick Hunter & Ann his wife, was married to Nancy Jackson daughter of Joab Jackson & Mary his wife, on the 7th day of October A.D. 1813.

80

(The New Testament ... with observations... composed by the Reverend Mr. Ostervald: Evert Duyckinck, John Tiebout, &c., New York, 1813. Owner unknown. Copied from a photostat owned by Fillmore Norfleet.

Note. Nansemond County Land Tax, 1784. "List of Alterations. From whom taken: Edward Riddick. To whom charged: Riddick Hunter. Acres: 1650." Edward Riddick (1735-1783), was the son of Lemuel Riddick (1711-1755.)

****

MATTHIAS JONES BIBLE.
(See Robert Moore Riddick - Matthias Jones Bible)

****

HUGH KELLY FAMILY RECORD.

Data obtained from a

"Sampler made by Margaret G. Kelly at Mrs. Cunningham's School 1818.

Margaret Goodman Kelly, daughter of Hugh and Margaret his wife, was born April 7, 1806.

Hugh Kelly was born November 19, 1756, and was married to Ann King and had the following children:

Elizabeth Kelly was born November 19, 1784 and departed this life.
Ann Kelly was born June 30, 1787.
Johanna Kelly was born August 16, 1790.
George Kelly was born October 2, 1793.
Mary Kelly was born October 2, 1795.

Ann the wife of Hugh Kelly departed this life.

Hugh Kelly was married to Margaret Holland December 16, 1800, who was born December 9th _____ and had the following children:

Hugh H. Kelly was born November 20, 1801.
Charity G. Kelly was born July 16, 1803.
Jacob M. Kelly was born April 12, 1807.
Martha J. Kelly was born February 18, 1809.
Herion W. Kelly was born September 8, 1811.
Eleanor C. Kelly was born November 8, 1813.
Elise K. Kelly was born May 17, 1815.
Frances H. Kelly was born May 21, 1816, and departed this life 1817.

Hugh Kelly departed this life September 16, 1817."

(Lee Pretlow Holland: The Lee Family of Nansemond County, typewritten, 40 pp.)

****

JACOB ELEY KELLY BIBLE.

Marriages

Jacob E. Kelly was married to Lucie E. B. Holladay on the 12th day of Jan. 1859.

Jacob E. Kelly was married to Hattie B. Rives on the 10th day of Sept. 1884.

Elizabeth H. Kelly (and) Ernest E. Goodrich married the 27th of Oct. 1897.

Jacob H. Kelly (and) Mamie Brothers were married Nov. 12th 1890.

Births

Jacob Eley Kelly was born on the 24th day of Feb. 1836.

Lucie Edith Ballard Holladay, wife of Jacob E. Kelly was born 5th day of Oct. 1839.

Jacob Holladay Kelly Son of J. E. & Lucie E. Kelly was born on the 7th day of Nov. 1859.

Lucy Holladay Kelly daughter of Jacob E. & Lucy E. B. Kelly was born 2d of October 1866.

Elizabeth Eley second daughter of Jacob E. & Lucy E. Kelly was born 4th Sept. 1868.

Births

Elizabeth Holladay third daughter of J. E. & Lucy E. Kelly was born 10th April 1870.

Edith H. fourth daughter of J. E. & L. E. Kelly was born 16th July 1873.

Fanny Day & Lydia Day (Twins) daughters of J. E. & L. E. Kelly were born on the 24th May 1876.

82

Joseph Holladay Kelly son of J. E. & L. E. B. Kelly was born on the ____
Feb. 1882.

Hattie Jake Virginia Kelly was born on the 29th day of August 1885, daughter
of J. E. & H. B. Kelly.

Deaths

Elizabeth Eley Kelly departed this life March 13th 1869.

Edith Holladay Kelly departed this life on the 16th October 1874.

Fanny Day Kelly departed this life on the 4th June 1876.

Lydia Day Kelly lived 11 mths.

L. E. B. Kelly the beloved wife of J. E. Kelly departed this life on the
21st day of Feb. 1882.

Joseph Holladay Kelly, son of J. E. & L. E. B. Kelly, departed this life
on the ___ Feb. 1882.

Jacob Eley Kelly departed this life on the 13th day of Jan. 1888.

Elizabeth Holladay Kelly Goodrich wife of Ernest C. Goodrich departed
this life April 8th 1899.

William Joseph Kelly son of Jacob H. & Mamie Kelly died Sept. 23d 1898.

Lyman Rudolph, son of Jacob H. & Mamie Kelly, died Nov. 13, 1902.

Edward Earle died Dec. 28, 1902 (twins).

Virginia Inez daughter of Jacob H. & Mamie Kelly died June 12th 1894.

Mamie B. Kelly departed this life Sept. 5, 1923.

Hugh Day Kelly, son of Jacob Holladay & Mamie B. Kelly departed this
life Dec. 6, 1928.

Hattie B. Rives Kelly departed this life June 10, 1908.

(The Bible, its title page torn out, is owned by Miss Mary Edith Kelly.
Transcribed: 1947).

****

SOLOMON KING BIBLE.

Michael King was born in Old England and Came out of the City of Norwich to Virginia and their Served his time With John Wright in Nansemond County after that he marred with Elizabeth Hiry (indistinct) and Lived in the upper Parrish of Nansemond County on the Southern branch of Nansemond River, &c--and he had by his wife Six Children Viz. Nathan William Michael Henry John & Elizabeth--and their he bought A plantation with Land in the year 1686 and Bult a Large Dwelling hous with Brick and Bought several Negro Slaves and also a larg Copper Still &c. Written by me Solomon King, son of Charles King the Said Charles Was Son of William Which was son of Michael the Older --

Charles King Father of Solomon King Departed this Life January the 15th 1762 --

Mary King Mother of Solomon King Departed this Life February the 2 Day 1762 --

Henry King Uncell to the Said Solomon King Departed this life December the 7 day 1771 --

Mary Hare aunt to the Said Solomon King Departed this life February the 11 Day 1774 --

John Lee Father in Law to the Said Solomon King Departed this life February 9 day 1770 --

Henry King Brother to Solomon King Departed this Life April the 15th Day 1782 --

Bathsheba Porter Daughter of Solomon King Departed this life march 10th, 1789.

(The Bible was published by Alexander Kincaid, His Majesty's Printer, Edinburgh, MDCCLXIX. The record was published in the Va. Mag., Vol. 36, pp. 194-195.)

****

"THE JOURNAL OF ABIGAIL LANGLEY, OF NANSEMOND COUNTY."
(Excerpts)

(Page 1)
Mr. Jones minnister of the loer parrish died July the 29 day in the year 1742 on Saterday an died suddenly.

84

(page 17)
Memo. made by John Granbery in Norfolk 23d June 1812.
Josiah Granbery, second son of Josiah Granbery & Christian his wife
was born 15 day. 1765 married Elizabeth Cowper, who was born in
Nansemond 8 Dec. 1766 & married the 17 Jany. 1784.

their children

Christian	-	16 May 1785 at Suffolk
Louis	-	19 Jany. 1788 at Carolina
William Francis	-	12 Mar. 1790 at Nansemond
Joseph Allen	-	1 Sept. 1792 died 21 Oct. 1799
Grissey	-	3 Nov. 1797
Richd Allen	-	3 Oct. 1802, Norfolk
Mary or Polly	-	20 Apr. 1795
John Gregory	-	27 Aug. 1807 Norfo. County
Elizabeth	-	27 Nov. 1804 Do.

Josiah Granbery the father of the above died decr 12, 1811 & Elizabeth
his wife died 9 March 1812 both buried at their plantation near Halls Mill.

(page 18)
James Granbery was the third son of Josiah & Christian Granbery - was
born   and married Mary Harvey, daughter of Col. Thos Harvey of
Perquimans, on the 31 May 1796 - they had children

born

Mary	23 Nov. 1797 died
Charles	13 Oct. 1800 "
Margaret	18 Apr. 1805
James	died in Edenton Oct. 1804

(page 22)
Josiah Granbery second son of Josiah Granbery was born 15 Augt. 1764
married Elizabeth Cowper who was born in Nansemond 8 Decr 1766, were
married 17 Jany. 1784. -

Their children

Christian G.	born	16 May 1785
Louis	"	19 Jany. 1788
William Francis	"	12 Mar. 1790
Josiah Allen	"	1 Sept. 1792 died. Oct. 1799
Gilby	"	3 Nov. 1797
Richard Allen	"	3 Oct. 1802
Mary or Polly	"	20 Apr. 1795
John Gregory	"	27 Aug. 1807
Betsey	"	27 Nov. 1804 died 1815

Josiah the father of the above died Dec. 12, 1811 at his plantation on Western
Branch Norfo Co. and his widow died at the same place 9 March 1812.

Suffolk burned by the British troops 13 May 1779.

(page 23)
Written in 1806 by John Granbery

Josiah Granbery left Nansemond 21 Oct. 1747 to go & keep store in Chowan
now Gates County for Riddick supposed Col. Leml Riddick - after this he
kept store at the Folly for his own acct., then at the place now called
Sunbury, which he purchased, about 7 miles on the south side of the Virginia
line where John & Polly were born -- about the year 1776, the family moved
to Suffolk; he entered into trade with James Gibson, in Suffolk were born
Josiah & James, - see Family Bible.

John married Susanna B. Stowe of Bermuda 23 Sept. 1789 - lived in Norfolk
from 1790 -

Their Children

Betsey	born 13 April 1791 married Jonas Hastings Aug.1810.
George	" 9 Sept. 1794
Julia	" 17 Jany. 1797
Polly	" 11 Mar. 1793 died Oct. 1804
John Gregory	" Oct. 1788 died 4 Aug. 1799
Caroline	" 3 Sept. 1800
Augusta	" 2 May 1802
Henrietta	" 2 Sept. 1804 died 9 May 1807
Mary	" 6 April 1806
Henry Augustus	" 24 March 1808
John Stowe H.	" 27 Sept. 1811 died 20 Oct. 1814

(page 26)
John Granbery was married to abigail Langley the 26 Day of february 1722/3.

Thomas Granbery son of John Granbery and abigail his wif was born the
twenty fourth day of June 1724.

Mary Granbery daughter of John Gran(bery) and abigail his wife was born the
eighth day of April 1726.

Josiah Granbery son of John Granbery and abigail his wife was born the 14the
day of October 1728.

died Jany. 7, 1814 nearly 88 years old, widow of John Cowper, the father
of Wills John & Robert by a first wife -- died at Suffolk Decr 1772

The father of John Granbery, the writer of the above in the city of Norfolk
July 1815

page parrin born April 1715.

(page 27)
John Granbery son of John Granbery and Abigail his wife was born the third day of October 1730.

William Granbery Son of John Granbery and abigail his wife was born the twenty third day of March 1731/2.

Margaret Granbery daughter of John Granbery and abigail his wife was born the twenty secon day of September 1733

In the year 1733 my dear an loving husband departed this lief on the 25 day of desember

Abigail Granbery

Note, has been married about 10 years, written by John Granbery (1759-1818)

(page 28)
hillary hargroves son of Robert and Abigail his wife was born the 6 day of marc 1736/7

(page 29)
Abigail Langley Hargroves daughter of Robert hargroves and Abigail his wife was born august the twenty day 1738 and died 19 of october 1747.

Margaret hargroves was born September the fifth day 1740 and died the 30 day of october 1740.

hillary hargrove died 2 day of November 1743.

(page 30)
november the 10 day Willies Hargroves was born 1741

bety Jenkins Born July 21 1743 an came to me April 1748

pagge granbery born Octob er the 6 day 1752

John Granbery born november the 1 day 1755

Josiah Granbery born March the 14, 1754
(written across the last three by John Granberry, 1759-1815, "These were the children of John Granbery."

My dear mother departed this lief november 19 day 1738

Abigail Hargroves

(page 31)
My dear father departed this lief the 5 day of October 1747

My father born desember 1654 an died october the 5 day 1747

my mother born august 1660 an died' november the 19 day 1738
Abigail Hargroves

(page 33)
John Granbery the Son of John Granbery was Borne in the year of our Lord
1755, november the 1 day

Peggy Granbery was Born in the Year 1752 October the 6 day

Peggy Granbery was born Octr 6th Day in the year of our Lord &
Christ 1752

(page 34)	(page 35)
The father of William, Wills, John, Robert & Gilby or Guzzel Cowper (written by John Granbery, 1754-1815)	John Cowper departed this life May 22nd 1768
	Abigail Hargroves wife of Robert Hargroves departed this life Feby. 29th 1763.

(page 39)
This John Cowper was the father of William, Wills, John, Robert & Gilby
Cowper - His second wife was Mary Granbery born 8 April 1726 - now
alive, - (my old Aunt Cowper) near Suffolk. -
William Cowper was married to my mother in 1777 or thereabouts she
being the widow Doeber. Abigail Hargroves was the wife of my Grandfather
John Granbery. - They lived (page 39) near Hargroves, now Huttons (could
be read Hattons) Mill, the House was off the road, on the Mill run - this
was the plantation or estate. - It appears that he John Granbery was a planter
& trader - that the farm produced Tobacco in those day - Hogsheads of 400
to 500 pounds - This book my old Aunt Cowper gave to me in 1806. It appears
to be written by my Grandmother Abigail Granbery whose maiden name was
Langley, see page 26. In December 1733 my Grandfather died, - his widow
married Robert Hargroves -- They had children, see page 28. --

John Granbery, born
7 Oct. 1759.

(A photostatic copy of "The Journal of Abigail Langley, of Nansemond County,"
made from the original formerly in the possession of Julian Hastings Granbery,
is in the files of the Virginia Historical Society. See the Chart of the Granbery
Family by Julian Hastings Granbery copies of which are in the Virginia Historical
Society and VSL.)

****

ISAAC LEE BIBLE.

Isaac Lee was born May 21, 1788, married Nancy Barnes April 6, 1808.

Isaac Lee and Mary Holland, daughter of Job Holland and his wife, were married March 23, 1815.

Births

Martha Elizer Lee was born April 1, 1817.

Talitha Ann Lee was born March 1, 1819.

Susannah Lee was born Nov. 18, 1820.

Cherry Lee was born Dec. 14, 1822.

Margaret Ann Rebecca Lee was born Jan. 25, 1825.

Mary Elizabeth Lee was born Nov. 1, 1827.

Richard Henry Lee, son of Isaac and Mary Lee, was born Oct. 15, 1829.

Isaac Holland Lee, son of Isaac and Mary Lee, was born April 23, 1833.

Marcelon Ann Holland, daughter of Hilliard Holland and Martha Elizer, his wife, was born Nov. 19, 1845

Deaths

Talitha Ann Lee died Oct. 17, 1819.

Susannah Lee died May 11, 1826.

Isaac Holland Lee died March 14, 1834.

Mary Lee, wife of Isaac Lee, died Aug. 25, 1835.

Richard H. Lee died Oct. 10, 1860.

Mary E. Norfleet died Oct. 4, 1882.

Isaac Lee died Oct. 1, 1869.

John Norfleet died May 18, 1895.

Mamie V. Rogers Norfleet, wife of R. C. Norfleet, was the daughter of Richard T. Rogers and his wife Almira Savage, daughter of Herman Savage.

Richard R. Rogers, was the son of James Rogers and his wife Emily, and he was born March 3, 1834.

(The record in this Bible, formerly owned by R. C. Norfleet, was transcribed in 1928.)

****

McCLENNY BIBLE.

William D. McClenny, son of Elijah and Polly McClenny was born July 3rd, 1798.

Judith Y. McClenny, daughter of Elijah and Polly McClenny was born March 5th, 1802.

Stephen G. McClenny, son of James and Polly McClenny, was born Decem. 21st, 1805.

James M. McClenny, son of James and Polly McClenny was born Feb. 25th, 1815.

William Stephen McClenny, son of James M. and Caroline McClenny, was born March 4th, 1837.

Lucy Ann Amelia McClenny, daughter of James M. and Caroline McClenny, was born June 15th, 1839.

Richard Henry McClenny, son of James M. and Caroline McClenny, was born Septm. 11th, 1841.

Judith Caroline McClenny, daughter of James M. and Caroline McClenny, was born January 25th, 1844.

Thomas Alphonso McClenny, son of James M. and Caroline McClenny, was born Dec. 12th, 1845.

James Alva McClenny, son of James M. and Caroline McClenny, was born March 9th, 1848.

John David McClenny, son of James M. and Caroline McClenny, was born October 6th, 1850.

Robert Edwin McClenny, son of James M. and Caroline McClenny, was born February 14th, 1855.

Was married on the 18th Decem. 1835, James M. McClenny to Eliza
Caroline Clayton, daughter of James and Amelia Clayton.

Eliza C. McClenny the wife of James M. McClenny departed this life June 3rd,
1870.

Lucy Ann Bradshaw, wife of Willis Bradshaw, departed this life December
the 29th, 1860.

James M. McClenny, the son of James and Polly McClenny, died the 12th
of October, 1881.

Mary Deans, daughter of Daniel and Judith Deans, was born April 1st, 1775,
and departed this life May 30th, 1859.

(This record was copied by Wilbur E. McClenny, Nov. 2, 1934, from a paper
in the possession of Mrs. A. L. Rawls.)

****

MILLS ROSS MINTON BIBLE
(Excerpts)

Marriages
Mills R(oss) Minton and Sarah Jane Campbell were married the 16th of
December 1852.

Births

Mills R. Minton was born 19th of January 1829, the son of John Minton and
Mary E., his wife.

Sarah J. Campbell was born 28th of February 1832, the daughter of William
Campbell and Eliza Jones, his wife.

Deaths

John Minton departed this life Tuesday Morning three o'clock Oct. 18th 1864
in the 78th year of his age.

Mrs. Eliza J. Minton departed this life Saturday evening half after six o'clock
September 15th 1866 in the 54th year of her age.

Mrs. Sallie Jane Minton wife of Mills R. Minton departed this life near
Knoxville, Tenn., en route to New Orleans, March 18th 1885, of heart
disease in the 53rd year of her age.

(Holy Bible, Jesper Harding, No. 57, S. Third St., Philadelphia, 1854.
Formerly owned by Mrs. Frank S. Bunkley.)

****

THOMAS MINTON BIBLE.

Benjamin Minton, son of Thomas (and) Martha his wife was born Jan. 12th
1711/12 and departed this life on Sunday the 3rd of April A.D. 1774, being
Easter Sunday about midnight.

Martha Minton, wife of the above Benjamin was born March 31st A.D.
1713/14, and departed this life Nov. 22, 1762.

Thomas Minton, son of Benjamin & Martha his wife, was born Sept. 26th,
1734.

Elizabeth Minton, daughter of Benjamin & Martha, his wife, was born May
20, 1741.

Mills Minton, my (grand-father) son of the above was born April 21,
1750, and died Dec. 28, 1815.

Martha Minton, daughter of Benjamin & Martha, his wife, was born 15th
Sept., 1753.

Mills Minton was married to Elizabeth Shepherd, July 22, 1788.

William Minton, son of Mills Minton and Elizabeth his wife was born Sept.
7th, 1789.

Martha Minton, daughter of Mills Minton & Elizabeth his wife was born
Feb. 27, A.D., 1791.

Elizabeth Minton (my mother) daughter of Mills Minton and Elizabeth his
wife, was born Feb. 26, 1793.

John Minton, son of Mills Minton & Elizabeth his wife was born June 4th,
1795.

Shepherd Minton, son of Mills Minton and Elizabeth his wife was born Nov.
4th A.D., 1796.

Thursday Minton, daughter of Mills Minton and Elizabeth his wife was
born Oct. 25, A.D., 1799.

Elizabeth Minton (my Grandmother), wife of Mills Minton departed this life Oct. 22nd, A.D., 1803.

Elizabeth Browne, daughter of Mills Minton & Elizabeth his wife (and wife of Dr. Samuel Browne) departed this life the 14th day of September A.D., 1822. (Buried at Mintonsville, Va.)

Dr. Samuel Browne, son of Edward Browne and Ann Knott, his wife was born Monday 1st day of Dec. 1788, died Jan. 3, 1829, A.D. (Buried at Mintonsville, Va.)

Dr. Elvington Knott Browne, son of Edward Browne and Ann Knott, his wife, was born Tuesday the 25th day of Oct. 1793.

John Minton, son of Mills Minton & Elizabeth his wife, died March 31, 1830. (Buried at Mintonsville, Va.)

(Copied in 1945 by Mrs. Henry Alvin Rawles, nee Virginia Browne Riddick, from the Minton Bible record contained in the Bible of James Samuel Browne owned by her.)

****

JOHN MURDAUGH BIBLE.

(677)
Family Record.

Marriages.

John Murdaugh son of James & Mary Murdaugh was married to Ann Jordan daughter of Robert and Elizabeth Jordan the 6th day of June 1816.

Jos. P. Hall Son of Wm & Olive Hall was married to Laura Ann Murdaugh daughter of Ann and John Murdaugh the 16th day of February 1859.

(678)
Family Record.

Births.

Mary Eliza Murdaugh daughter of John and Ann Murdaugh was born on the twenty ninth day of March 1818 between 9 & 10 o'clock A.M.

Ann Jordan Murdaugh, daughter of John and Ann Murdaugh, was born on the thirty first day of March 1819 between 11 & 12 o'clock, P. M.

Laura Ann Murdaugh, daughter of John & Ann Murdaugh, was born on the 17th day of June 1820, about six o'clock, A. M.

Martha Jordan Murdaugh, daughter of John & Ann Murdaugh, was born on the 22nd day of September, between 5 & 6 o'clock A. M. , 1822.

(679)
Family Record.

Births.

Jerusha Walke Murdaugh, daughter of John & Ann Murdaugh, was born on the 15 day of March 1824 between 7 & 8 o'clock A. M.

Virginia Washington Murdaugh, daughter of John & Ann Murdaugh, was born on the 4 day of April 1829 between 7 & 8 o'clock A. M.

Deaths.

Ann Jordan Murdaugh, daughter of John and Ann Murdaugh, departed this life on the twelfth day of August 1819, between ten and elven o'clock, P. M.

Doctr John Murdaugh departed this life the 14th day of January 1830 between 9 & 10 o'clock, A. M. I can with truth say he was a tender & affectionate husband, a too fond & indulgent parent & a sincere friend.

Virginia Washington Murdaugh, daughter of John & Ann Murdaugh, departed this life on the 11th of September 1830 between 3 & 4 o'clock, A. M.

(680)
Family Record.

Deaths.

Departed this life in the 71st year of his age Mr Wm. Sumner at a quarter past 12 o'clock at night on the 7th November 1865. (He) was confined only about a week with pneumonia. Ah how uncertain is human life. Little did I think I should be deprived of my companion in life so soon but he is gone to rest. He died a Christian perfectly resigned.

Departed this life in the 74th year of her age Ann Sumner at 10 min. of 4 o'clock on the afternoon of July 22nd 1873. (She) was confined to her bed 3 1/2 months of pulmonary comsumption. Never have I seen such a patient sufferer; perfectly resigned to the will of the Master. She was only waiting this call. Oh, my precious loved ones gone before me, but I trust I shall meet them again when my pilgramage on this troublous journey is ended, and with songs of joy to greet them where no farewell tear is shed.

(The Bible record of Dr. John Murdaugh consists of four numbered pages taken from the Bible and inserted in the Bible of Joseph Patton Hall, Sr., now owned by Mrs. Harvey M. Holland, nee Eloise Walton Jordan.)

****

CORDALL NORFLEET BIBLE.

Joseph Norfleet son of Cordall and Mary Norfleet was born the 13th October 1772.

Elizabeth Norfleet was born 20th August 1774.

John Norfleet was born the 20th Sept. 1776.

Sarah Norfleet was born the 12th Sept. 1780.

Cordall Norfleet died (no date).

James Gee and Mary Norfleet was married 18th Ma(torn edge) 1794.

James Henry Gee son of James and Mary his wife was born the 13th June 1795. Ob. 30th Sept. 1795.

William Henry Gee was born 18th April 1797.

Lovinia N. Gee was born 21st August 1798.

Sarah Jones formerly Norfleet died 22nd Sept. 1798.

John Norfleet died the 14th July 1798.

Lovinia N. Gee died 30th Sept. 1798.

Mary Gee, wife of James Gee, died the 9th November 181_ (torn off).

William N. Blunt and Elizabeth Norfleet was marred the 24 of November 1790.

Mary Wilkerson Blunt daughter of Wm. and Elizabeth Blunt was born 7th of Sept. 1791.

Ann Gilliam Blunt was born 23rd Jan. 1793.

Sarah Norfleet Blunt was born 19th Jan. 1795.

Louisa Rebecceh Blunt was born 8th July 1796.

Eliza Norfleet Blunt was born 14th April 1798.

John Norfleet Blunt was born 5th March 1800.

Martha Priscilla Blunt was born 5th March 1802.

William Cordall Blunt was born 22nd July 1804.

Sarah Norfleet Blunt died 24th Aug. 1807.

William Blunt, Sen., died 27th April 1807.

William Blunt, Jun., died 17th Nov. 1807.

Elizabeth Johnston formerly Blunt died 6th March 1813.

Nathaniel Wilkerson and Ann G. Blunt was married 18th January 1810.

John Wilkerson son of Nathaniel and Ann G., his wife, was born 17th January 1811.

Nathaniel Wilkerson was born the 28th July 1813.

Nathaniel Wilkerson, Sen., died 15th May 1813.

Nathaniel Wilkerson, Jun., died 18th Jan. 1814.

John Wilkerson died 13th Sept. 1814.

Thomas Ridley and Ann G. Wilkerson was married 24th July 1816.

(Va. Mag., Vol. 37, pp. 67-68. For further genealogy, see the case of Blunt & al. v. Gee & al., Munford's Reports, Vol. 5, pp. 481-531.)

****

96

ELISHA NORFLEET BIBLE.

Elisha Norfleet was born Nov. 15, 1800, in Nansemond County, and died December 25, 1869. He married twice: (1) Dec. 30, 1824, Sarah Ann Lassiter (1804-1850), daughter of Jason and Elizabeth Lassiter, and (2) Nov. 20, 1851, Sarah Elizabeth Riddick (1833-1910), daughter of Jethro Riddick (1803-1874), and his wife Elizabeth Vaughan (1806-1880).

By his two wives Elisha Norfleet had issue twenty-one children. Hamlin Lassiter (1836-1928), of Brazil, Elisha Adolphus (1842-1867), and Margaret Jennette (1845-1865) were the surviving children of the first marriage. By the second marriage, he had issue, surviving: Alida (1852-1899), Sarah Katherine (1858-1941), Annie Riddick (1860-1948), Robert Jethro (1866-1945), John Ballentine (1866-1955), and Elizabeth Elisha (1870-1915).

A transcription of the entire Bible record, together with a genealogy, will be found in Elisha Norfleet, 2-5, 39-44.

****

JOHN AND ELIZABETH RIDDICK NORFLEET BIBLE.

(John) Norfleet, son of John Norfleet and his wife was born July 21st 1699.

Elizabeth Riddick Daughter of Abraham and Pleasant Riddick born April 5, 1710.

John Norfleet and Elizabeth Riddick was married May 28 Day in the year 1727.

Abraham Norfleet son of John and Elizabeth Norfleet was born Aug. 28th in the year 1728.

.... Norfleet was born Oct. 30, 1729

Pleasant Norfleet was born Aug. 14, 1732.

.... Norfleet was born March 18, 1734.

Esther Norfleet was born Jan. 13, 1736.

.... Norfleet was born June 30 (?), 1737.

.... Norfleet was born May 30, 1739.

.... Norfleet was born May 19, 1741.

.... Norfleet was born Aug. 17, 1743.

.... Norfleet was born Oct. (?) 6, 1745.

.... Norfleet was born Aug. 23, 1747.

.... Norfleet was born March 28, 1751.

.... & Esther Norfleet were Baptized Sept. 26, 1753.

.... Baptized Dec. 22, 1753.

(This greatly weathered and mutilated Bible, found in a barn on a farm once owned by Abram Norfleet, 1776-1827, near Box Elder, Nansemond Co., was formerly owned by Mrs. John Eppes Martin, nee Virginia Jenkins. The entries given are all that are legible.

In the Gates County, N. C. Settlement of Estates (1780-1790; N. C. Historical Commission, Raleigh) is an order of the court dated Feb. 18, 1784, dividing the estate of John and Elizabeth (Riddick) Norfleet, naming eleven children and restricting sale to each other. An inventory of the estate of Elizabeth (Riddick) Norfleet is dated May 16, 1784. The Gates County Recorder's Office has deeds from eight of the children each conveying his allotted inheritance. These documents reveal the eleven children:

1. Abraham Norfleet (b. Aug. 28, 1728; will dated Oct. 25, 1784, but not probated), of Chowan Co., N. C. He m. Sarah Lewis, and had issue: 1. Isaac (who sold to Jacob Gordon, Feb. 3, 1808, 21 acres "in the White Marsh," Gates Co. "being the same land bequeathed to Isaac Norfleet by the last will & Testament of his father Abm Norfleet." Gates Co. Deed, Vol. 7, p. 135); 2. Elisha; 3. Benjamin; 4. Abraham; 5. Mary; 6. Sarah; 7. Elizabeth.

2. John Norfleet, of Nansemond Co., married Judith ___, and with her conveyed by Gates Co. deed dated Jan 10, 1780, to Jacob Gordon, of Gates Co., 20 acres, part of the estate of John and Elizabeth Norfleet, Gates Co. Deed, Vol. I. Issue: Abram Norfleet (1776-1827), on whose Nansemond County farm the Bible was found. He married Elizabeth Ashburn. For their descendants see, Nettie Hale Rand: Hale, Strong and Allied Families.

3. James Norfleet, of Nansemond Co. (patented 537 acres in Nansemond Co., 1763, Vol. 35, p. 109), married his cousin Philisia Norfleet. Their son John Norfleet, of Northampton Co., N. C., on Jan. 6, 1787, conveyed his father's share of 20 acres to Elisha Darden, of Southampton Co., Va. (Gates, Co. Deed, Vol. I, p. 293; Ibid, Vol. 2, p. 261).

4. Hezekiah Norfleet, of Nansemond Co., married Mary ____, and with her conveyed to Jacob Gordon, of Gates Co., by deed dated Feb. 2, 1786, 20 acres "lying on the ninth lot" (Ibid, Vol. I, p. 185). Issue: 1. Bathsheba, m. Arthur Jones, of Nansemond Co.; 2. John, to whom his father Hezekiah Norfleet gave, Feb. 1, 1800, by deed of gift, 123 acres in Nansemond Co. (see mss. in Riddick Papers, Va. State Library).

5. Elisha Norfleet (d. unmarried), of Gates Co., conveyed to Jacob Gordon, by deed dated May 19, 1794, 21 acres in Gates County "Known by the name of Island and White Oake Spring Marsh, being the fifth lot in a Division of a tract of land patented by John Norfleet," (Ibid, Vol. 3, p. 167). He also conveyed, Nov. 13, 1797, to Kinchen Norfleet, his nephew, a tract of marsh land "near the Orepeak Swamp, being part of a tract formerly Belonging to John Norfleet decd and by him given to his Eleven children" by will "which tract is the Eight, Ninth, Tenth and Eleventh part" according to the division (Ibid, Vol. 3).

6. Jacob Norfleet (will dated Chowan Co., Dec. 12, 1778, prob. Aug. 1780, Vol. I, pp. 7-8), m. Elizabeth _____ (see "Account of Sales of Estate of Jacob and Elizabeth Norfleet, Dec. 15, 1790"). Issue: 1. Kinchin; 2. Ester; 3. Elizabeth; 4. Pleasant Lawrence; 5. Mourning.

7. Pleasant Norfleet (b. March 18, 1734), m. John Twine, of Perquimans Co., N. C. (his will dated Gates Co., May 13, 1781, prob. April 24, 1784), the two conveying to Elisha Norfleet, of Gates Co., by deed dated Feb. 5, 1783, 21 acres, "Being the fifth lot: (Gates Co., Record A., No. 98).

8. Ester Norfleet (b. Jan. 13, 1736), m. James Winborn, of Nansemond Co., and with him conveyed 21 acres ("the fourth Division"), in Gates Co., to Jethro Ballard, of Gates Co., by deed dated Jan. 19, 1782. (Ibid. Vol. 4, p. 304).

9. Elizabeth Norfleet, concerning whom no record is available. However, a John Baker and Nancy, his wife, of Gates Co. conveyed to Elisha Norfleet, 21 acres "being the eighth lot of the division of John and Elizabeth Norfleet" (Ibid, Vol. 2, p. 182). Since Elizabeth Norfleet was the only daughter not married at the time of the division in 1784, it is possible that she and "Nancy Baker" are one and the same.)

10. Bathsheba Norfleet married Jacob Gordon, of Gates Co. (his will, Gates Co., dated Sept. 22, 1817, prob. Feb. Court, 1820, abstract in N. C. Hist. and Gen. Register, Vol. 2, p. 50), who eventually sold the first, fifth, and sixth lots in the division to Kinchin Norfleet (Gates Co. Deeds, Vol. 4, p. 114).

11. Mary Norfleet married John Ellis (Gates Co. will dated Nov. 8, 1810, prob. Feb. Court, 1811, abstract in N. C. Hist. and Gen. Register, Vol. 2, p. 47), and had issue: 1. Marmaduke Norfleet Ellis, 2, Sarah Norfleet Ellis; 3. Elizabeth Riddick Ellis.

For further information concerning this family see, Stuart H. Hill, The Hill Family, of Bertie Co., &c., the Norfleet section being in Vol. 2, pp. 221-263, and John Bennett Boddie, Southside Virginia Families, Vol. I, pp. 330-340).

****

JOSEPH NORFLEET BIBLE.

John Norfleet, son of Joseph Norfleet and Nancy his wife, was born Jan. 15, 1783.

Polly Rawls, daughter of John Rawls and Mary his wife, was born May 1, 1788.

(Issue of John Norfleet and his wife Polly Rawls)

Ann Norfleet, daughter of John Norfleet and Polly his wife, was born Jan. 10th, 1808.

Jos. Norfleet, son of John Norfleet and Polly his wife, was born Jan. 24, 1810.

Mary Ann Norfleet, daughter of John Norfleet and Polly his wife, was born Apr. 25, 1812.

Emaline Norfleet, daughter of John Norfleet and Polly his wife, was born March 5, 1814.

Jeremiah Norfleet, son of John Norfleet and Polly his wife, was born April 8, 1816.

John Norfleet, son of John Norfleet and Polly his wife, was born Dec. 29, 1817.

James Nelson Norfleet, son of John Norfleet and Polly his wife, was born Dec. 16, 1819.

Margaret Susan Norfleet, daughter of John Norfleet and Polly his wife, was born Aug. 27, 1822.

Richard G. Norfleet, son of John Norfleet and Polly his wife, was born April 14 1825.

Justin R. Norfleet, son of John Norfleet and Polly his wife, was born Oct. 21, 1826.

John Norfleet and Polly his wife were married April 1, 1807.

Polly Norfleet, wife of John Norfleet, died May 11, 1837.

Mary Ann Norfleet, daughter of John Norfleet and Polly his wife, was married to Robt. Rawls, April 22, 1830.

Ann Norfleet, daughter of John Norfleet and Polly his wife, was married to Jethro Sumner, June 8, 1824.

Emeline Norfleet, daughter of John Norfleet and Polly his wife, was married to Samuel Ethridge, Sept. 10, 1833.

Jeremiah Norfleet and Matilda Jane Darden were married Jan. 30, 1838.

John Norfleet and Margaret Lee were married May 6, 1841.

(The Bible was formerly owned by Wilbur E. McClenny.)

****

NATHANIEL NORFLEET I (RECORD)

Nathaniel Norfleet (1780-1836) married Priscilla Milner (1780-1835) Jan. 23, 1800, in Louisburg, N. C. Edward (Norfleet), only brother, died 5-26-1806, in Nansemond County, Va., age 37 years 8 months. Jacobina Milner died 7-28-1827.

Norfleet-Milner issue in order of age:

Sophia Norfleet, 1800-1856, married John G. Willson, of Louisburg, N.C.

Jacobina Norfleet, 1802-1858, married Randolph Barksdale.

James L. Norfleet, 1804-1842, married Ursula McNeile.

Edward W. Norfleet, 1805-1878, married Elizabeth Read, of Rutherford, Tenn.

Thomas M. Norfleet, 1807-1835, married Ann Berman, of Rutherford, Tenn.

Maramduke Norfleet, 1809-1838, married Mary C. Roan, of Caswell Co., N. C.

John H. Norfleet, 1813-1844, married Susan Verell, of Caswell Co., N. C.

Albert Allen Norfleet, 1814 - ? (no record).

Medicus Norfleet, 1816- ? (no record).

Nathaniel Norfleet, 1818-1844 (no record).

(The above "are the recordings of the old Norfleet family Bible, whi ch was found in our family by me last summer while visiting relatives in the east. ... This has the dates of birth and death as well as the dates of marriages, also the names of their children and birth dates. ... My grandfather Nathaniel Willson, oldest of seven children of John and Sophia, 1822-1902, was a Baptist minister, and this family came to Marshall Co., Miss.ı Sophia buried in Chulahoma, Miss., but no mention is made of John. " Quoted from a letter dated Feb. 14, 1950 from Milton Barksdale, Fullerton, California, to Fillmore Norfleet.
  Notes from the Raleigh Register: Issue of July 19, 1836, "Marriage Notice. John H. Norfleet to Susan M. Verrell, Person Co., June 6. " Ibid, issue of Oct. 13,, 1835, "Death Notice. Died. Dr. Thomas Norfleet, of Person Co., in Sept. Rutherford Co., Tenn. "

****

NATHANIEL NORFLEET (II) BIBLE.

Nathaniel Norfleet and Mary Ann Benn were married on 18th of Nov. 1819.

Nathaniel Norfleet and Joanna Darden were married Aug. the 29, 1822.

Nathaniel Norfleet and Sophia Ann Riddick were married on Tuesday the 4 day of May 1841.

Joseph Henry Yates and Sophia Ann Norfleet, 2nd daughter of Wilson and Clara Norfleet, were married Jan. 20, 1897, at Suffolk, Va.

Edward Norfleet and Jane his wife was married May 27th 1790.

Edward T. Allen and Ann his wife was married July 18th, 1807.

Wilson Norfleet and Susan Clara Hunter were married 12th Jan. 1873.

Lewis Kemper Kirby and Julia Riddick Norfleet were married December 19th, 1901, at Suffolk, Va., 1st daughter of Wilson and Clara Norfleet.

Ann Norfleet, daughter of Edward and Jane, was born March 26th, 1791.

Nathaniel Norfleet, son of the above, was born Nov. 14, 1792.

Thomas Norfleet, son of the same, was born Aug. 25th, 1794.

Jane Norfleet, daughter of the same, was born June 5th, 1795.

Mary Norfleet was born Jan. 19th, 1798.

John C. Norfleet was born Jan. 15th, 1800.

Wilson Norfleet was born Dec. 25th, 1801.

Julia Norfleet was born Aug. 5th, 1806.

Belson Jordan, the son of Belson and Jane Jordan, half brother of the above named, was born Oct. the 7, 1808.

Horatio Gates Norfleet, the son of Edward and Jane Norfleet, was born Oct. 7th, 1803.

Nathaniel Norfleet, son of Edward and Jane Norfleet, was born 14th Nov. 1792.

Mary Ann Benn, the wife of Nathaniel Norfleet, was born Nov. 24th, 1798.

Stella M. Allen, daughter of Edward and Ann, was born the 31 May, 1810.

Edward N. Allen, the son of Edward and Ann, was born April the 20, 1813.

Edward J. Allen, the son of Edward and Ann, was born March 20th, 1815.

James W. Allen, the son of Edward & Ann, was born November 16, 1817.

Wilson Norfleet, son of Nathaniel Norfleet, Sr., and Sophia Ann, his wife, was born Nov. 18th, 1849.

Maria Louisa Norfleet, daughter of Nathaniel Norfleet, Sr., and Sophia Ann, his wife, was born July 17th A.D., 1846.

Mary Jane Norfleet, the daughter of Nathaniel and Joanna Norfleet, was born June 10th, 1823.

Janette Norfleet, the daughter of Nathaniel and Joanna Norfleet, was born Wednesday the 15th of April,, 1825.

Nathaniel G. Norfleet, the son of Nathaniel and Joanna Norfleet, was born Thursday the 21 day of Dec. 1826.

Margaret Jane Norfleet, the daughter of Nathaniel and Joanna, was born Aug. 31, the day Thursday1828.

Robert E. Norfleet, the son of Nathaniel and Sophia Ann Norfleet, was born the 30 day of Sept. 1843.

Mary Louisa Norfleet, daughter of Nathaniel and Sophia Ann, was born July 17, 1846.

Mary Ann Norfleet, the wife of Nathaniel Norfleet, departed this life on Saturday morning the 30th of September, 1820.

Mary Jame Norfleet, the daughter of Nathaniel and Joanna Norfleet, departed this life July the 23, 1824.

Margaret Ann Darden, the daughter of Elijah and Joanna Darden, departed this life Sept. 9th, 1824.

Joanna Norfleet, the companion of Nathaniel Norfleet, departed this life Friday morning the 6 day of January, 1837.

Nathaniel Norfleet, Sr., departed this life on Monday the 27th day of June A.D. 1853, at an early hour in the morning age 61 years.

Jane Mizzell departed this life Sept. 7th 1846.

R. E. Norfleet (Uncle Bob) died Sept. 24, 1908.

Wilson Norfleet died Sept. 14, 1926, age 78.

Clara Hunter Norfleet, his wife, died on the 8th of April, 1921, age 74.

Edward Norfleet departed this life May 26, 1806.

Jane Norfleet, his wife, departed this life October 19th 1808.

Mary Norfleet departed this life October 8th 1799.

John C. Norfleet departed this life Sept. 7th 1803.

Horatio Gates Norfleet departed this life August 1804.

Thomas Norfleet departed this life Oct. 22, 1807.

Edward T. Allen departed this life 14th April 1819.

Wilson A. Norfleet, the son of Edward and Jane, departed this life the 4th day of May, 1828.

Ann Hargraves (Norfleet), sister to the above named and wife of Edward T. Allen, departed this life on Thursday the 8 of Sept. 1842.

Lemuel R. Hunter was married to Julia Parker the 1st day of January 1829.

Wilson Norfleet was married to S. Clara Hunter the 12th January, 1873.

Walter Scott Hunter was married to Lucy J. Jackson the ____June, 1873.

Mark W. Smith was married to Julia A. Hunter Oct. 31st 1876.

Julia N. Norfleet, born Oct. 28, 1873.

Sophia A. Norfleet, born Mar. 17, 1876.

Lemuel H. Norfleet, born Feb. 15, 1879.

Robert E. Norfleet, born June 26, 1883.

Willard W. Norfleet, born Feb. 7, 1886.

Alvah Norfleet, born Oct. 10th 1888.

Nathaniel Norfleet, born Oct. 25th 1881.

Nathaniel Norfleet, 2nd son of Wilson and Clara, his wife, died Nov. 13, 1881.

Mary E, Norfleet, daughter of Nathaniel G. and Mary E. Norfleet, married
Dec. 5, 1883, Elbridge G. B. Dumville, son of Benjamin B. and Sarah
Dumville.

(The Bible was formerly owned by Mrs. Lewis Kemper Kirby, nee Julia
Riddick Norfleet. The copy of the record was made by Wilbur E. McClenny.)

****

THOMAS NORFLEET BIBLE.

Thomas Norfleet, the son of Abram and Lottie (Duke) Norfleet, was
born in Nansemond County, Feb. 14, 1824, and died in Washington, D. C.,
March 4, 1889. On Nov. 14, 1848, he married in Washington, Susanna Dawson
(1821-Nov. 5, 1889), daughter of Hugh Dawson (born in Musselborough,
Scotland) and Ann Rawline, his wife, and widow of Thomas Williams (d. Aug.
1844, in Washington, D. C.). The children of Thomas and Susanna (Dawson)
Norfleet were: 1. Lottie Anne Norfleet (1851-1915), m. 1869, George Millard
Fillmore (issue surviving: Susie Juliette (1873-1914), m. Guy William Arthur
Camp; 2. Lottie Norfleet (1875-1945), m. Robert Jethro Norfleet; 3. Edward
Valentine (b. 1885), m Ina Griffin; 2. Mildred Norfleet (1853-1927), m. 1884,
Horace V. Bisbee; and 3. Margaret Jane Norfleet (1856-1931), m., 1874, John
Kunkle Robinson.

A transcript of the entire Bible record will be found in Elisha Norfleet,
pp. 10-11.

****

WILSON NORFLEET BIBLE.

Married in Suffolk on Thursday, 16th day of November, 1843, by the Rev.
Allen R. Bernard, Wilson Norfleet to Miss Caroline Virginia McGuire.

Wilson Norfleet, son of Abram and Elizabeth Norfleet, was born the 10th day
of May in the year of our Lord 1819,

Caroline Virginia McGuire, daughter of James and Emily McGuire, was born
the 6th day of December in the year of our Lord 1826 and Baptised in July by Dr.
Waller.

Virginia Wilson Norfleet was born the 29th day of September in the year of
our Lord 1844, and Baptised by the Rev. Allen R. Bernard, 1845.

Emily Riddick Norfleet, daughter of Wilson and Caroline Virginia Norfleet,
was born 26th June in the year of our Lord 1847 and Baptised by the Rev.
Allen R. Bernard, 1848.

Willie Anna Norfleet, daughter of Wilson and Caroline Virginia Norfleet, was born the 16th day of February 1850, in the year of our Lord, and Baptised by the Rev. William J. Norfleet in 1851.

Emily Riddick Norfleet, daughter of Wilson and Caroline Virginia Norfleet, was born the 22nd day of March, 1852 and Baptised by the Rev. ___ _____.

Cornelius Riddick Norfleet, son of Wilson and Caroline Virginia Norfleet, was born the 1st day of July 1854, in the year of our Lord, and Baptised by the Rev. James A. Riddick.

Lizzie Fletcher Norfleet, daughter of Wilson and Caroline Virginia Norfleet, was born the 10th of September 1856, and Baptised by Rev. E. W. Peterson.

Eddie Alston Norfleet, son of Wilson and Caroline Virginia Norfleet, was born the 20th November in the year of our Lord 1859.

Pattie Louise Norfleet, daughter of Wilson and Caroline Virginia Norfleet, was born 22nd March in the year of our Lord, 1862.

Son -- unnamed, born 6th Oct., 1864.

Emily Riddick Norfleet, daughter of Wilson and Caroline Virginia Norfleet, departed this life the 6st day of June 1857.

Cornelius Riddick Norfleet departed this life 8th day of October, 1856.

Willie Anna Norfleet departed this life 7th of August, 1864.

(The record in the Bible, formerly owned by Miss Lillian Gertrude Norfleet, was copied in 1951.)

****

DAVID PARKER BIBLE.

David Parker was born June 2nd, 1782.

Jennett (Carter) Parker, his wife, was born ___, 1791.

Mary Eliza Parker, daughter of David and Jennett Parker, was born April 1st, 1808.

Lazarus Parker, son of David and Jennett Parker, was born November 3rd, 1809.

Martha Amanda Parker, daughter of David & Jennett Parker, was born May 5th, 1811.

Dawson C. Parker, son of David & Jennett Parker, was born December 24th, 1812.

Elizabeth Parker, daughter of David and Jennett Parker, was born November 19th, 1814.

Jennett Parker, daughter of David and Jennett Parker, was born April 29th, 1816.

Mary Ann Parker, daughter of Lazarus and Felicia Parker, was born October 6th, 1837.

George W. Parker, son of Lazarus & Felicia Parker, was born April 6th, 1839.

Margaret E. Parker, daughter of Lazarus & Felicia Parker, was born November 28th 1840.

William Dawson Parker, son of Lazarus & Felicia Parker, was born July 25th, 1841.

Lazretta Parker, daughter of Lazarus & Felicia Parker, was born November 24th, 1843.

William Dawson Parker, son of Dawson C. and Felicia Parker, was born July 26th, 1846.

Julia Carter Parker, daughter of Dawson C. and Felicia Parker, was born August 16th, 1849.

David Parker and Jennett Carter were married May 19th, 1807.

Mary Eliza Parker, their daughter, and Victor Geffroy, were married 1827.

Lazarus Parker and Felicia Freeman were married December 25th, 1836.

Martha Amanda Parker and Jackson Brinkley were married March 4th, 1832.

Dawson C. Parker and Felicia Freeman-Parker were married June 26th, 1845.

Elizabeth Parker and David P. Wright were married November 17th, 1839.

Jennett Parker died April 30th, 1816.

David Parker died April 8th, 1850.

Mary Eliza Geffroy died July 31st, 1831.

Lazarus Parker died September 1st, 1843.

Felicia Parker died July 26th, 1872.

George W. Parker, son of Lazarus Parker, died June 5th, 1844.

Wm. Dawson, son of Lazarus Parker, died Sept. 9th, 1841.

Wm. Dawson, son of Dawson C. Parker, died Aug. 22nd, 1846.

Dawson C. Parker died Octo. 27th, 1879.

Mrs. Lazretta Costen died Sept. 22nd, 1880.

Mrs. Julia C. Costen died Aug. 16th, 1895.

Mrs. Margaret Parker Doughtie died November 7th, 1910.

(Copied from the notes of Miss Julia Amanda Brinkley, 1947).

****

WILEY PARKER BIBLE.

Births

James Robert Parker son of Wiley and Ann P. Parker'was born 16th day of June A. D. 1827.

Wiley Williams Parker son of Wiley and Ann P. Parker was born the 3rd day of June A. D. 1849.

Alexina Parker daughter of Wiley Parker and Ann Pleasant, his wife, was born on the 11th day of August, 1852.

Margaret Ann daughter of Wiley Parker and Ann Pleasant his wife was born on the 17th day of March 1855.

Francis Edward Parker, son of Wiley Parker and Ann Pleasant Parker was born _____ (1858).

(Recorded on a page torn from a Bible. Former owner: Francis Edward Parker Transcribed: 1946).

****

DIXON PINNER BIBLE.

(Inscribed on flyleaf): This Book I wish Retained in my family. D. P. 1821.

Dixon Pinner son of John Pinner and Mary his wife was born March 23rd 1775.

Emily Everitt Daughter of Thos Everitt and Martha his wife was born Novr 5th 1788.

Marriages

Elizabeth M. Pinner Daughter of Dixon & Emily Pinner was married to Josiah C. Parker March 4th Anno Domini Eighteen Hundred and Twenty Three by the Rev. Allen R. Bernard.

Martha Ann Pinner daughter of Dixon and Emily Pinner was married to Col. Joseph Holladay March 18th 1831 by the Rev. Jacob Keeling.

Josiah Pinner was married the 30th of Jany. 1834 to Mrs. Ann T. R. Green.

Emily S. Pinner Daughter of Emily & Dixon Pinner was married to Francis D. Holladay Jany. 4th 1837 by the Rev. Jacob Keeling.

Margaret F. Pinner daughter of Dixon & Emily Pinner was married to William R. Ellis March 11, 1852.

Joseph Francis Holladay son of Francis D. & Susan Holladay was married to Carrie Tynes daughter of Henry L. Tynes Nov. 15, 1859.

Jeremiah D. Pinner and Elizabeth Sumner were married May the 7th 1846.

Maud S. Pinner, daughter of Jeremiah & Elizabeth Pinner was married to Archibald Riddick September 4th 1888.

Ida S. Pinner daughter of Jeremiah & Elizabeth Pinner was married to Dr. A. W. Eley September 28th 1886.

Millard T. Pinner, son of Jeremiah & Elizabeth Pinner was married to Clara P(auline) Walker Jan. 21st 1897.

Births

William D. Pinner, son of Dixon & Nansy Pinner his wife, was born April 4th, 1802, Sunday 6 o'clock, P. M.

Edward D. Pinner, son of Dixon Pinner & Nansy his wife, was born Sept. 10th, 1803.

110

Elizabeth M. Pinner, daughter of Dixon Pinner & Emily his wife, was born Wednesday 12th August 1807.

Josiah Pinner Son of Dixon and Emily his wife was born Sunday the 26th of June 1809.

Martha Ann Pinner daughter of Dixon Pinner and Emily his wife was born Thursday the 22nd August 1811.

John Pinner Son of Dixon Pinner and Emily his wife was born Wednesday 7th April 1813.

Births

Sarah Everitt Pinner, daughter of Dixon Pinner & Emily his wife was born Friday 17 March 1815.

Emily Susanah Pinner daughter of Dixon Pinner and Emily his wife was born Feby. 27, 1817.

Thomas Dixon Pinner Son of the above was born April 3rd 1819.

Margaret Frances Pinner, Daughter of the above was born Oct. 12th 1821.

Jeremiah Pinner Son of the above was born August 18th 1823.

Jeremiah D. Pinner son of Dixon Pinner was born Friday 7th of January 1825.

Bushrod Pinner was born 5th day of May 1827.

Births

Theodore S. Pinner, son of Jeremiah D. Pinner and Elizabeth, was born the 2nd day of December __o'clock A.M. 1847.

Ida S. Pinner, daughter of Jeremiah D. Pinenr and Elizabeth his wife, was born Wednesday the 13th December 8 o'clock P.M. 1848.

Millard T. Pinner, son of Jeremiah D. & Elizabeth Pinner, was born on Sunday the 10th November 9 o'clock A.M. 1850.

Martha S. Pinner, daughter of Jeremiah D. Pinner and Elizabeth his wife, was born on Monday July 26th 1852.

Maud S. Pinner, daughter of Jeremiah D. Pinner and Elizabeth, his wife, was born Tuesday the 24th of January 1854.

Lizzie Pinner, daughter of Jeremiah D. and Elizabeth Pinner, was born December 28th 1856.

Ellen Eudora Riddick, daughter of Archibald A. and Maud S. Riddick, was born Dec. 20th 1889, Friday 8 p. m.

William Ellis Pinner, son of Millard T. and Clara, born Jan. 14th 1898, 6 1/2 o'clock P. M. Friday.

Mary Walker Pinner, daughter of Millard and Clara Pinner, born Jan. 11th 1901.

Josiah Parker son of Eliza Parker was born Sunday the 4th of January 1824.

Bushrod Wills Pinner, was born May 7th 1830 at 10 o'clock P. M. & died Sept. 14th 1831, he was the 2nd son of that marriage.

Josiah Dixon, son of Josiah and Ann T. R. Pinner, was born Nov. 22, 1834.

Emily Ann Hancock, daughter of Josiah and Ann T. R. Pinner, was born April 31, 1837.

Joseph Francis, son of Francis David and Emily Susan Holladay, was born 16th May 1839.

Monimia Elizabeth Simson, daughter of Josiah and Ann T. R. Pinner, was born March 27th 1841.

Alto F., son of Francis D. and Emily S. Holladay, was born 26 June 1844.

Deaths

Edward D. Pinner departed this life 11th Oct. 1803.

Nansy Pinner, wife of Dixon Pinner, departed this life 22nd Oct. 1803.

Jeremiah Pinner Aged 47 departed this life 20th Dec. 1820.

Sally Applewheat, the wife of H. W. Applewheat, departed this life Sept. 18 Dec. 1820 (sic) aged 33 years.

112

Jeremiah Pinner, son of Dixon Pinner, departed this life Aug. 31, 1823.

Elizabeth M. Pinner departed this life January 31, 1825, aged 17 years 5 months & 19 days.

Bushrod Pinner, son of Dixon Pinner, died July 3rd 1829, aged 2 years and 2 months.

Departed this life on Sunday the 2nd Septr 1827, Sarah B. Jordan, wife of Joseph G. Jordan, aged 24 years.

William David Pinner died Sept. 21, 1832.

Sarah Eliza Emily Holladay died Sept. 1833 aged one year & ten months.

Martha Ann Holladay died 5th February 1834 aged 23 years 5 months and 24 day

Dixon Pinner departed this life the 20th of June 1838, aged 63 years 2 months and 25 days.

Sarah E. Pinner Departed this life the 21st day of Nov. 1841, aged 26 years 8 months & 4 days.

Deaths

Josiah Pinner departed this life the ___ April 1843 aged 33 years.

Emily Pinner, wife of Dixon Pinner, Departed this life the 25th of January 1844, Aged 55 years 2 months 4 days.

Jeremiah D. Pinner, son of Dixon & Emily Pinner, departed this life July 9, 18_5.

Elizabeth A. L. Pinner, wife of Jeremiah D. Pinner, died Oct. 16, 1857.

Joseph Francis Holladay died Jan. 13th 1861.

John G. Pinner died June 27th 1880.

Margaret F. Pinner Ellis died Feby. 6, 1896.

Martha Susan Pinner died Nov. 6, 1914.

Dr. Alphonso White Eley, husband of Ida Pinner Eley, died May 7, 1917.

(Bible published by D. Hill and T. Ware, For the Methodist Connexions in the United States, Paul and Thomas, Printers, 1815. Formerly owned by Mrs. Millard Thomas Pinner. Transcribed: 1947).

****

JAMES HUNTER PINNER RECORD.

(Inscribed on flyleaf):

James H. Godwin / Pembroke

Mr. Jas. H. Pinner / Chuckatuck / Nansemond Co., Va.

Jas. H. Pinner / was born Sept. / 1852.

Rosa V. Webb / wife of the above / was born March 11 / 1852.

Lizzie Cotten Pinner / daughter of the / above was born / Oct. 21st 1880.

Jeremiah Arthur / son of the above / was born May 20th '82.

James Hunter / son of the / above was / born Sept. 21, '83.

Gibson Webb Pinner / son of J. H. & Rosa / V. Pinner, was born / Oct. 14th 1884.

John Webb Pinner / son of J. H. and R. V. / Pinner was born / Apr. 1st 1886.

Agnes Godwin / Pinner daughter / of J. H. & R. V. / Pinner was born / Jan. 7, 1888.

Richard Heath / Pinner son of J. / H. & H. & R. V. Pinner / was born Nov. / 23, 1889.

Katherine H. / Pinner daughter / of J. H. & R. V. / Pinner was born / Mar. 24th 1893.

Deaths

Gibson Webb Pinner / Died Sept. 26th 1885.

Richard H. / Pinner died Jan. / 10th 1891.

114

James H. Pinner / Sr. died Dec. / 13th 1894.

James Hunter Pinner, Jr. died June 1934, buried St. John's, Chuckatuck.

John Webb Pinner died March 19, 1936, buried Cedar Hill, Suffolk.

(The Family Prayer Book or The Book of Common Prayer, Published by
Alexander B. Blake, No. 54 Gold Street, corner of Fulton, New York,
MDCCCXLI.
    Note: Rosa Virginia Webb was the daughter of Samuel Webb and Katherine
Heath, his wife.)

****

JOSEPH PRENTIS BIBLE.

(Written on flyleaf:)   Joseph Prentis / Suffolk, / Va.

Family Record.

Marriages.

Joseph Prentis, son of Judge Joseph Prentis of Williamsburg, and Susan
Caroline Riddick, daughter of Colo Robert M. Riddick, of Nansemond
County, were married on the 18th day of January 1810 by the Revd Jacob
Keeling an Episcopal Clergyman, at the residence of Matthias Jones, Esq.,
in the Town of Suffolk, Nansemond County, Virginia.

Joseph Prentis died on the 29th day of April 1851, aged 68 years, 3 months and
5 days.

Susan Caroline Prentis died on the 19th day of October 1862 at 12 1/2 o'clock
P. M. (Sunday), aged 71 years and 13 days.

Marianna Saunders Riddick died at the University of Virginia, on Saturday
the 16th day of April 1864, about 4 o'clock P. M., aged 51 years, 4 months
& 22 days.

Dr. Robert H. Webb and Margaret Susan Prentis were married on the 22 day
of January 1834.

Richard H. Riddick, jr. and Marianna Saunders Prentis were married on the
25th day of June 1834.

Peter Bowdoin Prentis and Eliza Wrenn were married on the 23 day of December
1841.

Robert Riddick Prentis and Margaret A. Whitehead were married on the 21st day of March 1844.

Capt: Charles Henry Causey and Martha Josephine Prentis were married on the 26th day of September 1864.

(Page 2)   Births.

Margaret Susan Prentis was born December 29th 1810.

Marianna Saunders Prentis was born November 24th 1812.

Eliza Jackson Prentis was born January 8, 1815.

Joseph Prentis was born July 20, 1816.

Robert Riddick Prentis was born April 11th 1818.

Peter Bowdoin Prentis was born April 5th 1820.

John Brooks Prentis was born June 20th 1822 and died September 30th 1862.

Elizabeth Riddick Prentis was born September 28, 1824.

Maria Louisa Prentis was born June 25, 1826.

Joseph Prentis born January 8th 1831.

Louisa Josephine Prentis was born October 29th 1833. Died September 17th 1844.

Births,
Of my Grandchildren

Joseph Prentis Riddick, Born August 12th 1836.

Margaret Susan Webb, Born October 3d 1836.

Mary Henning Webb, Born 11 September 1838 (died 31 May 1840).

Robert Fisher Webb, Born November 3d 1841. Died 28 Sept. 1844.

Joseph Prentis Webb, Born 30 Octo 1843.

Joseph son of Ro. R. Prentis was born 15 Jany. 1845, and died on the 1st day of July 1862, on the field of battle before Richmond.

Walter Prentis, son of Marianna S. Riddick, was born 22 Jany. 1847.

Catharine Flynn Prentis, daughter of my son Robert R. Prentis, born 27th day of January 1847.

Elliot Whitehead Prentis, son of same, was born on the 28th day of March 1848.

Robert Riddick Prentis, son of same, born Jany. 20, 1830, & died the 4th August 1854.

Deaths.

Eliza Jackson Prentis died August 28th 1815.

Joseph Prentis died August 10th 1829.

Elizabeth Riddick Prentis died October 7th 1824.

Maria Louisa Prentis died September 26th 1833.

Joseph Prentis died July 16th 1831.

Louisa Josephine Prentis died the 17th Septr 1844.

John Brooks Prentis died the 30th day of September 1862, aged 40 years, 3 months, and 10 days.

Joseph Prentis died on the 29th day of April 1857, **aged 68 years,** 3 months & 5 days.

Susan Caroline Prentis died on the 19th day of October 1862, at 12 1/2 o'clock P (Sunday) aged 71 years & 13 days.

Marianna Saunders Prentis died at the University of Virginia on Saturday the 16th day of April 1864 about 4 o'clock, P.M., aged 51 years, 4 months & 22 days.

Deaths
Of my Grandchildren

Margaret Susan Webb died May 4th 1837, aged 7 mo. & 1 day.

Joseph Prentis Riddick died October 14th 1838, aged 2 years 2 mos. & 2 days.

Mary Henning Webb died May 31st 1840, aged 1 year, 8 mos. & 20 days.

Robert Fisher Webb died the 28th Septr 1844.

Catharine Flynn Prentis died 20th April 1847.

Robert Riddick Prentis died 4th day of August 1854.

Joseph Prentis was killed on the battle field before Richmond on the 1st day of July 1862. He was 2nd Sergeant in Capt. John T. Kilby's Company - his age was 17 years., 5 months & 25 days.

(On sheet of paper attached:)

Ages of Servants belonging to the family of Joseph Prentis,

Mariah Parker was born in 1799 (this is followed by fifteen names with birthdates).

(The Holy Bible, containing the Old and New Testaments: Together with the Apocrypha. Published and sold by H. & E. Phinney, Cooperstown, N. Y.; Sold also by I. Tiffany, Utica, 1840. The Bible, owned by Mrs. Robert Henning Webb, was transcribed in 1962.)

****

JOSEPH PRENTIS RECORD.

(Page 2)
Joseph Prentis son of Joseph & Margaret Prentis of Williamsburg, was married to Susan Caroline Riddick daughter of Robert Moore Riddick and Elizabeth his wife by the Revd Jacob Keeling, at the house of Matthias Jones in Suffolk, on the Evening of the 18th January 1810.

1. Margaret Susan their first child born 29th Decemb. 1810.

2. Marianna Saunders Prentis was born 24th November 1812.

3. Eliza Jackson Prentis born 8th January 1815 and died on the 28th of August following, on her passage to Baltimore where she was going for her health. She was buried by Bishop Kemp, in the new Episcopal burial ground.

4. Joseph Prentis, born on the 20th July 1816 - died on the 10th day of August 1829, at Colo. Willis H. Woodley's school in Isle of Wight County, aged 13 yrs. 20 dys.

5. Robert Riddick Prentis born 11 April 1818.

6. Peter Bowdoin Prentis born 5th April 1820.

7. John Brooks Prentis born 20th June 1822.

8. Elizabeth Riddick Prentis born 28th Sepr 1824, died 7th Octo following.

9. Maria Louisa Prentis born June the 25th 1826. (died 26 Sepr 1833)

On the twentieth day of Octo 1823, Margaret Susan, Marianna Saunders, Joseph, Robert Riddick, Peter Bowdoin and John Brooks were baptized by the Revd Jacob Keeling, in my dining room, without any company or parade, about 10 o'clock in the forenoon.

I have purchased a small piece of ground at Jerico for a burial ground. It is now enclosed, deed recorded, from Jac. Keeling, in Nansd Co.

Maria Louisa Prentis was baptized in the front room of my dwelling by the Rev. W. G. H. Jones, on Monday afternoon July the 13th 1829. (died in same room, Septemr 26, 1833)

10. Joseph Prentis born January 8th 1831. (Died the 16 July 1831).

11. Louisa Josephine, born Octo 29th 1833. (died 17th Sepr 1844).

(Page 3)
The following was taken from a small Family Bible, belonging to my father and which is now in the possession of my brother John B. Prentis, of Richmond It is in my father's handwriting, and (covers?) the period of his marriage with my mother, together with the births, and deaths of his children, viz:--

Joseph Prentis & M. Bowdoin married 16th Decr 1778.

William B. Prentis born 17th April 1780 - died 15th Octo 1783.

Joseph Prentis born 24th Jany. 1783.

William Prentis born 13th Jan. 1785. Died 9th Aug. 1790.

John B. Prentis born 15th Feb: 1787. Died 13th feb. 1789.

John Brooks Prentis born 1 Feby. 1789.

Eliza Prentis born April 14th 1791.

Mary Ann Prentis born 19th March 1796.

Robert W. Prentis born the 6th Nov. 1794. Died 18th ____.

On the 12th Nov. 1827, my dear Susan and myself ratified and confirmed the baptismal vow which had been made for us, when unable to answer for ourselves and she took the sacrament at the same time in the Isle of Wight, old church, Bishop Moore of the Prot. Epis: Church performing the ceremonies.

On the 20th Feby. 1828, at St. Paul's church on the hill, near the Town of Suffolk, by devine grace, I entered into my Sacramental Covenant with my blessed Lord & master, and my prayers are fervently and continually offered up, for my love to God, and trust I may love him more and serve him better. Bishop Moore, on same day admitted to the order of Priesthood the Revd Jacob Keeling, the Rd W. G. H. Jones was admitted to the same order of Priesthood in the sd I. of W. Church, when I was confirmed.

(Page 4)
Margaret Prentis my beloved mother died at Green Hill, the old mansion in the City of Williamsburg, the 27th August 1801.

Joseph Prentis my father, the late Judge Prentis, died at the same place, on the 18th June 1809.

(Taken from The Account Book of Joseph Prentis II, a manuscript volume bound in brown buckram with 1815 inked on the spine, VSL. For a complete genealogy, see Frederick Adams Virkus, Compendium of American Genealogy, Vol. III, p. 230.)

****

BENJAMIN BRIDGER RIDDICK BIBLE.

Births.

Benjamin (Bridger) son of Archibald Riddick and Priscilla Bridger, his wife, born at Mossy Swamp Farm in Nansemond County, Sept. 8, 1809.

Eliza J(erusha) daughter of Timothy and Eliza D(igges) Porter was born Oct. 14, 1812.

Benjamin Riddick and Eliza Jerusha Porter were married Dec. 15, 1830.

Jerusha Frances, daughter of Benj. and Eliza J. Riddick, was born March 22, 1832.

Eudora Porter, daughter of same, was born September 28, 1833.

Frances Marietta, daughter of same, was born May 29, 1835.

Eliza Priscilla, daughter of same, was born August 19, 1838.

Louisiana S(umner), daughter of same, was born March 21, 1840.

Ellen Custine, daughter of same, was born January 25, 1845.

Archibald Allen, son of same, was born March 15, 1848.

Ellen Eudora Riddick, daughter of Archibald A(llen) and M(aud) S(umner) Riddick, was born December 20, 1889.

Marriages.

Benjamin Riddick and Miss Eliza Jerusha Porter were married Decr 15, 1830.

Exum B(ritton) Britt and Miss Eudora Porter Riddick were married Novr 22, 1855.

Richard Seth Eley and Miss Eliza Priscilla Riddick were married Feby. 13, 1866.

Exum B. Britt and Miss Ellen Custine Riddick were married April 3, 1867.

Archibald A. Riddick and Miss Maud Sumner Pinner were married Sept. 3, 188

Deaths.

Jerusha Frances, daughter of Benjamin and Eliza J. Riddick, died Sept. 22, 1832.

Frances Marietta, daughter of same, died July 22, 1837.

Eudora P. Britt died on Oct. 21, 1865.

Howard Eley, son of R(ichard) S(eth) and Eliza P(riscilla) Eley, died August 18, 1869.

Ellen Custine Britt, wife of E. B. Britt and daughter of Benj. and Eliza J. Riddick, died Saturday morning, December 15, 1883.

Mrs. Eliza D. Porter died 25th day of Jany. 1843.

Mrs. Eliza J. Riddick, wife of Benj. Riddick, died the 29th day of May, 1882.

Mrs. Priscilla Riddick, mother of Benj. Riddick, died the 11th day of ___.

Benjamin Riddick died April 6, 1892.

Exum B. Britt died March 1, 1916, at the age of 85 years and 22 days.

(The Holy Bible, published by Andrus and Judd, Hartford, Ct. Sterotyped by James Conner, New York, 1832. Owned and transcribed by Miss Frances Louise Britt, 1962.)

****

EDWARD RIDDICK BIBLE.

Polly Riddick War born in December the 7th / Day 1800 the Daughter of Edward and Nancy / Riddick.

(A single excerpt cut from the Bible and formerly owned by Marmaduke Eppes Woodward. Mary (Polly) Riddick, who died "Sept. 3rd 1884 Age 84 years," married twice: (1) Oct. 1, 1816, Job Rawles Saunders, and (2) Solomon J. Holland.)

****

EUPHANE FIVEASH RIDDICK BIBLE.

(Written on flyleaf:)　　　Euphan T. Honey

Thomas Fiveash Riddick was born 5th June 1781.

William Honey was married to Mrs. Euphan Riddick 2nd October 1787.

John William Honey son to the above was born 2nd October, 1789.

William Honey, Husband to the above Euphan & Father to John William, departed this life on Thursday even, 23rd December 1790 in Suffolk, Virginia.

(The preceding entries are written on a blank page on verso of "The End of the Apocrypha," bearing the following bibliography: The Holy Bible. Printed by David Niven; For / J. Duncan and J. & M. Robertson, Booksellers, / Glasgow / MDCCLXXXIX. This separately printed version of the Apocrapha, inserted between the Old and New Testaments, is an integral part of The / Holy Bible / containing the Old and New / Testaments: / Newly Translated out of the / Original Tongues, / and with the Former Translations / Diligently Compared and Revised, / By His Majesty's Special Command. / Appointed to

be Read in CHURCHES. / Edinburgh. / Printed by the Assigns of Alexander
Kincaid, His / Majesty's Printer. / MDCCLXXXV.

For the remaining entries contained in this Bible, see the Robert Moore
Riddick - Matthias Jones Bible.

Note. Euphane Fiveash married twice: (1) Jason Riddick, and (2) William
Honey.

Jason3 Riddick (died 1784, at "Green Hill," near Cypress Chapel,
Nansemond Co.; Moses2, John1) served in the Continental Line, being appointed
lieutenant April 2, 1776, and captain, January 6, 1778, serving with this rank
until February 13, 1781, when his request for permission to resign was granted
by Major-General Baron von Steuben, at Chesterfield Courthouse. Jason and
Euphane Fiveash Riddick had one child, Thomas Fiveash Riddick (1781-1830),
who received June 9, 1784, Virginia Bounty Land Warrant No. 3140 (for 4,000
acres of land in Kentucky), settled in St. Louis, Missouri, about 1804, and
married August 12, 1812, in Lexington, Kentucky, Eliza Minor Carr.)

****

JAMES EDWARD RIDDICK BIBLE.

Marriages

James E. Riddick and Harriet D. Rabey was married April 22nd A. D. 1852 by
A. M. Craig.

Charles C. Riddick and Martha E. King was married January 5, 1881 by
C. G. Ralston.

Etta M. Riddick and W. A. King was married July 7th A. D. 1881 by C. G.
Ralston.

Claudius J. Riddick & Emily S. Wingfield was married Oct. 3rd A. D. 1893
by Rev. R. W. Forsyth of Phila. Penn. & J. B. Funsten of Portsmouth, Va.

Dora Riddick and John W. King was married November 28th A. D. 1893 by
H. H. Butler.

Adrian Riddick was married to Mrs. Jennie H. Thorpe October 27, 1892,
Petersburg, Va.

Charles C. Riddick and Mary Edna Pearce was married March 15, 1917,
by H. H. Butler.

Births

Charles C. Riddick son of James E. Riddick & Harriet D., his wife, was born 22nd day of January 1853.

Adrian Riddick son of James E. Riddick & Harriet D., his wife, was born the 9th of July A. D., 1858.

Claudius Riddick son of James E. Riddick & Harriet D., his wife, was born the 10th of November A. D., 1858.

Henrietta Riddick daughter of James E. Riddick & Harriet D., his wife, was born the 17 of December A. D., 1861.

Dora Riddick daughter of James E. Riddick & Harriet D., his wife, was born the 21st of July A. D., 1871.

Dana C. Riddick daughter of James E. Riddick and Harriet D., his wife, was born April 5, A. D., 1874.

Emma May Riddick daughter of Charles C. and Martha Emma Riddick was born Oct. 24, 1881.

Sue Wingfield Riddick daughter of Claudius J. Riddick and Emily S., his wife, was born the 25th of September A. D., 1894 4:10 A. M.

Claudius James Riddick, Jr., son of Claudius J. Riddick and Emily S., his wife, was born the 2nd of June A. D., 1901 11:30 P. M.

John Walter King, Jr., born August 12, 1897 (son of J. Walter King & Dora his wife).

Edward Riddick King born Sept. 30th 1899, Son of J. Walter King & Dora his wife.

Births

Harriet Elizabeth Riddick daughter of Charles C. and Mary Emma Riddick, his wife, was born Sept. 14, 1918 2:30 p. m.

Deaths

Jethro Riddick departed this life January 17th 1874 aged 70 years, 4 mos. & 3 days.

Willis S. Riddick departed this life Decem. 13th 1875.

Dana C. Riddick daughter of James E. Riddick departed this life December 4th 1879.

Elizabeth Riddick wife of Jethro Riddick departed this life Sept. 19th 1880 Age 74 years & 6 days.

Dempsey Jones departed this life April 21st 1881.

Infant son of Charles C. Riddick departed this life July 24th 1883 aged 26 days old when he died.

Martha E. Riddick departed this life July 5th 1883. She was the wife of Charles C. Riddick.

Mary Holland departed this life Sept. 3rd 1884 Age 84 years. She was the sister of Jethro Riddick.

Jethro B. Riddick departed this life Decem. 11th A.D. 1887, 48 years 4 months & 27 days old.

James E. Riddick departed this life March 19th 1895 aged 68 yrs. 5 months & 5 days - son of Jethro Riddick "Requiescat in Pace."

Harriet Deborah Riddick departed this life May 17th 1896 Aged 70 yrs. wife of Jas. E. Riddick.

Edward Riddick departed this life Oct. 10th 1849 aged 84 years. The father of Jethro Riddick.

Nancy Riddick the wife of Edward Riddick departed this life Oct. 25th 1855, 72 yrs. 7 mos. & 16 days old. The mother of Jethro Riddick.

Nancy J. Eley departed this life May 24th 1894 aged 57 yrs. 2 mos. & 12 days. Daughter of Jethro & Elizabeth Riddick.

Wm. Thomas Riddick departed this life Dec. 11th 1890 aged 62 yrs. 9 mos. & 23 days. Son of Jethro & Elizabeth Riddick.

Ellen Katherine Brothers departed this life 1895 aged 53 years, daughter of Jethro & Elizabeth Riddick.

Adrian Riddick departed this life in Richmond, Va. Aug. 2nd 1904, son of Jas. E. Riddick and Harriet D.

Charles C. Riddick departed this life Dec. 5th 1922 aged 69 years.

(Bible owned by Miss Sue Wingfield Riddick).

****

JETHRO RIDDICK BIBLE.

Marriages

Married on the 28 of February 1850 Mary A. to W. S. Riddick by the rev. W. B. Welons.

Married on the 20 of November 1851 Sarah E. Riddick to Elisha Norfleet by the rev. W. B. W.

Married on the 22 of April 1852 James E. Riddick to Harriet D. Rabey by the rev. Craig of N. C.

Married on the 30th of November 1853 Nancy Jane Riddick to James E. Ames by the rev. W. B. Wellons.

Married on the 31st of January 1861 Nancy Jane Ames to Walter H. Ealey by the Rev. W. B. Wellons.

Births

John Walter King, jr. Born August 12th 1897, Son of J. Walter King and Dora his wife.

Edward Riddick King, Born Sept. 30th 1899. Son of J. Walter King and Dora his wife.

Marriages

Dora Riddick & J. Walter King was married Nov. 28th 1893 by Rev. H. H. Butler.

John Walter King, Jr. & Sallie Ophelia Brinkley was married Oct. 24th 1928 by Rev. H. S. Hardcastle.

Births

James E. Riddick was born the 14th day of October 1826 the son of Jethro Riddick and Elizabeth his wife.

William T. Riddick was born the 18th day of February 1828 the son of Jethro Riddick and Elizabeth his wife.

Charles J. Riddick was born the 3d day of July 1829 the son of Jethro Riddick and Elizabeth his wife.

Mary Ann Riddick was born the 17th day of April 1831 the daughter of Jethro Riddick and Elizabeth his wife.

Sarah E. Riddick was born the 14th day of November 1833 the daughter of Jethro Riddick and Elizabeth his wife.

Nancy J. Riddick was born the 12th day of March 1837 the daughter of Jethro Riddick and Elizabeth his wife.

Jethro Bal(l)entine Riddick was Born the 14th day of July 1839 the son of Jethro Riddick and Elizabeth his wife.

Ellen C. Riddick was Born the 14th day of May 1842 the daughter of Jethro Riddick and Elizabeth his wife.

Margaret L. Riddick was born the 28th day of October 1844 the daughter of Jethro Riddick and Elizabeth his wife.

Deaths

Jethro Bal(l)entine Riddick departed this life December the 11th A.D. 1887, 48 years 4 months & 27 days, the son of Jethro Riddick.

Wm Thomas Riddick departed this life December 11th A.D. 1890, age 62 years 9 months & 23 days, son of Jethro & Elizabeth Riddick.

Nancy J. Eley departed this life May 24, 1894, age 57 years, 2 mos. 12 days, daughter of Jethro & Elizabeth Riddick.

James E. Riddick departed this life March 19th A.D. 1895 age 68 years 5 months & 5 days. "Requescat in pace," C.J.R.

H. D. Riddick departed this life May 17th 1896 age about 70 years, wife of James E. Riddick.

Adrian Riddick departed this life in Richmond, Va., Aug. 2nd 1904.

Sarah E. Norfleet departed this life June 9th 1910, age 76 years 6 months & 25 days.

Charles C. Riddick departed this life Dec. 5th 1922, age 70 years, the son of James E. Riddick and Harriet D., his wife.

J. Walter King, son of John G. & Martha A. King. Born Dec. 12, 1846, Died April 3rd 1927, age 80 yrs. 3 mos. & 24 days.

Dora Riddick, wife of J. Walter King. Born July 21st 1871. Died May 4th 1935, age 63 yrs. 9 mos. 8 days, by Edward R. King, her son.

Charles J. Riddick departed this life the year 1833 February ____

Margaret L. Riddick departed this life September 5th day 1851, six years 10 months & 7 days old.

James E. Ames departed this life September 18th day, 1855, twenty four years of age, the husband of Nancy J. Riddick, the daughter of Jethro & Elizabeth Riddick.

Henry Skinner departed this life January 8th day 1858, 38 years old.

Catharine Duke departed this life June 10th 1861, 68 years of age.

Edward Riddick Departed this life October the 10th 1849, Eighty four years old. The father of Jethro Riddick.

Margaret J. Brinkley departed this life December 28th 1853.

Margaret Skinner departed this life August 3d day 1855.

Nancy Goodman Riddick the wife of Edward Riddick, Sr. departed this life October 25th day 1855 Seventy Two years 7 months & 16 days old, the mother of Jethro Riddick.

James Goodman departed this life August 29th day 1861 Seventy-one years 10 months & 23 days old when he died.

Barnes Goodman departed this life February 29th 1862 Sixty four years of age when he died 64 years.

Elisha Norfleet departed this life December 25th 1869, Sixty nine years when he died.

Mary A. Riddick departed this life April 21st 1871, the wife of W. S. Riddick and was 40 years & 4 days old and was the daughter of Jethro & Elizabeth Riddick.

Jethro Riddick closed his earthly pilgrimage on the 17th day of January A. D. 1874, age 70 years 4 months 5 days.

Elizabeth Riddick wife of Jethro Riddick breathed her last on Sunday morning September 19th 1880 age 74 years & 6 days.

(On a separate sheet):

Charles C. Riddick son of James E. Riddick and Harriet D. his wife was born 22nd day of January 1853.

Adrian Riddick son of James E. Riddick and Harriet D. his wife was born the 9th of July 1855.

Claudius J. Riddick son of James E. Riddick and Harriet D. his wife was born the 10 of November A. D. 1858.

Henrietta M. Riddick, daughter of James E. & Harriet D. his wife was born the 17 of December 1861.

Dora Riddick daughter of James E. Riddick and Harriet E. his wife was born 21 of July 1871.

Dana C. Riddick, daughter of James E. Riddick & Harriet D. his wife was born April 5, 1874.

Emma Maie Riddick daughter of Charles C. & Martha Emma Riddick, born Oct. 24th 1881.

Marriages

James E. Riddick & Harriet D. Raby was married April 22nd 1852 by A. M. Craig.

Charles C. Riddick & Martha E. King was married Jany. 5th 1881 by C. J. Ralston.

Etta M. Riddick and W. A. King was married July 17th 1881, by C. J. Ralston.

Claude J. Riddick &·Emily S. Wingfield were married Oct. 3, 1893, by Rev. R. W. Forsyth of Phila. Penn. & Rev. J. B. Funston, of Portsmouth, Va.

Dora Riddick & J. Walter King were married Nov. 28th 1893 by Rev. H. H. Butler.

(Bible published by Kimber & Sharpless, at their book store, No. 8 So. 4th St., Philadelphia, Stereotyped Edition; no date. Owned by Edward Riddick King.
   For a partial genealogy of the Jethro Riddick family, see, Elisha Norfleet, pp. 11-12.)

****

JOHN ROBERT RIDDICK BIBLE.

Married on the 3rd January 1856,
John R. Riddick to Mrs. Julia D. Allen, youngest daughter of William Drew and Margaret Roberts, of Norfolk, Va., by Rev. Dr. Minnegerode.

Born 11th day May 1827, John R. Riddick, oldest son of Mary and Henry Riddick.

Born on 31st Aug. 1829, Julia D. Roberts, youngest daughter of William Drew and Margaret Roberts.

Born 8th day of Nov. 1856, Eliza Roberts, 1st daughter of John R. and Julia D. Riddick.

Born 9th June 1859, Margaret Holloway, 2nd daughter of John R. & Julia D. Riddick.

Born the 17th day of April 1862, Cornelius Robert Riddick, 1st son of John R. & Julia D. Riddick.

Born the 13th day of Jan. 1864, Julia Anna Lassell Riddick, 3rd daughter of John & Julia D. Riddick.

Born 9th April 1867, John Robert Riddick, 2nd son of John R. & Julia D. Riddick.

Born 11th day of Jan. 1870, Willis Starr Riddick, youngest son of Julia & John R. Riddick.

Died on Friday about 7 o'clock the 12th day of Dec. A. D. 1862, Cornelius Robert, infant son of John R bert & Julia D. Riddick, age 7 mos. 25 days. Funeral services Sunday the 14th by Rev. Allen R. Bernard of the Va. M. E. Conference. Text 28v. of 12th Chap. Hebrews, Suffolk, Nansemond Co., Va.

Died on Sunday at 1 o'clock the 31st day of May 1868, John Robert Riddick, infant son of J. R. & J. D. Riddick.

John R. Riddick, Father, died Dec. 1891.

Julia D. Riddick, Mother, died Jan. 30, 1912.

Eliza Freeney, Sister, died Oct. 14, 1923.

(Bible owned by Mrs. Robert G. Blackwell.)

****

JOSIAH HENRY RIDDICK BIBLE.
(Excerpts)

(Inscribed on flyleaf:)
> William Henry Harrison Riddick / "Pleasant Hill" Gates County, North Carolina / 1876

Deaths

Lavinia Riddick, Consort of Josiah H. Riddick, died Feb. 3, 1880, aged 70 years.

Virginia Adeline Riddick died Dec. 29, 1891. Consort of William Henry Harrisc Riddick.

Departed this life Jan. 9, 1906, William Henry Harrison Riddick, son of Josiah H. and Lavinia Riddick, in the 65 year of his age.

Marriages

William Henry Harrison Riddick, son of Josiah H. and his wife Lavinia Riddick was married to Virginia Adeline Wright, daughter of James and Martha Ann Wright, by the Methodist Preacher, March 16, 1865.

Lillian Ethel Jeannette, daughter of William H. H. and Virginia Adeline Riddick, was married April 17, 1895, aged 18, to the Rev. George White (Bapti minister), aged 23, (at) Rocky Creek, Chowan County, N. C.

Births

Willis Edward Holmes, son of William H. H. and Virginia Adeline Riddick, born Dec. 14, 1865.

Claudia Ethel McCall, daughter of same, born April 3, 1867.

Mary Irene Sumner (daughter of same) born Aug. 15, 1870.

Sarah Virginia Chapman (daughter of same) born Aug. 15, 1868.

Clarence Summerfield (son of same) born Apl. 18, 1874.

Sidney Virginius, son of Wm. H. H. and Virginia Adeline Riddick, born March 2, 1872.

Ethel Jeannette, daughter of above Wm. H. H. and Virginia Adeline Riddick, born Feb. 20, 1873.

(Holy Bible. Published by Thomas Mason & George Low, New York, 1837. Owned by Mrs. Cecil Riddick.)

****

LEMUEL RIDDICK BIBLE.

Lemuel Riddick was born August 23rd in ye year 1711.

Anna Riddick wife of Lemuel was born April 9th, 1715.

Lemuel and Anna was married Dec'r 17, 1729.

James Riddick, son of Lem'l and Anne, was born Nov'r 17th, 1731.

Lemuel Riddick, son of Do. was born Jany 5th, 1733-4.

Edward Riddick (son of Do.) was born Jan. 29, 1735-6.

Anna Riddick, Daughter of Do. was born Sept'r 17, 1738.

James Riddick married Mildred, the Daughter of Colo. Will Baker, 1753, August 28th. They have had two daughters, both dead after Nov. 17, 1760.

Lemuel died at sea with the small-pox, on his passage home from Antigua & buried in the Sea, April 1756.

Ann married Mr. Stephen Wright in July 1756, & died Nov. 11, 1759, in child-bed, having brought a dead female child, both buried at the White Marsh in one Cofin.

Edward married Margaret, the Daughter of Capt. Henning Tembte, Jan. last she was delivered of a female Child on the third Day of this Instant, Nov'r 1760 & she, the Mother Departed this Life Saterday Morning Last, the 15th inst. & is this day buried at her fathers plantation.

My Dearly Beloved Wife Ann, departed this Life this morning five of the Clock, after a Violent Sickness of Nine Weeks Leaving me a Disconsolate Widower, with few of my posterity to be a Comfort. What more may happen If (I) live I perhaps may write down here for the Satisfaction of those I Leave behind. This is the 17th day of Novr. 1760. Signed by Lemuel Riddick.

James Riddick, Son of Lemuel Riddick departed this Life at his Own House at Sleepy Hole, the 16th day of December 1760, Leaving his Widdow with child.

Lemuel Riddick married a second time unto Esther Pugh, the Widdow of Theophilus Pugh, Esquire, the 5th day of May, 1761. She was born in North Hampton County, the 10th Nov. 1722, being the daughter of Colo. John Robbins & Katherine, his wife.

The widow of Son James, was delivered of a female Child, on the third day of June, 1761 & Baptised the ___day of July by the name of Anne & at the Same time my son Edward's Daughter was baptised and named Margarett.

Lemuel Riddick, the son of Lemuel Riddick and Esther his wife, was born the 1st day of July 1763, at four of the Clock in the morning & Baptised the Monday after.

Colo. Lemuel Riddick, Departed this Life Dec. 2nd, 1775.

Esther, his Wife Departed this Life 23rd of Sept. 1775.

Colo. Edward Riddick Departed this Life Sept. 1783.

Lemuel Riddick, Son of Lemuel Riddick and Esther, his wife, Departed this Life the 19th day of February, 1811, About four o'clock of the Night.

Births

Samuel Barron Cunningham, was born July 26, 1757.

133

Margaret Cunningham, wife of Samuel B. Cunningham, was born Novem. the 3rd, 1760.

Edward Riddick Cunningham, Son of Samuel B. Cunningham and Margaret his wife, was born the 26 Sept. 1779.

Ann Cunningham, Daughter of Samuel B. Cunningham & Margaret, his wife, was born 13th of October, 1781.

Samuel Barron Cunningham, son of Samuel B. Cunningham and Margaret his wife, was born the 28th day of February 1784.

David Cunningham, Son of Samuel B. Cunningham and Margaret, his wife, was born 9th March, 1786.

Lemuel Riddick Cunningham, Dito, was born 18th of June, 1791.

Henning Tembte Cunningham, "   "   " 21st of March, 1793.

William White Cunningham, Son of Samuel B. Cunningham and Elizabeth, his 2nd wife was born 15th Sept. 1795.

Washington Smith, Son of Thomas Smith and Anne Smith, his wife, was born the 11th August 1772.

Margaret Anne Smith, Daughter of Washington Smith and Ann, his wife, was born the 10th of October, 1799.

Henning Tembte Smith, Dito - 3rd of January, 1803.

Mary Jane Smith,   "   1st day of August, 1805.

Robert Riddick Smith   "   16th day of January, 1808.

Thomas Smith   "   13th of November, 1810.

Sophia Emmeline Smith, Daughter, Dito, 3rd of January, 1813.

Anne Cunningham Smith   "   21st of May 1816.

William Louis Parham, Son of Thomas Parham and Elizabeth his wife, was born the 25th of May, 1808.

William Cunningham, son of William L. Parham and Anne C., his wife, was born Dec. 24th, 1837.

Sallie Jackson, daughter of Henning E. Smith and Jennie W., was born December 19, 1866.

Willie Anna, Daughter of Henning E. Smith and Jennie W., was born August 21st, 1868.

Robert Riddick, Son of Henning E. Smith and Jennie W., was born June 8, 1871

Jennie Wilson, daughter of Henning E. Smith and Jennie W., was born June 17, 1879.

Marriages

Samuel Barron Cunningham and Margaret Riddick were married 27th of Sept. 1778.

Samuel Barron Cunningham was married to Elizabeth White, his second wife, the 18th of December, 1793.

Washington Smith, of Somerton, Virginia, & Anne Cunningham were married the 3rd of January, 1799.

William Lewis Parham and Anne Cunningham Smith were married 17th of March A.D., 1836.

Robert Riddick Smith and Sarah J. Powell were married on the 18th of March, 1834.

Burwell Riddick and Margaret Anne Smith were married the 1st day of Jany 1818.

Henning Tembte Smith and Martha G. Pipkin were married on the 5th of July, 1825.

Doct. James Harrison and Mary Jane Smith were married on ____.

John D. Hart and Sophia Emeline Smith were married on the 18th of October, 1834.

Henning E. Smith and Jennie V. Norfleet were married 13th of Febry 1866.

R. R. Smith and Laura Boswell Daughtrey were married March 20, 1866.

Thomas W. Smith and Harriett G. Borland were married on the 27th of October, 1870.

Mills C. Daughtrey was married to Anne Cunningham Hart at Canton, Miss., 24th of Feb. 1863.

Frank T. Jones and Sallie Jackson Smith were married on Oct. 17, 1888, Suffolk, Virginia, Nansemond County.

Deaths

David Cunningham, son of Samuel B. Cunningham and Margaret, his wife, departed this life this 6th day of August, 1787.

Margaret Cunningham, wife of Samuel B. Cunningham, Departed this life the 5th of August, 1793.

Henning Tembte Cunningham, Son of Samuel B. Cunningham and Margaret his wife, departed this life 27th of August, 1794.

William White Cunningham, son of Samuel B. Cunningham and Elizabeth his wife, departed this life the 1st of October, 1795.

Samuel B. Cunningham, son of Samuel B. Cunningham and Margaret his wife, departed this life the 10th of October, 1795.

Samuel B. Cunningham, Senr Departed this life the 8th of June, 1796.

Lemuel Riddick Cunningham, Son of Samuel B. Cunningham and Margaret his wife, departed this life in Suffolk, Virginia, the 5th of August, 1812, and (was) buried at the Retreat.

Anne Smith, Consort of Washington Smith of Somerton, departed this life the 4th day of June, 1816, Leaving a husband with 6 small children, the youngest a daughter two weeks old.

Thomas Smith, son of Washington Smith and Anne his wife, departed this life the 10th of August, 1814, about 10 o'clock at night after a long illness.

Washington Smith, departed this life April 14, A.D. 1835, Leaving a Second Wife and eleven children to lament his loss.

Anne Cunningham Parham, departed this life January 8, 1838, who was the wife of William Lewis Parham.

Doct. William Lewis Parham departed this life July 18, 1838, Leaving a son near seven months of age to lament his loss.

Major Robert R. Smith, departed this life September 13, 1845.

Sarah J. Elliott, wife of Major Robert R. Smith, departed this life August 29, 1868.

Washington C. Smith, son of Robert and Sarah his wife, departed this life, June 28, 1865.

Sophia Emeline Hart departed this life Feb. 1885, at Canton, Miss.

Robert Riddick Smith, son of Robert Riddick Smith and Sarah Jackson, his wife, departed this life April 7, 1925, (12:30 o'clock A.M.) in Suffolk, Virginia.

(Marginal entries in pencil:)

Mills Riddick, son of James ____ and Christian his wife was born Septr 25th___.

Joseph Riddick, son of Do born July 5th _____.

(Entries on a separate sheet of paper:)

Laura Boswell Smith, wife (widow) of Robert Riddick Smith, departed this life on February 3rd, 1933 (at 8:15 o'clock P.M.), in Suffolk, Virginia.

Henning Ezekiel Smith, son of Robert Riddick Smith and Sarah Jackson, his wife, departed this life June 22nd, 1913, Suffolk, Virginia.

Virginia Wilson Smith (called Jennie), his wife, departed this life Sept. 13th, 1925, Suffolk, Virginia.

Frank C. Wurdemann, and Jennie Wilson Smith married December 26, 1907.

(Entries on a separate sheet of paper:)

Sarah J. Powell, Daughter of Ezekiel Powell, was born the 9th March, in the year 18___.

Sarah J. Powell, Daughter of Ezekiel Powell and Elizabeth, her mother, the 13th day of May in the year 1808.

_illy Powell, daughter of Ezekiel and Rachel her mother, was born June 8th day in the year 1812.

Jackson Powell, Sun of Ezekiel and Rachel, his mother, was born December 11th day, 1817.

Capt. John Drew Hart and Sophia Emeline Smith were married on the 18th day of Oct. 1824.

John Drew Hart, son of John Hart & Susan Boone, was born Jan. 12th, 1802, in Southampton Co., Va.

Their children

John W. Hart, born Oct. 13th, 1835, died 1848.

Robert H. Hart, born Jan. 17th, 1838; married Agnes Cornelia Magette, 1862.

James E. Hart, born May 24, 1840.

Ann C. Hart born April 10th, 1842; mar. Mills C. Daughtrey, 1864; she died 1904.

Susan Emeline Hart, born April 17th, 1844; married James Dinkins of Mississippi, 1866, Nov. 15th at Canton, Miss.

Mary S. Hart, born Dec. 6th, 1846, m. Rev. Wallace Carnahan, 1871; d. 1902.

Sarah Jane Hart, b. Sept. 27th, 1848; m. Hugh W. Virden.

John D. Hart, b. April 3, 1850; d. 1855.

Children of Susan Emeline Hart (5th child of John Drew Hart and Susan Boone) and James Dinkins.

Lynn Hamilton Hart, b. Madison Co., Miss., Aug. 15, 1867.

Myriam Cynthia, b. Madison Co., Miss., Dec. 1870; mar. C. G. Robinson, of Charlottesville, Va., 1903.

Lynn Dinkins Robinson was born in Charlottesville, Va., Sept. 22, 1905.

(The Holy Bible / containing the Old and New Testaments / newly translated out of the / original tongues / Diligently compared and revised. / By his Majesty's Special Command / Appointed to be read in Church / Oxford / Printed by John Baskett, Printer to the University, MDCCXXVII. / Price thirty-six shillings in quires.

The Bible, leather-bound with Lemuel Riddick's name stamped in gold on the spine, was transcribed by Mrs. Marion Kelly Kendrick in 1933. The record is printed in James Dinkins, The Dinkins and Springs Families, New Orleans, 1908. For Riddick genealogy, see Henning Tembte.

Note. The will of Henning Tembte (b. c. 1700-d. 1771. Oct. 9, 1771; Nov. 1771) is in the Halifax County Records, Historical Commission, Raleigh, N.C., Will Book, 1755-1782, Part III, p. 13). "To granddaughter Pegge Riddick my land in Tuckers Neck Nansemond Called the Little Pasture." Residue of personal estate to be equally divided between his two daughters Mary Fisher and Elizabeth Murden and his housekeeper Elizabeth Davis. Executor: David Sumner. Witnesses: Mary Whitley, Mary Smith.)

****

MILLS AND MARY (TAYLOR) RIDDICK BIBLE.

(Written on the flyleaf:)

Mrs. Mary A. Riddick Suffok Virginia
September 20th 1840

This Bible presented to Nathaniel Riddick Withers Great Grand Son of Mills and Mary Riddick by Wm David Riddick Wood who inherited it from his mother Juliana Wood daughter of Mills and Mary Riddick and who inherited it from her mother Mary Riddick.
Suffolk, Va.
May 10, 1911.

(On a blank page facing Family Record:)

Births.

Mills Riddick son of Josiah and Ann Riddick was born Apr. 5th 1780.

Mary Taylor daughter of Richard and Diana Taylor was born March 20th 1788.

Josiah Riddick father of Mills Riddick & son of Mills Riddick brother of Col. Willis Riddick was born Sept. 5th 1748. Married Ann Riddick his cousin.

(Page 1)   Family Record.

                            Marriages.

Mills Riddick and Mary Taylor was married, Oct. 27, 1803.

Richard H. Riddick son of Mills and Mary Riddick was married to Martha
M. Jordan Augt. the 23, 1827.

Mary Allen Riddick daughter of Mills and Mary Riddick was married to
Richard D. Webb, Nov. the 28, 1827.

Diana Tabb Riddick daughter of Mills and Mary Riddick was married to
Gabriel P. Disosway, Dec. the 25th, 1828.

(Page 2)   Marriages.

Josiah Riddick son of Mills and Mary Riddick was married to Elizabeth Wright
Oct. 23, 1833.

Juliana Riddick daughter of Mills and Mary Riddick (was) married to (Rev.)
David Wood Jan. the 21, 1834.

Maria Taylor Riddick daughter of Mills and Mary Riddick was married to
William Henry McGuire Jan. the 21, 1834.

Nathaniel Riddick son of Mills and Mary Riddick was married to Missouri
A. J. Kilby Dec. 19, 1839.

Cornelia Riddick daughter of Mills and Mary Riddick was married to Daniel
H. Hatton Feb. the 16, 1841.

(Page 3)   Deaths.

Margaret Ann Riddick departed this life to live in heaven July 29, 1809.

Ann Eliza Riddick departed this life to live in heaven Feb. the 2, 1815.

Robert William Riddick departed this life to live in heaven Oct. the 29,
1823.

The son not named died the 27 Sept., 1827.

Diana T. Disosway died on Staten Island April 1st 1883.

140

Maria T. McGuire died in Suffolk May 8th 1883.

Juliana Wood died in Suffolk, Va., Jan. 30, 1893.

Cornelia Hatton died in Suffolk, Va., Dec. 9, 1889.

Mills Edward Riddick died in Nansemond Co., April 15th, 1891.

(Page 4 is blank).

Page 5)   Marriages

Mills Edward son of Mills and Mary Riddick was married to Clara Ann Judkins Feb. 8, 1844.

Washington Lafayette son of Mills and Mary Riddick was married to Frances Marion Blount August 18, 1844.

Amelia Ann Eason daughter (of) Henry and Elizabeth Eason was married to Daniel Ayres Dec. the 11, 1839.

(Page 6)   Births.

Richard Henry son of Mills and Mary Riddick was born May 27, 1806.

Margaret Ann daughter of Mills and Mary Riddick was born March the 7, 1808.

Mary Allen daughter of Mills and Mary Riddick was born Augt. the 3, 1809.

Diana Tabb daughter of Mills and Mary Riddick was born Augt. 29, 1810.

Josiah son of Mills and Mary Riddick was born August the 13, 1812.

Ann Eliza daughter of Mills and Mary Riddick was born January 31, 1814.

Juliana daughter of Mills and Mary Riddick was born April the 6, 1815.

(Page 7)   Births.

Maria Taylor daughter of Mills and Mary Riddick was born Nov. the 12, 1816.

Mills Edward son of Mills and Mary Riddick was born January the 23, 1818.

Nathaniel son of Mills and Mary Riddick was born March the 19, 1819.

Cornelia daughter of Mills and Mary Riddick was born October 28, 1820.

Robert William son of Mills and Mary Riddick was born March the 16, 1822.

Washington Lafayette son of Mills and Mary Riddick was born Augt. 15, 1825.

Mills and Mary Riddick had a son born not named Oct. 26, 1826.

(Page 8)   Deaths.

Mills Riddick Died in Suffolk September 5th 1844.

Mary Riddick Died in Suffolk August 8th 1875.

Josiah Riddick, died at "Soldiers Hope" May ___, 1848.

Richard Henry Riddick Died at Pantego, N. C., January 14th 1868.

Washington L. Riddick Died in New Orleans February 3rd 1871.

Mary Allen Webb Died in Suffolk January 1873.

Nathaniel Riddick died in Suffolk Dec. 30, 1882.

(The Holy Bible Containing The Old and New Testaments: Translated out of
the original Tongues, &c. Stereotyped by L. Johnson, Philadelphia. Alexander
Towar, 19 St.-James-St. and Hogan & Thompson, 139 1/2 Market-st.,
Philadelphia, 1833. This Bible, formerly owned by Miss Anna Mary Riddick,
is now in the possession of Mrs. John Franklin Pinner. Transcribed: 1962.
     Note. See the Riddick family genealogy in Kilby, pp. 30-32. For the
ancestry of Mary Taylor (Riddick), see, Suffolk, p. 88, and "Redwood vs.
Riddick and wife," March 1814, in Munford's Reports, Vol. 18, pp. 222-227.)

****

MILLS EDWARD RIDDICK BIBLE.

(Inscribed on flyleaf:)
          Mills E. Riddick / May 12, 1848 / Presented / by / Mary Riddick /
          His Mother

Marriages

Married in Suffolk, Va., February the 8th, 1844, By the Rev. Allen R.

Bernard, Mills Edward Riddick son of Mills and Mary Riddick to Clara Ann
Judkins, Daughter of Jarratt and Content Judkins.

Married in Nansemond Co., Va., Sept. 18th, 1879, By the Rev. James Crowde
Mills J. Riddick son of Mills and Clara Riddick & Ella L. Franklin, daughter of
Javan and Jane Franklin.

Births

Mills Jarrett son of Mills Edward and Clara Ann Riddick was born on the 5th
of September 1848.

William Edward son of Mills Edward & Clara Ann Riddick was born the 26th
of October 1852.

Mary Whitehead Daughter of Mills Edward & Clara Ann Riddick was born the
22nd of May 1855.

Josiah Riddick son of Mills Edward & Clara Ann Riddick was born the 7th day of
February 1858.

Emmett Hatton son of Mills Edward and Clara Ann Riddick was born on the 31st
of January 1860.

Cornelia Taylor Daughter of Mills Edward and Clara Ann Riddick was born on
the 13th day of December 1861.

Mills Edward Riddick son of Mills and Mary Riddick was born on the 23d of
January 1818.

Clara Ann Judkins daughter of Jarratt W. and Content Judkins was born on the
12th day of May 1825.

Mills Jarratt & William Edward Riddick were baptised by the Rev. E. Peterson
August 9th 1857.

Josiah and Emmett Hatton Riddick were Baptised by the Rev. Wm. E. Judkins
August 30th, 1861.

Mary Content Riddick was Baptised by the Rev. Wm. E. Judkins Dec. 14th 1880

Deaths

Died on the 13th day of July 1856, Mary Whitehead daughter of Mills E. and
Clara Ann Riddick.

Died on the 12th day of June 1862 Cornelia Taylor daughter of Mills E. Riddick and Clara Ann Riddick.

Died on the 2nd day of July 1864 William E. Riddick son of Mills E. and Clara Ann Riddick.

Died on the 2nd day of June 1865 Emmett Hatton Riddick son of Mills E. Riddick and Clara A. Riddick.

Died on the 4th of Sept. 1884 Mary C. daughter of Mills J. and Ella L. Riddick, Age 4 years 2 months & 16 days.

Died July 24, 1902 Age 77 years Clara A. Riddick wife of Mills Edward Riddick.

Died May 17, 1923 Mills Jarratt Riddick in his 75th year.

Died on May 22nd 1925 Emmett J. Riddick son of Mills J. and Ella Riddick in his 43rd year.

Died on July 10, 1935, Ella L. Riddick in her 84th year.

Marriages

Emmett J. Riddick and Ursula Williams were married Nov. 11, 1909.

Effie Jane Riddick and James Brittain were married Sept. 1907.

Gertrude L. Riddick and John Brooke Pruden were married June 8, 1910.

Arthur Elliott (sic).

Mills Allen Riddick and Margaret Corbitt were married ...

Births

Emmett J. Riddick, son of Emmett J. and Ursula W. Riddick was born Aug. 21, 1911.

Virginia Williams Riddick daughter of Emmett J. & Ursula W. Riddick was born Oct. 1, 1914.

Virginia Riddick Brittain daughter of Effie Jane Riddick & James Brittain was born Oct. 13, 1908.

James Riddick, son of Effie Jane Riddick & James Brittain was born Oct. 21, 1909.

John Brooke Pruden, son of Gerturde L. Riddick & John Brooke Pruden was bo
Aug. 20, 1916.

Mills A. Riddick son of Mills A. Riddick and Margaret Corbitt (was born).....

Mary Ann Riddick, daughter of Mills A. Riddick and Margaret Corbitt (was bor

(On sheet attached)

Married in Portsmouth, Va., on the 24th of January, 1884, by the Rev. A. E.
Owen, Josiah Riddick & Jeanette Bensten.

Born in Nansemond Co., Va., on the 6th of December 1884, Sat.   1/2 past nin
A.M. Christal Clara, daughter of Josiah and Jeanette Riddick.

Born in Nansemond Co., Va., on the 2nd of Nov. 1885, Monday at 11 o'clock
A.M., Josiah Judkins, son of Josiah & Jeanette Riddick.

Born in Norfolk Co., Va., on May 14th, 1888, Monday 10 o'clock P.M., Maria
Jeanette, daughter of Josiah & Jeanette Riddick.

Born in Portsmouth, Va., March 22nd 1890, Richard Hamlette, son of Josiah &
Jeannette Riddick.

Died in Portsmouth, Va., on 7th April, 1890, Mrs. Jeanette Riddick, wife
of Josiah Riddick.

Died in Portsmouth, Va., on the 15th of June, 1890, Richard Hamlette, infant
Josiah & Jeanette Riddick.

Died in Portsmouth Oct. 1902 Josiah Riddick, son of Mills E. and Clara
Riddick.

(The Bible, printed in New York in 1845, is owned by Mrs. John Brooke Pruden
nee Gertrude Lee Riddick. For this branch of the Riddick family, see Kilby, p.

****

NATHANIEL RIDDICK BIBLE.

(Written on flyleaf:)

Nathaniel Riddick   Suffolk, Va.   1843

Presented to Jno. T. Riddick son of Nathaniel Riddick by his father at his
death 1882.

Presented to Nathaniel Riddick Withers by his uncle Jno. Thompson Riddick
at his death 1884.

Presented to Nathaniel Riddick Withers, Jr. by his father Nathaniel Riddick
Withers at his death Dec. 4th 1920.

(Page 1)   Family Record.

Marriages.

Nathaniel Riddick, Son of Mills & Mary Riddick, & Mis(s)ouri Ann Jones
Kilby, daughter of John Thompson & Ann Newton Kilby, were married 19th
December A. D. 1839.

Austin Chin(n) Withers, Son of Robert W. & Susan D. Withers and Missouri
Taylor Riddick, daughter of Nathaniel & Missouri A. J. Riddick, were
married at Suffolk, Virginia, on the first day of June, 1871.

Arthur Woolford, Son of Arthur G. & Annie P. Woolford and Missouri Kilby Withers,
daughter of Augstin C. and M. T. Withers, were married at Suffolk, Va., on the
21st day of June, 1893.

Jno. Thornton Withers son of Austin Chinn & Missouri Taylor Withers was
married to Phoebe Jones daughter of Wm. H. Jones and Sarah Virginia (Jones)
in Suffolk, Va. Oct. 25, 1905 (last number indistinct).

Anne daughter of Mills Riddick & Josiah Riddick son of Mills Riddick son of
Josiah Riddick.

Capt. Mills Riddick & Mary Taylor daughter of Capt. Richard Taylor were
married Oct. 27th 1803.

Nathaniel Riddick Withers, son of Austin Chinn and Missouri Taylor Withers
and Mary Rosa Etheredge, daughter of C. Melville & Mary Washington Etheredge
were married Dec. 14th 1898, at Charlotte, N. C.

(Page 2)   Births.

Anna Mary, daughter of Nathaniel & Missouri Ann Jones Riddick, was born 21st
July 1841.

Mills, son of Nathaniel & Missouri Ann Jones Riddick was born 8th October, 1843.

John Thompson, son of Nathaniel & Missouri Ann Jones Riddick was born 1st
August, 1845.

Missouri Taylor, Daughter of Nathl & Missouri Riddick, was born 4th August 1848.

Deaths.

Cordelia Kilby, Daughter of Nathl & Missouri Riddick, departed this life 7th Oct. 1852.

Mills Riddick, son of Nathl & Missouri A. J. Riddick, departed this life at Suffolk, Virginia, August 7th 1877.

John Thompson Riddick, son of Nathl & Missouri A. J. Riddick, departed this life at Suffolk, Virginia, on the 18th day of July 1884.

Nathaniel Henley Riddick (died) in Norfolk, Va., February 14, 1901.

(Page 3)   Births.

Nathaniel Henley & Cordelia Kilby, twin children of Nathaniel & Missouri Riddick, were born 19th July 1852.

Sons and Daughters of Missouri Taylor (Riddick) Withers & A. C. Withers, her husband:

Nathaniel Riddick,	Aug. 2, 1872
Missouri Kilby,	Sept. 24, 1873.
Robert Walter,	Sept. 7th, 1875
John Thornton,	June 15th 1877
Jennet Alexander	April 22, 1879
Anna Chinn,	June 5th 1881

(Here follow four entries each of which includes the children's names and birth dates):

Sons and Daughters of Missouri Kilby (Withers) Woolford & Arthur Woolford, her husband:

Sons & Daughters of Nathaniel Riddick Withers and Mary Rosa (Etheredge) Withers:

Sons & Daughters of Janet A. (Withers) Darden & W(illiam) H(erbert) Darden:

Sons & Daughters of Jno. Thornton Withers & Phoebe (Jones) Withers his wife:

(Page 4)   Births.

Nathaniel Riddick, son of Mills & Mary Riddick was born in Suffolk, Va. 19th March 1819.

Missouri Ann Jones Kilby daughter of John Thompson & Ann Newton Kilby was born in Suffolk, Va. 16th November, 1821.

(Page 5)   Deaths.

Robert Walter Withers, second son of A. C. & M. T. Withers, died at Suffolk Nov. 15th 1912.

Anna Chinn Withers, youngest child of the above parents, died at Suffolk Aug. 17th 1916.

Mary Washington (Riddick) Etheredge wife of C. Melville Etheredge (mother of Mary Rosa (Etheredge) Withers, wife of Nathaniel Riddick Withers) died at Charlotte, N. C., May 28, 1899.

Christopher Melville Etheredge father of Mary Rosa Etheredge, wife of N. R. Withers, died at Charlotte, N. C., Dec. 31, 1916.

Missouri Kilby (Withers) Woolford, first daughter of A. C. & M. T. Withers, died at Suffolk,   Va., June 4, 1925.

(The Holy Bible. S. Andrus and Son. Hartford, 1843. Owned by Mrs. Nathaniel Riddick Withers. Transcribed: 1962).

    Note. Christopher Melville Etheridge and Mary Washington Riddick, his wife, had issue (surviving): 1. Melville Riddick (m. Emmy Pargo); 2. Frank Hunter (m. Eva Markham); 3. Mary Rosa (m. Nathaniel Riddick Withers); 4. Frances Marion (m. John M. Berkley); 5. Leoline Catharine (m. Tscharner H. De Graffenreid); 6. Laura Fraser (m. John Franklin Pinner).)

                    ****

        ROBERT MOORE RIDDICK - MATTHIAS JONES BIBLE.

(Entries written at the end of the Old Testament):

Robert M. Riddick & Mary his wife was maried March 24, 1798.

Robert M. Riddick Son of Robert M. Riddick & Mary was born Jany 29, 1801.

148

Richard W. Riddick Son of the above was born April 24, 1802.

Eliza G. Riddick daughter of Robert M. Riddick & Mary was born March 30, 1805.

Richard W. Riddick died January 30th 1853.

(Entries written on verso of the above transcribed page):

Matthias Jones son of Matthias Jones and Bethsheba his wife, was born 19th March 1772 and married to Polley Riddick daughter of Ro: Moore Riddick 11th day of August 1796 who was born the 1st February 1781.

Bethsheba Byrd Jones daughter of Mathias & Polley his wife, was born 21st May 1797.

Nancy Newton Jones daughter of Matthias & Polley his wife, was born 25th April 1800.

Robert Jones son of Matthias & Polly his wife was born 3rd April 1802 & died 7 November 1802.

Mary Prentis Jones daughter of Matthias & Polly his wife, was born the 6th of Nov. 1803.

Susan Swepson Jones daughter of Matthias & Polly his wife, was born 28th February 1806 and departed this life August 1806.

Bethsheba Byrd Jones daughter of aforesaid departed this life 3rd Oct: A.D. 1826.

Nancy Newton Jones was married to Joseph B. Baker 26 Oct: 1815, who died 23 December 1815, Nancy was married again 1 May 1817 to John Thompson Kilby.

Mary Prentis Jones was married to Ro: H. Webb 8th Aug: 1822 and departed this life the 9th September 1832.

Matthias Jones departed this life the 6th of May 1834.

(Entries written on sheets of paper sewed to the page beginning Malachi, Chapter III, verse 16):

Memorandum of Negros ages, a part of which is taken from an old Prayer Book formerly belonging to Col: Robert Moore Riddick, the Father of my wife Mary 31 December 1822 by Matthias Jones.

(The preceding entries are followed by a list of twenty-one names of Negro slaves, with birth dates, chiefly the children and grandchildren of "Jack & Lucy." Among the more interesting entries are the following):

Jack Old & Infirm died August 1804 A.D.

Lucy Old & Infirm died 2nd day of November 1819.

Billy, son of "Old Will," was born in 1799, the property of Jeremiah Godwin of whom I bought & sold to Herman, Mar: 1830. $600.

Charles bought of the heirs of Sarah Lewis was born the month of November 1803.

Amy bought of Darden Davis was born Oct. 1794 by his account.

Lucy Daughter of Matilda was born 18 Nov. 1830 the day of layin(g) the foundation of the new fire proof Clerks Office.

(For the complete bibliography of this Bible, published in Edinburgh in 1785, see the note under Euphane Fiveash Riddick Bible.
        The Bible evidently belonged first to Mrs. Euphane Fiveash Riddick and became, after her death, the property of her son, Thomas Fiveash Riddick (1781-1830),whose legal guardian was Robert Moore Riddick (d. 1804), there being no relationship so far as is known. When Thomas Fiveash Riddick settled in St. Louis, Missouri, about 1804, he undoubtedly left many of his superfluous possessions in Suffolk. This makes understandable the continuance of entries by Robert Moore Riddick and by the family of his daughter, Mary (Polly) Riddick, who married Matthias Jones. Their granddaughter Missouri Ann Jones Kilby (1821-1873) married Nathaniel Riddick (1819-1882,) son of Mills Riddick (1780-1844), builder of the three-story, brick house (between 1837 and 1843) now known as the Withers House.
        In 1862, when Suffolk was occupied by Federal troops, this Bible was taken from a Suffolk house and "forwarded" to Massachusetts, where the Lowell Daily Citizen & News (November 15) printed the following, in part:
        "Rebel Relics. A soldier in the Sixth Regiment, at Suffolk, Va. has forwarded to his friends in this city, some curious relics from that locality,

150

among which is an Edinburg edition of the Bible, bearing the imprint of His Majesty's Printer, 1785. The volume evidently was part of the household effects of the Riddick family. ... Turning to the last chapter of Malachi, we find a fly leaf of old-fashioned machine-paper, well covered with memoranda beginning with a record of 'Negroes' ages,'' a part of which is taken from an old Prayer-book, formerly belonging to 'Col. Robert Moore Riddick, the father of my wife Mary.' '' Here follows part of the record of slaves births. "It is an open question whether our boys in Virginia should be allowed to treat the Bible as contraband of war. We really hope the Riddicks will all become loyal and by some fair means get possession of the time-worn volume now noticed.''

Robert Moore Riddick (d. Dec. 4, 1804), of "Jericho,"Nansemond Co., married three times: (1) Theresa2 Riddick (b. 1754; Willis 1), and had issue Mary, who m. Matthias Jones, and Anne, who m. Thomas Swepson (1765-1819); (2) Elizabeth2 Riddick (1747-1793; Willis1), widow of Samuel Carr. of Albemarle Co. and had issue, Susan Caroline (1791-1862), who m. Joseph Prentis: and (3) Mary _____, whose children are listed in this record.

For further Riddick information, see the bound booklet, 48 pp., titled: "The Estate of Robert M. Riddick, Decd / under the administration of Joseph Prentis, left unadmi - / nistered, by Thomas Swepson," owned by Mrs. Peter Prentis Causey, and available on microfilm No. 2227, Alderman Library, the University of Virginia.

The Bible, now owned by Mrs. Nathaniel Riddick Withers, was returned to Suffolk at some unknown date and stored in the attic of the Mills Riddick (now Withers) house, from which it has been retrieved in recent years. It was transcribed in December, 1961, by Mrs. Henry B. Crocker, nee Katherine Beamon West.)

****

SOLOMON RIDDICK BIBLE.

Solomon Riddick son of Solomon Riddick and Mary his wife and Mary Smith daughter of Thomas Smith and Ann his wife were married on the 10th day of November A. D. 1800.

Robert Riddick son of Solomon and Mary his wife and Mary Riddick widow of Solomon Riddick was married on the 10th day of November A. D. 1803.

Solomon Riddick, son of Solomon Riddick son of Solomon and Mary his wife, departed this life May 1st 1883.

Richard Riddick and Margaret Copeland were married Sept. 30, 1830.

Solomon Riddick, son of Solomon and Mary his wife, departed this life on the 4th day of December A. D. 1802.

Robert Riddick, son of Solomon and Mary his wife, departed this life on the 27th day of Sept. A.D. 1843.

Mary, wife of Robert Riddick, departed this life Jan. 1857.

Virginius S. Bracy and Annie Smith Riddick were married May 7th 1873.

Solomon Riddick, son of Solomon and Mary his wife, was born in the month of March A.D. 1771.

Mary Riddick his wife, daughter of Thomas and Ann Smith his wife, was born on the the 18th day of January A.D. 1782.

Robert Riddick, son of Solomon Riddick and Mary his wife, was born on the 10th day of May A.D. 1783.

Solomon Riddick, son of Solomon and Mary his wife, was born Sept. 21st A.D. 1803.

Archibald Riddick, son of Robert and Mary his wife, was born Sept. 26th 1820.

Mary Louisa Riddick, daughter of Robert and Mary his wife, was born October 29th 1823.

Margaret Copeland was born May 7th, 1800.

Margaret Elizabeth, infant daughter of Virginius and Annie Smith Bracy, was born June 9th 1874, died July 7th 1877.

Solomon Riddick, son of Solomon and Mary his wife, and husband of Mary Riddick, departed this life December A.D. 1802.

Lemuel Riddick, son of Robert Riddick and Mary his wife, departed this life in the month of August, 1815.

James Smith Riddick, son of Robert and Mary his wife, departed this life April 1st, 1818.

Robert W. Riddick, son of Robert and Mary his wife, departed this life April 2nd, 1827.

Mary Eliza Riddick, daughter of Robert and Mary his wife, departed this life April 8th, 1818.

Richard T. Riddick, son of Richard and Margaret his wife, died Sept. 10th, 1855.

Sallie C. Riddick, daughter of Richard and Margaret his wife, died Aug. 22nd, 1855.

Robert H. Riddick, son of Richard and Margaret his wife, died Dec. 25th, 1867.

Margaret, wife of Richard Riddick, departed this life Nov. 6th ____ .

Richard Riddick departed this life Nov. 27th _____ .

Annie S. Riddick was born the 31st of October, 1831.

Sallie C. Riddick was born the 10th January, 1837.

Robert H. Riddick was born the 14th February, 1839.

Richard T. Riddick was born the 30th of September 1840.

Richard T. Riddick died Sept. 10th, 1855.

Willie Jamerson was born the 30th of December, 1820.

(This Bible record was among the papers of Wilbur E. MacClenny).

****

WILLIS RIDDICK (I), RECORD A.

Willis Riddick was born June 23d, 1725 (in ink) and married Mary.

James Riddick, Son of Willis and Mary, his Wife, was born September 14th, 1745.

Elizabeth Riddick was born November 22d, 1747.

Priscilla Riddick was born February 15th, 1749.

Anne Riddick was born August 28th, 1752.

153

Theresa Riddick was born March 25th, 1754.

Willis Riddick was born April 21st, 1757.

Christian Riddick was born November 10th, 1759 (in ink) died March 22, 1822,
aged 62, 4 mo 12 days, and married Archibald Richardson.

(In ink) Venerable, and Most amiable Mother departed this life Jany 26, 1801, a
aged ab. 60 years.

(These Bible entries were printed and pasted to the flyleaf of the Arthur
Smith - Susan Richardson Bible, formerly owned by Bradford Kilby.
    Note. The will of Col. Willis Riddick, I, was dated April 10, 1781,
and proved in Nansemond County Court, April 8, 1782. Willis Riddick, II
(b. 1757) died Oct. 10, 1800 (see his obituary in Supplementary Statistical Data),
"at his seat near Suffolk" ("The Retreat," subsequently called "Old Place").
Theresa Riddick (b. 1754), m., as 1st wife, Robert Moore Riddick. Elizabeth
Riddick (1747-1793) married twice; (1) Capt. Samuel Carr (see their marriage
bond in Supplementary Statistical Data), and (2) as 2nd wife, Robert Moore
Riddick. Her portrait, painted in 1774 by John Durand, is in the possession
of Mrs. Robert Henning Webb. The last item in the above record probably
refers to Mary Faulk or Folk, wife of Willis Riddick, I.)

****

WILLIS RIDDICK (I), RECORD B.

"1. Willis Riddick, born June 25, 1725.
 2. James Riddick, born Sept. 14, 1745.
 3. Elizabeth Riddick, born Nov. 22, 1747.
 4. Priscilla Riddick, born Feb. 15, 1749.
 5. Anne Riddick, born Aug. 28, 1752.
 6. Theresa Riddick, born March 25, 1754.
 7. Willis Riddick, born April 21, 1757.
 8. Christian Riddick, born Nov. 10, 1759.
 9. Josiah Riddick, born Sept. 5, 1748.
10. Nathaniel Riddick, born Feb. 2, 1768.
11. Elizabeth Riddick, born Feb. 5, 1770.
12. Anne Riddick, born Aug. 28, 1752.
13. Josiah Riddick, born Oct. 6, 1772.
14. Christian Riddick, born Jan. 24, 1775.
15. Anne Riddick, born Sept. 14, 1777.
16. Mills Riddick, born April 5, 1780.
17. Anne Riddick, born Oct. 16, 1783.
18. Henry Riddick, born Dec. 15, 1786.
19. Henry Riddick, born April 6, 1789.

154

Memoranda

Furnished by Mrs. Dr. Ned (Edward Dove) Phillips, mother of Mamie (Mary Claudia) Baker, in April 1871.

Nos. 2, 3, 4, 5, 6, 7, 8 were children of Willis Riddick and Mary (Foulk or Folk) Riddick.

No. 2. Grandfather of Caroline Walters.

No. 3. Mother of Susan Prentis who was the mother of Margaret S. Webb, Marianna Riddick, Robert Riddick Prentis, Peter B. Prentis and John B. Prentis.

No. 4. _____.

No. 5. Mother of Josiah Riddick and Mills Riddick, and wife of Josiah Riddick.

No. 6. Mother of Ann Swepson, who was mother of Mary Allen who was mother of Mary Swepson Darden, Lucy Murray, Edward Archibald Allen and Robert Riddick Allen.

No. 7. Married a Miss Simms (Anna Maria Syme) of Hanover Co., and was father of Mills and Lemuel Riddick.

No. 8. Married Archibald Richardson.

No. 9. Father of Col. Josiah Riddick, of "Soldier's Hope," and of Capt. Mills Riddick, and son of Mills who was a son of Josiah Riddick.

No. 10 and 11. Children of Josiah Riddick and Elizabeth Godwin, his first wife. No. 10 died when quite a young man, not having married. No. 11 became wife of Henry Eason and mother of Amelia Ayers, of New York.

No. 12. Wife of Josiah Riddick as before mentioned and owner of Prayer Book referred to.

No. 13, 14, 15, 16, 17, 18, and 19. Children of Josiah Riddick and Anne, his second wife.

No. 13. Col. Josiah Riddick, of "Soldier's Hope," who was the father of Josiah Henry Riddick.

No. 14, Wife of Thomas P. Smith and mother of Mrs. Virginia Cowper, Mrs. Dr. Arthur Smith, and Mrs. Evelina Purdy, and Thomas P. Smith, Jr.

No. 15, Died in infancy.

No. 16. Married Mary Taylor, of Williamsburg, Va., and was the father of Richard H., Josiah, Mills E., Nathaniel, and Washington Lafayette Riddick, and of Mrs. Mary Allen Webb, Diana T. Disosway, and Julianna Wood, Maria T. McGuire, and Cornelia Hatton.

No. 17. Died in infancy.

No. 18. Died in infancy.

No. 19. Died in infancy.

Anne Riddick, daughter of Col. Willis Riddick, and the mother of Col. Josiah Riddick and Capt. Mills Riddick, survived her husband, Josiah Riddick, many years. They resided at the 'Old Place,' on the Whitemarsh Road. This record is copied from her prayer book which was printed in the city of Edinburgh, Scotland, in 1788."

****

ROGERS BIBLE.

Philip Rogers and Emeline Riddick, the daughter of Edward and Eunice
Rid. were married January the 12, 1850.

Maria P., the daughter of Philip and Emeline Rogers, was born January
22nd 1856.

Deaths

William W. Rogers died November 2nd 1856.

Blanch Rogers, the daughter of Philip and Emeline, his wife, died July
17th 1858.

(From the Bible formerly owned by Edward (Ned) Rogers, son of Philip
Rogers and Emeline Riddick, his wife.)

****

THOMAS SWEPSON SHEPHERD BIBLE.

Family Record.

Births.

Emma Allen, daughter of / Thos S. & M. Fanny Shepherd / was born at
Suffolk, Va. / July 29th 1853.

Marriages.

Thos S. Shepherd & Maria F. / Allen were married at the / M.E. Church
Suffolk, on / Thursday 21st Octo 1852.

Deaths.

Maria F. Shepherd, the fond, / confiding, & truly affectionate / wife, died at
Suffolk / on Friday the 11th July 1856, / after a protracted illness, / borne
with a christian forti-/tude & resignation. / The God of Peace is hers.

T. S. S.

(The Comprehensive Bible; containing the Old and New Testaments, according
to the Authorized Version, &c. London: Printed for Samuel Bagster, Paternoster

Row. Philadelphia: Republished by J. B. Lippincott & Co., 1850.

Note: Thomas Swepson Shepherd (son of Dr. William Shepherd, 1770-1860, and Frances H. Swepson, his wife, married, as 2nd wife, Maria Frances Allen, daughter of Thomas William Gilbert Allen, 1807-1857, and Emeline Sumner, his wife.)

****

SIMONS BIBLE.

Kinchen Simons was born November 29th, 1770, and Decst this life the 29th day of August, 1825.

Elizabeth Simons, wife of Kinchen Simons, departed this life the 15th day of August, 1862. May she rest in peace.

Peggy Milteer, daughter of Kinchen and Elizabeth Simons, his wife, deceased this life the 18th of April, 1836.

William Augustus Simons Decst this life the 17th day of August, 1843.

Mary Eliza Simons Decst this life the 21st day of September, 1843.

John Hunter Simons Decst this life the 15th day of September, 1843.

The third son of Margaret Ann and Joshua Simons, not named, departed this life the 9th day of September, 1844.

Margaret Ann Simons Decst this life the 22nd day of May, 1850.

Parthenia Pierce departed this life the 7th day of November, 1857, age 46 years, 9 months, 25 days.

Elizabeth, wife of Kinchen Simons, departed this life the 15th day of August, 1862, age 83 years.

Joseph Simons departed this life the 4th day of September, 1870, age 24 years, 5 months, 10 days.

Virginia C. Simons departed this life the 25th day of December, 1870, age 21 years, 11 months 23 days.

Joshua Simons departed this life the 21st day of July, 1892, age 77 years, 3 months, 23 days.

Margaret E. Simons departed this life the 21st day of June, 1893, age 64 years, 3 months, 2 days.

Maggie (Simons) Rogers departed this life July 8th, 1919, age 64 years.

William Joshua Simons departed this life May 17, 1926, age 66 years.

Kinchen Simons and Elizabeth, his wife, daughter of William Powell, were married February 6th, 1803.

Joshua Simons and Margaret Ann, daughter of Jacob Daughtrey, were married October 31st, 1839.

Peggy Simons, daughter of Kinchen Simons and Elizabeth, was born November 13th, 1803.

John (Jack) Simons, son of said K. & E. Simons, was born October 23rd, 1806.

Winnie Simons, daughter of the same, was born August 19th, 1808.

Parthenia Simons, daughter of the same, was born January 12th, 1811.

Joshua Simons, son of the same, was born March 28th, 1815.

William Augustus Simons, son of Joshua Simons and Margaret Simons, his wife, was born August the 7th, 1840.

Mary Eliza Simons, daughter of the same, was born November 28th, 1841.

John Hunter Simons, son of same, was born April 1st, 1843.

The third son of the same was born the 1st of September, 1844, not named.

Joseph Kinchen Simons, son of Joshua Simons and Margaret Ann Simons, his wife, was born the 25th of March, 1846.

Elmedian Elizabeth Simons, daughter of Joshua Simons and Margaret Emeline, his wife, was born the 6th of April, 1852.

Samuel Huston Simons, son of Joshua and Margaret E. Simons, was born the 4th of August, 1854.

Margaret Henrietta Simons, daughter of Joshua and Margaret E. Simons, was born the 24th of October, 1857. (Maggie)

William Joshua Simons, son of Joshua and Margaret E. Simons, was born the _th day of September, 1859.

Martha John Simons, daughter of Joshua and Margaret E. Simons, was born the 28th day of July, 1865. (Mollie)

Sarah Barshaba Simons, daughter of Joshua and Margaret E. Simons, was born the 28th day of October, 1868. (Sally)

Mary Eliza Simons, daughter of Joshua and Margaret E. Simons, was born the 28th of October, 1865.

Joshua Simons and Margaret Ann Daughtrey were married the 31st of October, 1839.

Joshua Simons and Margaret Emeline King were married the 6th day of March, 1851. (Second wife)

Joshua Simons was born the 28th of March, 1815.

Margaret Ann Daughtrey, now Simons, was born the 13th of February, 1821.

Margaret Emeline King, now Simons, was born the 2nd of March, 1829.

Clarence Nelms and Mary Eliza Simons were married June 8th, 1892.

Paul J. Powell and Sarah Barshaba Simons were married December 28th, 1898.

William Joshua Simons and Lottie Hunt Phillips were married September 14th, 1900.

Robert Walter Ashburn and Martha J. Simons (Pat) were married April 25th, 1906.

Robert Walter Ashburn departed this life the 29th of August, 1919.

Annie J. Darden departed this life August 28th, 1917.

Leonard S. Darden and Lizzie King were married August 2nd, 1917.

(The Bible record was copied by Wilbur E. McClenny May 6, 1929. Inscribed on the flyleaf is "Price of Bible $3.75 / Bought January 1837.")

****

BENJAMIN DEVANIA SMITH BIBLE.

Benjamin D. Smith and Fanny R. Day were married Jan. 27th 1846.

James B. Norfleet and Fanny R. Smith were married November 19th 1872.

Jesse Bruce Brewer & Elizabeth Frances Smith were married in the Town of Suffolk by Rev. A. R. Bernard on the night of the 19th December 1849. at B. D. Smith's.

Births

Fanny Devania daughter of Fanny and Benjamin Smith was born April the eighth 1847.

Benjamin Devania Smith was born Feb. 14th 1822 at Summerton, Va.

Fanny R. Day was born Nov. 16th 1827 at Lerclgrun (?), Va.

Jesse B. Brewer (son of) Jesse B. & Elizabeth Frances Brewer was born in ____ 18_____ .

Deaths

Fanny Devania, daughter of Fanny R. and Benjamin D. Smith died Oct. 1st, 1851.

Elizabeth F. Brewer consort of J. B. Brewer died at Musk Rat Farm on the ___ 18 ___ .

Benjamin Devania Smith died December 8th 1869 in Suffolk.

(Bible Published by E. H. Butler & Co., Philadelphia, 1847. Owned by Miss Mary Edith (Mamie) Kelly. Transcribed Aug. 11, 1947.)

****

ARTHUR SMITH - SUSAN RICHARDSON BIBLE.

(Page one)   Family Record

Marriages

Arthur Smith and Susan Richardson were married on the 22nd December, 1804.

Rev. James Morrison and Almira Smith were married Feby. the 5th 1829.

Doctr Arthur R. Smith and Anna Maria Smith were married November 10th 1829.

Arthur R. Smith and Jane E. Herbert was married May 8th 1839.

Anna Maria Smith died Aug. 5, 1838.

John Richardson Kilby and Martha Jane L. Smith were married December 5th 1838.

(Page two)   Births   Deaths

Arthur Smith was born Oct. 9, 1779. Died 6th October, 1849, aged 69 years, 11 months & 27 days.

Susan Smith was born May 27, 1781. Died January 28, 1845, aged 63 years, 8 mos. 4 days.

Arthur Richardson Smith was born Nov. 8, 1805. Died Sept. 13th 1865, aged 59 yrs 10 mos 5 days.

Albert Smith was born Feby. 4, 1807. Died Sept. 1, 1807, aged 6 mos 28 days.

Almira Smith was born Sept. 9th 1808. Died March 5, 1846, aged 37 years 5 mos 26 days.

Alexander Smith was born Oct. 28, 1810. Died Aug. 12, 1814, aged 3 yrs. 9 mos 15 days.

Mary Eliza Smith was born March 12, 1813. Died July 15, 1815, aged 2 yrs 4 mos 3 days.

Delia Anna Smith was born Jan. 16, 1815. Died Octr 14, 1815, aged 8 mos 29 days.

(Page three)

Martha Jane Louisa Smith was born December 5th 1816. Died 7th Feby. 1888, aged 71 years, 2 months and 2 days.

_____ was born Aug. 17, 1821. Died Aug. 17, 1821.

Theodora Smith was born Octr 6, 1823. Died October 21, 1823, aged 15 days.

Anna Maria Morrison, daughter of James and Almira Morrison, was born April 6, 1830. Died Oct. 7, 1832, aged 18 months 1 day.

Indiana Smith, daughter of Arthur & Anna Maria Smith, was born November 6, 1830.

(Page four)

Susan Fletcher Morrison was born April 12, 1832.

Virginia Smith was born October 20, 1832.

Armirella Morrison was borned July 16th 1834. Died Sep. 17, 1836, aged 2 years 2 mos 1 Day.

Edward Livingston Smith was born June 16, 1835. (Followed by printed obituary:) Died Dec. 22, (1859) Mr. Edward L. Smith, son of Dr. Arthur R. Smith, aged 25 years. In Portsmouth.

James Arthur Morrison was born Sep. 10th 1836.

Anna Maria Smith was born Dec. 3, 1837. Died Aug. 6, 1838, aged 8 mos 3 days.

William Francis Morrison was born Sep. 17, 1838.

Walter Glazebrook Kilby son of Jno. R. & Martha J. L. Kilby, was born 10th of Jany 1840. Died 29th September 1840, aged 8 months, 19 days.

Arthur Smith, son of Arthur R. & Jane E. Smith was born 19th of Aug. 1840. Died in New Orleans of yellow fever ____day of 1867.

(Page five)   Births

Herbert Smith, son of Arthur R. and Jane E. Smith, was born 4th March 1842.

Worthington Smith, son of Arthur R. and Jane E. Smith, was born December 24, 1843.

Elizabeth Baughan Smith, daughter of Arthur S. and Jane E. Smith, was born ____1845. Died the 19th of March 1846 - aged

(Printed obituary)   Died
At Millwood, Norfolk County, on the 6th of July, Arthur Smith, son of Robert and Virginia Keeling, aged 6 months.

(Page six)

Willis Riddick, son of Archibald & Christian Richardson, was born March
1st, 1783.

William Richardson, son of Archibald & Christian, was born April 16th
1785, Died the 10th Nov. 1820, was burried at Bells Mills, Norfolk
County, Va.

Archibald Richardson, son of Archibald & Christian, was born Augt 26th
1788.

Dead

Betsey Richardson Daughter of Archibald & Christian was born Jan. 4th 1791.
Was burried at the Old Brick Church, in Isle of Wight Co., Oct. 19th 1864.

Mary Ann, Daughter of Archibald & Christian. Born Oct. 28th 1793. Mary
Ann Hill, Died Feb. 21st 1852, burried at Sunsbury, Gates Co., N.C.

Archibald Richardson, son of Archibald & Christian Richardson, Born Feb.
27th 1796. Died April 16th 1829, burried at the Retreat, near Suffolk.

Patrick Henry, son of Archibald & Christian Richardson, Born Jan. 10th
1798. Died in Philadelphia June 16th 1871.

(Page seven)

Leroy Richardson, 2d child of Jno. R. & Martha J. S. Kilby, was born 20th
May 1841.

Wallace Kilby (3d child of above) was born 22d February 1843.

Susan Smith Kilby, daughter of John R. & Martha J. L. Kilby, was born
27 May 1845.

Arthur Turpin Kilby, son of Jno. R. & M. J. L. Kilby, born 2d July 1847.
Died 2d Jany. 1857, aged 3 years & 6 months.

Wilbur Jno. Kilby, son of Jno. R. & M. J. L. Kilby, was born 18th April,
1850.

Livingston Clay Kilby, son of Jno.R. & M. J. L. Kilby, was born 6th April,
1852.

Annette Maria Kilby, daughter of Jno. R. & M. J. L. Kilby, was born 27 Dec. 1853.

(Page five)

Joseph Smith Morrison, son of James & Almira Morrison, was born 21st Decem. 1840.

Sarah Caroline Morrison, child of above, was born 7th April, 1843.

Edwin Smith Morrison, son of James & Almira Morrison, was born April 6th 1845. Died May 4th 1845, aged 1 year 28 days.

(Bible published by M'Carty & Davis, No. 171 Market Street, Philadelphia: I. Ashmead & Co., Printers, 1830. Formerly owned by Bradford Kilby. For a genealogy of the Smith, Riddick, and Kilby families, see Kilby, pp. 7-14, 28-29, 37.)

****

THOMAS SMITH BIBLE.

Family Record

Births

Thomas Smith was married to Ann Smith Nov. 26th 1772.

Mourning Smith, daughter of Thomas and Ann Smith, was born Nov. 10th, 1773.

Elizabeth Smith, daughter of Thos. and Ann Smith, was born Nov. 4th, 1775.

Washington Smith, son of Thos. and Ann Smith, was born Aug. 11th, 1777.

Clary Smith, son of Thos. and Ann Smith, was born Oct. 15th, 1779.

Mary Smith, daughter of Thos. and Ann Smith, was born Jany. 18th, 1782.

Thomas P. Smith, so of Thos. and Ann Smith, was born Jany. 26th, 1784.

John S. Smith, son of Thos. and Ann Smith, was born June 23rd, 1786.

Benjamin Smith, son of Thos. and Ann Smith, was born May 22nd, 1788.

Richard B. Smith, son of Thos. and Ann Smith, was born April 4th, 1790.

Nancy C. Smith, daughter of Thos. and Ann. Smith, was born March 24th, 1792

Charles Smith, son of Thos. and Ann Smith, was born Sept. 10th, 1794.

James C. Smith, son of Thos. and Ann Smith, was born April 11th, 1796.

William Smith, son of Thos. and Ann Smith, was born March 10th, 1798.

Thomas Smith and Ann his wife lived together 33 years and 3 days.

(page 2)   Deaths

James C. Smith departed this life July 21st, 1837, in the 42nd year of his age.

William J. Smith departed this life the 12th day of June 1870, age 55 years.

Elizabeth Smith departed this life March 27th 1872 in the 75th year of her age.

James Thomas Smith, son of James C. Smith, departed this life the 25th day Sept. 1843 in the 13 year of his age.

William J. Smith departed this life the 12 day of June 1870.

(page 3)   Marriages

James C. Smith and Elizabeth Odom were married the 17th July, 1815.

Richard B. Smith and Mary L. Riddick were married _____

James Thomas Smith, the son of Richard and Mary Smith, was born the 24th of Feb. 1849.

James Thomas Smith, the son of Richard and Mary Smith, departed this life the 21 of Sept. 1859.

(page 4)   Births

William Jackson Smith, son of James C. Smith and Elizabeth his wife, was born the 5th April, 1816.

Lucy Jane Smith, daughter of the above couple, was born the 18th Oct. 1818.

Frances Ann Smith, daughter of the above couple, was born the 23rd Sept. 1820.

James Monroe Smith, son of the above couple, was born the 10th March, 1822.

Richard Bowling Smith, son of the above couple, was born the 16th January, 1823.

Lucy Frances Smith, Daughter of the above couple, was born the 23rd May, 1826.

James Thomas Smith, son of the foregoing couple, was born the 23rd January, 1831.

Dianna Smith, daughter of the above couple, was born the 17th January, 1834.

(page 5)

James Thomas Smith, the son of Richard and Mary Smith, was borned the 24th of February A.D., 1849.

William B. Smith, the son of Richard and Mary Smith, was borned January the 25th, 1851.

Walter B. Smith, the son of Richard and Mary L. Smith, was borned the 14th of June A.D., 1853.

Charles C. Smith, the son of Richard and Mary Smith, was borned the 28th of March, 1855.

Arther H. Smith, the son of Richard and Mary Smith, was born the 11 of February A.D., 1857.

Richard T. Smith, the son of Richard B. Smith and Mary L. Smith, was borned the 8 of March, 1859.

Edgar G. Smith, the son of Richard B. Smith and Mary L. Smith, was borned May the 19th, 1861.

Archibald R. Smith, the son of Richard B. Smith and Mary L. Smith, was borned December the 10, 1863.

(page 6)   Marriages

Richard B. Smith was married to Mary L. Riddick the ninth of May A.D., 1848.

166

Richard B. Smith, son of James C. and Elizabeth Smith, was born Jan. the 16th, 1826.

Mary L. Smith, the Daughter of Robert and Mary Riddick, was born October the 29, 1823.

(page 7)   Deaths

James T. Smith, the son of Richard and Mary Smith, departed this life September the 20,   1851.

Arther H. Smith, the son of Richard and Mary Smith, departed this life July the 16, 1867.

Richard T. Smith, the son of Richard and Mary L. Smith, departed this life Feby. 24th, 1889.

Archie R. Smith, the Son of R. B. S. and Mary L. Smith, departed this life July the 22, 1892.

James C. Smith departed this life the 21 of July, 1837.

Elizabeth Smith departed this life the 27th of March, 1872.

W. J. Smith Departed this life the 12 Day of June, 1870.

(page 8)

Archie R. Smith, Son of Richard and Mary L. Smith, Departed this life July 22, 1892.

Richard B. Smith Died the 7th July, 1906.

William J. Smith Departed this life the 12 day of June, 1870.

Thomas P. Smith departed this life the 16 day of June, 1870.

(Bible published by Jesper Harding, No. 57 South Third Street, Philadelphia, 1848. Owned in 1945 by Mrs. Surry Parker.)

****

JETHRO SUMNER BIBLE.

Jethro Sumner Son of Jethro Sumner was Born in the year of our Lord 1798 And was Married unto Elizabeth Mary Lawrence the 29th day of June 1820-- The said Elizabeth M. Lawrence was born in the year of our Lord 1796.

Dempsey L. Sumner son of Jethro Sumner and Elizabeth his wife was born
August 1st, 1823.

Elizabeth Mary Sumner Departed this life December 13th 1823.

Jethro Sumner Departed this life March the 10, 1836.

Jethro Sumner Son of Jethro Sumner was Married with Ann Norfleet the 11th
of June 1824.

Mary Elizer Sumner Daughter of Jethro Sumner and Ann his wife was born
July 11th 1825.

Mariah Ann Sumner was born January 1st 1827.

Martha Jane Daughter of Jethro Sumner and Ann Sumner was born the
5th of September, 1829.

Charles Edward Sumner was born Oct. the 4th, 1831.

(Bible printed by Alexander Kincaid, His Majesty's Printer, Edinburgh,
MDCCLXIX. Copied by Wilbur E. McClenny and published in Va. Mag.,
Vol. 36, pp. 194-195.)   .

****

WEBB RECORD:
(Entries from the Gunn and Scott Bibles)

1.

Miles Gunn was born January 17th, 1797

Miles Gunn was married on the 10 of August 1819 to Tembte F(isher) Webb

Martha Caroline Miles Gunn Daughter of Miles & Tembte F(isher) Gunn was
born Nov. 12, 1820

Miles Gunn Decd. July 30th day 1821

2.

S. H. Scott and Martha C. M. Scott was maried the 10th of Jany. 1836

Tembte F(isher) Watkins the mother of Martha C. M. Scott departed this life the 11th of August 1848 in the 47th year of her age.

(1. Excerpts from the Bible of the Rev. Thomas Gunn, 1770-1859, who died in Robertson Co., Tenn. Original leaves owned by Mrs. Alice E. Clement. 2. Excerpts from the Bible of Dr. S. H. Scott, 1812-1883, who died in Robertson Co., Tenn. Photostat owned by Mrs. Clement.
    Note. Richard Webb (d. 1760), of "Hill's Point, " on the Nansemond River, married Mary Tembte (see, Henning Tembte), and had issued: 1. Henning Webb, and 2. Daniel Webb (ante 1760-ante 1806), m. in 1793, Mary Darden Gardner, and had issue:

    1. Robert Henning Webb. M. D. (1795-1866), m. twice: (1) Mary
       Prentis Jones (see, Robert Moore Riddick-Matthias Jones Bible),
       and (2), in 1834, Margaret Susan Prentis (see, Joseph Prentis Bible).
    2. Richard Daniel Webb (1797-1836).
    3. Mary Webb (1800-1858), m. c. 1819, William Lewis Anderson.
    4. Tembte Fisher Webb (1802-1848), m. twice: 1. Miles Gunn, M. D.,
       and 2. Ballard Watkins.
For the Webb family, see Suffolk, p. 101).

****

SWEPSON WHITEHEAD BIBLE.
(Excerpts)

Anne Swepson married Alexander Boyd and lived in Mecklenburg Co., Va. Her sister Elizabeth Swepson married Benjamin Whitehead.

Swepson Whitehead, son of Benjamin & Elizabeth Whitehead, was born in Mecklenburg County, Virginia, the 17 day of September 1777.

Margaret, daughter of Nathaniel and Mary Hoggard, was born in Princess Anne Co., Virginia, the 15 day of March 1784.

Swepson Whitehead, son of Benjamin and Elizabeth Whitehead, was married to Margaret Hoggard, daughter of Nathaniel and Mary Hoggard, Sunday June 1, 1800 .

Mary Hoggard, daughter of Swepson and Margaret Whitehead, was born the 19th day of July 1801 - married first Dr. Anson Brooks and afterwards Capt. James Cornick - died in Norfolk, Virginia, the 16 day of February 1879.

Elizabeth Swepson, daughter of Swepson & Margaret Whitehead was born at Portsmouth, Virginia, the 6th day of February 1804 - christened at Broad Creel by Rev. Mr. Whitehead - married Rev. J. H. Wingfield, and died in Portsmout. Virginia, June 1858.

Benjamin, son of Swepson and Margaret Whitehead, was born at Portsmouth, Virginia, January 28, 1806. Died September 15, 1807.

Swepson Whitehead departed this life in Norfolk, Virginia, on the 6th day of October 1839. Aged 63 years. Baptized August 1839 by Rev. J. H. Wingfield.

Margaret Whitehead departed this life in Norfolk, Virginia, on the 30th day of January 1840. Aged 56 years, leaving . . . two daughters.

This record was copies from the Bible by Susan V. Bagnall in July 1898.
   Note. The Reverend John Henry Wingfield, rector of Trinity Protestant Episcopal Church, Portsmouth, gave much aid to the Reverend Jacob Keeling "during the latter yearx of his ministry." Mr. Wingfield married Elizabeth Swepson Whitehead. Their granddaughter was Emily Swepson Wingfield who married Claudius James Riddick, M. D.)

****

WILLIAMS - GWINN - CHERRY BIBLE.

Marriages

William H. Gwinn and Louisa Williams married the 1st day of March A. D. 1843.

William Cherry and Louisa, his wife, was married the 6th day of Dec. 1849.

Births

William Gwinn was borned April 10, 1783, Peggy M. Saunders the wife of Wm. Gwinn was borned October 27th 1792.

Moses Williams was borned the 15th day June 1775.

Jemina Hines the wife of Moses Williams was borned January 11th, 1776.

William H. Gwinn the son of Wm. Gwinn was borned the 4th day January A. D. 1817.

Louisa Williams the daughter of Moses Williams and Jemina his wife was borned 7th December A. D. 1815.

Eldora Gertrude Gwinn the daughter of Wm. H. Gwinn and Louisa his wife was borned the 23 day April 1844.

Mary Louisa Jordan daughter of William Cherry and Louisa his wife was born the 21st day of October 1850.

Samuel son of William Cherry and Louisa his wife was born the 12th day of November 1851.

Emily Ann daughter of William Cherry and Louisa his wife was born 20th day of March 1853.

Olivia W. daughter of Wm. and Louisa Cherry was born the 15th day of July 1855.

Deaths

Eldora Gertrude Gwinn died Sunday morning the 22nd of July 1849, Aged 5 years 2 months 29 days.

Mr. Wm. Cherry the son of Wm. Cherry died May 3rd 1878 aged 55 years.

170

Mary Louisa J. daughter of Wm. Cherry and Louisa his wife departed this life the 31st day of July 1851 Aged 9 months and 10 days.

Samuel son of Wm. Cherry & Louisa his wife departed this life 31st day July 1852 aged 8 months and 19 days.

Emily A. daughter of Wm. & Louisa Cherry departed this life 15th day of July 1854 aged 1 yr. 3 mo. 25 days.

Olivia W. daughter of Wm. & Louisa Cherry departed this life the 20th day of July 1859. Aged 4 years 55 days.

Mr. Wm Cherry the son of Kater Cherry departed this life 30th day April 1878.

(Bible, sterotype edition published and sold by Kimber and Shrapless at their Bookstore No. 50 North Fourth Street, Philadelphia; impressions from the Oxford edition of 1784 by Jackson & Hamilton; the Cambridge edition of 1668 by John Field with the Edinburg edition of 1775 by Kincaid with the London edition of 1772 by Eyre & Straten.
The Bible, formerly owned by Mrs. Eulahline Knight, is now in the possession of Mr. and Mrs. J. T. Williams.)

****

WOODWARD BIBLE.

James Woodward son of Richd Woodward & Jamymay his wife was Born in Septr 19, 1791.

John Woodward Son of Richd Woodward & Jamymay his wife was Born Octr 27th 1793.

William Woodward son of Richd Woodward & Jamymay his wife was born Sept. 23d in the year of our Lord 1797. (Last figure indistinct).

(Bible Printed by the Assigns of Alexander Kincaid, His Majesty's Printer, MDCCLXXXIX, Edinburgh, 1799. Formerly owned by Marmaduke Woodward.)

****

DAVID PIERCE WRIGHT BIBLE.

Marriages

David P. Wright and Elizabeth Parker, 5th of Nov. 1839.

Married at the residence of David P. Wright on the 29th day of April, 1867, Cornelius F. Savage and Mary Jennett Wright, Eldest daughter of David P. Wright.

Married by Rev. Wm. B. Wellons, on the 10th day of October, 1875, Cephas King and Maria Louisa Wright, daughter of David P. Wright and Elizabeth Wright, his wife.

At the residence of R. R. Owens, David P. Wright and Miss Ida Parker, July 28th, 1887.

Births

Francis Wright, the son of David P. Wright and Elizabeth Wright, was born 29th August, 1840.

Thomas J. Wright, the son of David P. Wright and Elizabeth Wright, was born July 29, 1843.

Mary J. Wright, the daughter of David P. Wright and Elizabeth Wright, was born the 3rd January, 1848.

Josephine and Maria Louisa Wright, daughters of David P. and Elizabeth Wright, was born 22nd October, 1855.

Genoa Columbus Wright, son of David P. Wright and Elizabeth, his wife, was born 24th day of September, 1858.

Robert Henry Wright, son of David P. Wright and Elizabeth, his wife, was born July 12th, 1860.

Deaths.

Departed this life 21st January, 1850, Francis M. Wright, the son of David P. and Elizabeth Wright.

Departed this life 5th May, 1858, Josephine Wright, the daughter of David P. and Elizabeth Wright.

Robert Henry Wright, the son of D. P. and Elizabeth Wright, his wife, departed this life 26th day of January, Eighteen Hundred and Sixty Three.

Thomas Jefferson Wright, son of D. P. and Elizabeth Wright, died of a mortal wound inflicted at the battle of Gettysburg on the 3rd day of July A. D., 1863.

David P. Wright died on February 7th, 1893, aged about 75 years.

Births

William P. Wright, son of Nathaniel and Mary his wife, was born February 17th in the year of our Lord 1825.

Margaret Ann Duke, daughter of Hardy and Christiann his wife, was born December 22nd in the year of our Lord 1829.

Marina D. Gay, daughter of Josiah and Mary his wife, was born June 30th in the year of our Lord 1834.

Births (Children)

Joseph Henry, son of William and Margaret Anne Wright, was born September 24th in the year of our Lord 1847.

Louisiana Wright, daughter of William P. and Margaret Ann Wright, was born April 22nd in the year of our Lord 1849.

Margaret Elizabeth Wright, daughter of William P. and Margaret Anne his wife, was born January 19th in the year of our Lord 1859.

Nathaniel Josiah Wright, son of William P. and Marina D. Wright, was born July 31st in the year of our Lord 1854.

Mary Alice Wright, daughter of William P. and Marina D. Wright, was born February _____ in the year of our Lord 1856.

Ida Virgilia Marian Wright, daughter of William P. and Marina his wife, was born January 5th in the year of our Lord 1859.

Marriages

William P. Wright was married to Margaret Anne Duke September 15th in the year of our Lord 1846.

William P. Wright was married to Marina D. Gay November 10th in the year of our Lord 1853.

William P. Wright was married to Amanda Anne Richardson December 12th in the year of our Lord 1860.

Births

Francis Jackson Wright, son of William P. and Amanda A., was born July 22nd in the year of our Lord 1862.

Deaths

Margaret Anne Wright departed this life October 30th in the year of our Lord 1852. Age 22, 10, 8.

Margaret Elizabeth Wright departed this life August 12th in the year of our Lord 1852. Age 1, 6, 25.

Deaths

Nathaniel Josiah Wright departed this life September 8th in the year of our Lord 1854. Age, 1 month, 8 days.

Mary Alice Wright departed this life August 5th in the year of our Lord 1857. Age 1, 6, 1.

Marina D. Wright departed this life February 3rd in the year of our Lord 1859. Age 24, 7, 4.

Ida Virgilia Marina Wright departed this life July 1st in the year of our Lord 1859.

William P. Wright departed this life June 22nd in the year of our Lord 1864. Age 37, 4, 5.

Amanda A. Wright departed this life February 5th 1924. Age 91, 5, 28.

Frank J. Departed this life August 30th 1938. Age 78, 1, 7.

Amanda A. Richardson was born August 12th, 1833, in Sussex Co., near Wakefield, Va.

(Bible owned in 1938 by David O. Savage.)

****

Supplementary Statistical Data.

1. Excerpts from the "Suffolk" and the "Upper Parish" sections of the 1860 Federal Census of Nansemond County, Virginia, in the National Archives.

2. Marriage Records.

3. Nansemond County Wills.

4. Obituaries.

5. Miscellaneous Items.

The statistical data contained in the following five sections will aid in clarifying some of the Bible records. Further information about many of these families will be found in the Census of 1850, being Volume I in a series entitled Nansemond County, Virginia (1949),

The statistical data contained in the following five sections will aid in clarifying some of the Bible records. Further information about many of these families will be found in the Census of 1850, being Volume I in a series entitled Nansemond County, Virginia (1949), edited and indexed by Fillmore Norfleet. To facilitate use in the entries extracted from the Census of 1860 and the Marriage Records, the "heads of households" and the "husbands" have been arranged alphabetically. The wives' surnames are given, when known, and are underlined.

1.

Federal Census of 1860

Free Inhabitants of the Town of Suffolk, in the County
of Nansemond, State of Virginia, enumerated by me, on
the 20th day of August, 1860. H. H. Kelly, Ass't Marshal.

22.
EMELINE (SUMNER) ALLEN, 50, F.; Maggie A. Allen, 14, F.; Tenant T. Allen,
12, M.

32.
JAMES S(AMUEL) BROWNE, 42, M., Physician; Frances G(reen) M(inton)
Browne, 15, F.; Octavia K(nott) Browne, 8, F.; Mary G(eorge) Browne,
6, F.; Jamesetta Browne, 3, F.

3.
WILLIAM J(OHN) COHOON, 31, M.; Sallie L(ouise Beamon) Cohoon, 28, F.

89.
ALGERNON S(IDNEY) DARDEN, 31, M.; Mary S(wepson Allen)Darden, 22,
F.; Lucy B(ernard) Allen, 19, F.; Edward A. Allen, 16, M.; Robert
R(iddick) Allen, 14, M.; Anna J(ordan) Darden, 2, F.

140.
JOHN RICHARD ELLIOTT, 37, M., Physician; Sarah J(ackson Powell) Elliott,
43, F.

76.
WILLIAM R. ELLIS, 52, M.; Margaret F(rances Pinner) Ellis, 44, F.; Hamlin
E. Franklin, 17, M.; Ida S(arah) Pinner, 12, F.; Millard T(homas) Pinner,
10, M.; Martha S(usan) Pinner, 8, F.; Maud S(umner) Pinner, 6, F.; Jerrie
E(lizabeth) Pinner, 3, F.

6.
OWEN R(IDDICK) FLYNN, 56, M., merchant; Martha E. Flynn, 40, F.; Jane
L. Perkins, 20, F.; Thomas W. Smith, 20, M., Clerk; James N. Harrell,
23, M., clerk (born: N.C.).

143.
GEORGE GODWIN, 74, M.; Fannie (Green) Godwin, 72, F.; Elizabeth King, 32,
F.; David Jordan, 59, M., Boarder; Washington C. Smith, 19, M., Boarder;
Henning E(zekiel) Smith, 17, M., Boarder; Robert R(iddick) Smith, 14,
M., Boarder.

18.

JOSEPH P(ATTON) HALL, 48, M., Druggist, (born: Conn.); Jerusha (Walke Murdaugh) Hall, 31, F.; Laura P(atton) Hall, 24, F.; Joseph P(atton) Hall, Jr., 17, M.; John M(urdaugh) Hall, 15, M.; Annie J(ordan) Hall, 12, F.; Jennie C(ooper) Hall, 9, F.; Emma E(ugenia) Hall, 6, F.; John Darden, 18, M., Clerk.

133.

FRANCIS D(AVID) HOLLADAY, 43, M., Hotel Keeper; Emily S(usan) Pinner) Holladay, 43, F.; Alto F(rancis) Holladay, 16, M.; Joseph F(rancis) Holladay, 21, M.; Caroline E(lizabeth) Tynes) Holladay, 20 F.; ... Mary Ann (Holladay) Harris, 32, F.; John C. Pinner, 47, M.; Edward M(inton) Browne, 39, M.; Elizabeth (Ellener Stone Maxwell Holladay) Browne, 39, F.

24.

LEMUEL C(ARR) HOLLAND, 47, M., Physician; Catharine B(ryant Woodley) Holland, 47, F.; Granville S(harp) P(atterson) Holland, 21, M., student; Charlotte (Holland) Keeling, 76, F.

79.

NANCY (NORFLEET) JAMES, 55, F.; Clotilda (Norfleet) Milteer, 41, F.; Martha S(arah) Brinkley, 16, F.

14.

MOURNING (SMITH RIDDICK)LASSITER, 45, F.; Susanna Lassiter, 24, F.; Mariah (Louisa) Lassiter, 18, F.

80.

WILLIAM D(EANS) McCLENNY, 62, M.; Martha (Ann Lankford) McClenny, 54, F.; Adolphus M. McClenny,. 21, M.; Walter M. McClenny, 15, M.

116,

JOSEPH B(ENSON) McGUIRE, 30, M.; Kate (Bruce Blamire) McGuire, 25, F.; Emily R(iddick) McGuire, 7, F.; Kate B. McGuire, 3, F.

136.

JAMES R(OBERT) McGUIRE, 36, M., Hotel Keeper; Georgiana (Godwin) McGuire, 36, F.; Georgiana G(odwin) McGuire, 13, F.; James R(obert) McGuire, 12, M.; Frederika B(rewer) McGuire, 9, F.; Ida R(iddick) McGuire, 8, F.; David E(mmett) McGuire, 6, M.; Euclid B(orland) McGuire, 3, M.; Emily L(ouise) McGuire, 2, F.; Almira W(ilkinson) Godwin, 32, F.; Cherry G. (Kelly) Godwin, 56, F.

81.
WILLIAM HENRY McGUIRE, 46, M. (born: N.C.); Mariah T(aylor Riddick) McGuire, 42, F.; Laura M(ills) McGuire, 14, F.; Joseph R(iddick) McGuire, 13, M.; Herbert H(enley) McGuire, 8, M.; Ada M(aria) McGuire, 6, F.; Richard N(athaniel) McGuire, 4, M.; Leonard T(aylor) McGuire, 2, M.

132.
JAMES B(UXTON?) NORFLEET, 48, M.; Julia(na) Norfleet, 21, F.; Frances E. Norfleet, 15, F.; Lucy E(vans) Norfleet, 12, F.; Charles B. Norfleet 9, M.; Jesse (Perry) Norfleet, 4, M.; Margaret E. Poole, 62, F.; Mourning Lawrence, 45, F.; Jesse Perry, 64, M., (born: N.C.).

23.
WILLIAM H(ENRY) NORFLEET, 29, M.; Jerusha (Brinkley) Norfleet, 29, F.; Wortley Norfleet, 1, F.; Mary (Norfleet) Brinkley, 68, F., Housekeeper.

16.
WILSON NORFLEET, 39, M., clerk; Caroline V(irginia McGuire) Norfleet, 33, F.; Virginia W(ilson) Norfleet, 15, F.; Willie A(nna) Norfleet, 10, F.; Emily R(iddick) Norfleet, 5, F.; Lizzie F(letcher) Norfleet, 4, F.; Edward A(lston) Norfleet, 7/12, M.; Emily (Riddick) McGuire, 67, F. (born: N.C.)

17.
JAMES W. PEDIN, 36, M., Merchant; Ellen P. (Whitlock) Pedin, 26, F.; James M. Bailey, 21, M., Clerk.

18 (sic)
JOHN F(RANKLIN) PINNER, 42, M.; Margaret P(atience Beale) Pinner, 42, F.; Jesse D. Daughtrey, 18, M.; Charles W. Daughtrey, 15, M.; Laura B(oswell) Daughtrey, 13, F.; Albert B. Daughtrey, 12, M.; Margaret A(nn) Daughtrey, 10, F.; William L(amb) Daughtrey, 8, M.; Harriet L. Beale, 44, F.; Susan Holland, 44, F.

35.
PETER B(OWDOIN) PRENTIS, 40, M., Clerk of Court; Eliza (Wrenn) Prentis, 40, F.; Martha J(osephine) Prentis, 15, F.; Sallie F. Segar (?), 28, F., Teacher; Abram T(homas) Norfleet, 28, M., Clerk.

33.
SUSAN (CAROLINE) R(IDDICK) PRENTIS, 68, F.; Elizabeth Doik, 58, F.

139.
ARCHIBALD C. RIDDICK, 39, M., Boarding House; Margaret E(lizabeth Sumner) Riddick, 29, F.; Archibald (Pascoe) Riddick, 7, M.; Margaret T. Riddick, 4, F.; Anna G. Riddick, 2, F.; George T. Williams, 30, M., Minister; Marmaduke Jones, 25, M., Boarder.

134.
BENJAMIN (BRIDGER) RIDDICK, 50, M.; Eliza J(erusha Porter) Riddick,
45, F.; Eliza P(riscilla) Riddick, 20, F.; Louisiana Riddick, 16, F.;
Ellen C(ustine) Riddick, 17, F.; Archibald A(llen) Riddick, 11, M.

87.
JOHN R(OBERT) RIDDICK, 33, M., (born: N. C.); Julia D(rew Roberts)
Riddick, 30, F.; Francis C. Allen, 6, M. (born: Missouri); Eliza R.
Riddick, 3, F.; Margaret Riddick, 1, F.; Mary L. Riddick, 11, F.
(born: N. C.); John H(enry) Riddick, 9, M. (born: New York).

34.
NATHANIEL RIDDICK, 41, M.; Missouri (Ann) J(ones Kilby) Riddick, 38,
F.; Anna Mary Riddick, 19, F.; Mills Riddick, 17, M.; John T(hompson)
Riddick, 16, M.; Missouri T(aylor) Riddick, 12, F.; Nathl H(enley)
Riddick, 8, M.; Elizabeth Richardson, 68, F.

77.
RICHARD T(AYLOR) RIDDICK, 25, M.; Alice M. (Keeling) Riddick, 20, F.;
Alice Godwin, 27, F.; Sallie W. Keeling, 10, F.

1.
WASHINGTON (LAFAYETTE) RIDDICK, 35, M., Atty. at Law; Fanny M(arion
Blount) Riddick, 35, F.; Julien F(razier) Riddick, 15, M.; (Mills) McDonal
Riddick, 10, M.; Mary W(ashington) Riddick, 7, F.

13.
WILLIS S(MITH) RIDDICK, 41, M., agent Dismal Swamp Land Co. a Mary A(nn
Riddick) Riddick, 29, F.; Margaret E(lizabeth) Riddick, 6, F.; Willis
S(mith) Riddick, 3, M.; Jethro (sic) (Ballentine) Riddick, 2/12, M.; Lucy
A(nn Riddick) Knight, 39, F.; Caroline V(irginia) Riddick, 28, F.; James
R. Knight, 18, M.; John R. Knight, 15, M.

61.
WILLIAM SHEPHERD, 76, M., Gentleman.

115.
BENJAMIN D(EVANIA) SMITH, 35, M.; Fannie R. D(ay) Smith, 32, F.; Fannie
D. Eley, 14, F.; Martha Powell, 55, F.; Edith (Eley Ballard) Holladay,
60. F.

21.
WILLIAM SUMNER, 56, M., gentleman; Ann (Jordan) Sumner, 61 F.; Frances
(Digges) Sumner, 27, F.; Mary E(liza) Murdaugh, 40, F.; Martha J(ordan)
Murdaugh, 35, F.

25.
ROBERT H(ENNING WEBB, 64, M., Physician; Margaret S(usan Prentis)
Webb, 49, F.; Joseph P(rentis) Webb, 16, M.

****

Federal Census of Nansemond County,
Virginia, July 30, 1860.

Upper Parish

312.
MARGARET ANN (WILLIAMS) BALLARD, 53, F.; Elisha L(awrence) Ballard,
23, M., Dep. Sheriff; Margaret S. Ballard, 21, F.; Lucy Ann Ballard, 17,
F.; Virginia L(ouisa Parker) Ballard, 23, Boarder; Walter W(ood) Ballard,
3, M.

21.
RICHARD H(ENRY) BEAMON, 43, M., Physician; Rebecca J(ane Applewhite)
Beamon, 35, F.; Thomas N(athaniel) Beamon, 14, M.; John R(ichard)
Beamon, 9, M.; Virginius C(incinnatus) Beamon, 9, M.; Mary A(nn
Applewhite) Lewis, 58, F., Boarder.

632.
ALLEN R(ODNEY) BERNARD, 65, M., Methodist Minister; Lucy (Swepson)
Bernard, 52, F.; Thomas S(wepson) Bernard, 30, M.; Mary L(ouisa)
Bernard, 23, F.; Lucy A(llen) Bernard, 21, F.

629.
(JOSEPH) NATHANIEL BOOTHE, 69, M.; Joseph Boothe, 27, M.; Andrew
Boothe, 61, M.

712.
JESSE B(RUCE) BREWER, 34, M., Surveyor; Elfrida (Charlotte Holland)
Brewer, 23, F.; Jesse (Bruce) Brewer, 8, M.; Elfrida (Bruce) Brewer, 3,
F.; Annie (Woodley) Brewer, 8/12, F.

463.
JACKSON BRINKLEY, 50, M.; Martha A(manda Parker) Brinkley, 49, F.;
Sarah Jane Brinkley, 24, F.; Lazarus (Parke) Brinkley, 16, M.; Joel
(Holloman) Brinkley, 13, M.; Philip S. P. Corbin, 22, M., Physician;
Martha E(liza) B(rown Brinkley) Corbin, 20, F.

672.
DANIEL BROTHERS, 36, M.; Henrietta (Briggs) Brothers, 25, F.; Florine
Brothers, 3, F.; Sarah (Jane Hortense) Brothers, 1, F.; Wm R(iddick)
Brothers, 31, M.

7.
JOHN C(OWPER) COHOON, (JR.), 70, M.; (Mary) Louisa (Everett) Cohoon,
67, F.; Willis E(verett John Cowper) Cohoon, 37, M.; Martha C. Cohoon,
F.; Indiana M. Denson, 21, F.

261.
SAMUEL ELEY, 58, M.; Susan L. (White) Eley, 37, F.; Adolphus (S.) Eley,
14, M.; Alphonso W(hite) Eley, 12, M.

353.
WM ELEY, 52, M.; Wm Eley, 23, M., Physician; Virginia (Priscilla) D(ay)
Eley, 21, F.; Monimia Eley, 19, F.; Edith W(ortley) Eley, 17, F.;
Fannie D(ay) Eley, 15, F.; Eudora (Lydia) B(allard) Eley, 14, F.;
Josephine (Florence) Eley, 12, F.; William (Francis) Eley, 10, M.;
Willis Eley, 9, M.; William W(alter) Eley, 7, M.; William A. Eley, 5, M.

671.
HAMLIN L(EE) EPPS, 66, M.; Christian (Skinner) Epps, 72, F.

612.
JAVAN R(IDDICK) FRANKLIN, 40, M.; Jane R(ebecca) L(ee Eppes)
Franklin, 38, F.; Armesia (C. E.) Franklin, 11, F.; Ella (Lee)
Franklin, 8, F.; Daniel Franklin, 5, M.; Horace(E.) Franklin, 2, M.

187.
JULIUS C(AESAR) GODWIN, 43, M., Clerk; Elizabeth (S. Powell) Godwin,
37, F.; Sallie J(ackson) Powell, 13, F.

622.
JAMES GOODMAN, 70, M.; Priscilla (Bridger) Goodman, 80, F. (born:
N. C.).

8.
EZEKIEL P(OWELL) KELLY, 21, M.; Mary C. (Flynn) Kelly, 22, F.

10.
JACOB E(LEY) KELLY, 24, M.; Lucy E(dith) B(allard Holladay) Kelly,
21, F.; F.; Jacob E. Kelly, Jr., 1, M.

267.
JOHN G. KING, 45, M.; Martha A(NN MILTEER) KING, 36, F.; Cornelia
King, 18, F.; Sarah King, 15, F.; John (Walter) King, 13, M.; Christopher
(C.) King, 11, M.; Margaret (E.) King, 9, F.; Woodville (Albinus) King, 8,
M.; Edwin King, 5, M.; Martha King, 3, F.; Francis King, 1, M.

165.
DANIEL H(ERRING) HATTON, 45, M.; Cornelia (Riddick) Hatton, 39, F.;
Clarence (Riddick) Hatton, 14, M.; Catharine (Hatton) Corbell, 40, F.

20.
EDWARD R(IDDICK) HUNTER, 73, M.; Edward B(everly) Hunter, 43, M.; Joseph
(Bridger) Dorlon, 63, M., Teacher; Beverly B(aker) Hunter, 21, M.,
Student of Medicine; Judith A(nn) Parker, 18, F.; Nannie C. Parker, 15,
F.; William H. Hunter, 19, M.

310.
LEMUEL R(IDDICK) HUNTER, 34, M.; Julia (Ann Parker) Hunter, 36, F.;
Frederick (W.) Hunter, 27, M.; Walter (Scott) Hunter, 24, M.; Callie (i. e.
Caroline) Hunter, 21, F.; Mariah (S.) Hunter, 19, School Teacher; Julia(na)
Hunter, 17, F.; Clara (S.) Hunter, 13, F.

731.
JAMES LASSITER, 55, M.; Emily (Ann) Lassiter, 17, F.; Ann (E.) Lassiter,
12, F.; Mary (Elizabeth) Lassiter, 9, F.; James (E.) Lassiter, 10, M.

122.
ISAAC LEE, 72, M., (born: N. C.); Richd H(enry) Lee, 32, M.; Mary Elizabeth
Lee, 27, F.; Eva (?) Lee, 6, F.; Isaac Lee, 4, M.; James (Wilson)
Lee, 1, M.

261.
JAMES M(ADISON) McCLENNY, 45, M.; Eliza (Caroline Clayton) McClenny,
45, F.; RICHARD H(enry) McClenny, 19, M.; Judith C(aroline) McClenny,
16, F.; Thomas A(lphonso) McClenny, 14, M.; James (Alva) McClenny, 12,
M.; John D(avid) McClenny, 10, M.; Robert E(dwin) McClenny, 5, M.

117.
JOSEPH C. MEADOR, 39, M.; Susanna J(eannette) H(olladay Godwin) Meador,
34, F.; Jennet M(cRae) J(ack Godwin) Godwin, 50, F.

720.
ELISHA NORFLEET, 59, M.; Sarah E(lizabeth Riddick) Norfleet, 26, F.;
Hamlin (Lassiter) Norfleet, 23, M.; Elisha (Adolphus) Norfleet, 18,
M.; Margaret (Jeannette) Norfleet, 14, F.; Alida Norfleet, 7, F.;
Sarah (Katherine) Norfleet, 2, F.; Jason Lassiter, 25, M.

182

240.
JOHN NORFLEET, 43, M.; Margaret (Ann Rebecca Lee) Norfleet, 33, F.;
Robert (J.) Norfleet, 16, M.; Mary (Frances) Norfleet, 15, F.; Martha (E.
Norfleet, 10, F.; Isaac (N. W.) Norfleet, 9, M.; William (H.) Norfleet,
7, M.; Lydia (A.) Norfleet, 2, F.

206.
JOHN NORFLEET, 77, M.; Lydia (Porter) Norfleet, 52, F.; Martha (Jane)
Norfleet, 20, F.; Rebecca (Jane) Norfleet, 19, F.; Thomas (H.) Norfleet,
18, M.; Elisha (Franklin) Norfleet, 13, M.

209.
JOSEPH NORFLEET, 49, M.; Louisa (Norfleet) Norfleet, 44, F.; Frances
Norfleet, 22, F.; James (H.) Norfleet, 21, M.; Edwin (Smith) Norfleet, 16,
M.; Joseph Norfleet, 13, M.; Laura Norfleet, 7, F.; Fulton B. Norfleet,
2, M.

213.
NATHL G(EORGE) NORFLEET, 33, M.; Mary E(lizabeth Darden) Norfleet, 28,
F.; Anna C(owper) Norfleet, 8, F.; Lucy H(olcomb) Norfleet, 6, F.; ____
A. Norfleet, 4, M.; Mary E. Norfleet, 2, F.

218.
SOPHIA A(NN RIDDICK) NORFLEET, 49, F.; Robert E. Norfleet, 16, M.; Mary
L(ouisa) Norfleet, 14, F.; Wilson Norfleet, 10, M.; Solomon Riddick,
57, M.

511.
WILEY PARKER, 60, M.; Ann P(leasant Brinkley) Parker, 40, F.; James (Rob
Parker, 12, M.; Wiley (Williams) Parker, 11, M.; Alexina Parker, 7, F.;
Margaret (Ann) Parker, 3, F.; Francis (Edward) Parker, 1, M.; Christian
(Parker) Norfleet, 70, F.

177.
EDWARD D(OVE) PHILLIPS, 30, M., Physician; Mary M(atilda Riddick) Phillip
22, F.

191.
JEREMIAH (ARTHUR) PINNER, 40, M.; (Julia) Agnes (Godwin) Pinner, 36,
F.; Hampden (P.) Pinner, 10, M.; James H(unter) Pinner, 8, M.; Arthur
Pinner, 6, M.; Charles (F.) Pinner, 2, M.; Julia A. Pinner, 2/12, F.

210.
ALBERT K(ELLY) RAWLS, 45, M.; Eliza(beth) A(nn Holland) Rawls, 42, F.;
Angeline Rawls, 18, F.; Hugh (Kelly) Rawls, 13, M.; (Mary) Ann Rawls,
10, F.; Martha Rawls, 6, F.; Eva(lina Maria) Finney, 27, F., Teacher;
Sarah (Ann) Finney, 23, F., Teacher; Lulie (i. e. Louisiana) Finney, 16, F

573.
EDWARD C(UNNINGHAM) RIDDICK, 51, M.: Eunice (Catherine Pierce) Riddick,
49, F.; Eunice (Catherine) Riddick, 16, F.; Robert (Edward) Riddick, 15,
M.; Catharine (Goodman) Duke, 60, F.; Mary Goodman, 56, F.; James E.
Skinner, 17, M.

723.
HENRY RIDDICK, 63, M., (born: N. C.); Mary (Brewer) Riddick, 60, F.;
John H(enry) Riddick, 8, M., (born: New York); Mary L(ouise) Riddick,
9, F., (born: N. C.)

662.
JAMES (EDWARD) RIDDICK, 34, M.; Harriet D(eborah Rabey) Riddick, 30, F.;
Charles (C.) Riddick, 7, M.; Adrian Riddick, 1, M.; Caleb Busby, 15, M.

603.
JETHRO RIDDICK, 56, M.; Elizabeth (Vaughan) Riddick, 50, F.; Jethro
B(allentine) Riddick, 21, M.; Ellen (Catherine) Riddick, 18, F.;
Nancy J(ane Riddick) Ames, 23, F.; Mary (Elizabeth) Ames, 5, F.;
Margaret (Edwin) Ames, 4, F.; Mourning Griffin, 43, F., Domestic;
John L. Humphlett, 16, M.

670.
MILLS E(DWARD) RIDDICK, 42, M.; Clara A(nn Judkins) Riddick, 35, F.;
Mills (Jarratt) Riddick, 11, M.; William Riddick, 7, M.; Josiah Riddick,
2, M.; Emmet Riddick, 6/12, M.

680.
PHILIP ROGERS, 29, M.; Emeline (Riddick) Rogers, 28, F.; Edward Rogers,
7, M.; Mariah (P.) Rogers, 6, F.

318.
RICHARD B(OWLING) SMITH, 36, M.; Mary L(ouisa Riddick) Smith, 36, F.;
William (B.) Smith, 9, M.; Walter (B.) Smith, 7, M.; Charles (C.) Smith,
5, M.; Arthur (H.) Smith, 3, M.; Richard (T.) Smith, 1, M.

61.
DEMPSEY L. SUMNER, 36, M.; Martha (C.) E(verett) Sumner, 28, F.; Elizabeth
Sumner, 5, F.; Mariah Sumner, 2, F.; Martha Sumner, 2/12, F.

676.
SARAH (BRINKLEY) SUMNER, 60, F.; Gillie (Riddick)   Brown-(Orpen) , 85,
F.; Margaret (Brown) Norfleet, 45, F.; Mildred (Brown) Norfleet, 21, F.;
Robert (Riddick) Norfleet, 15, M.; Jesse Norfleet, 8, M.

168.
ROBERT H(ENRY) TYNES, 31, M., Physician; Mary C(atherine) Tynes, 4, F.;
Robert H(enry) Tynes, 2, M.

184

677.
DAVID P(IERCE) WRIGHT, 42, M.; Elizabeth (Parker) Wright, 45, F.; Thomas (Jefferson) Wright, 17, M.; Mary (J.) Wright, 12, F.; Mariah (Louisa) Wright, 8, F.

2.
Marriage Records.

Excerpts from the Nansemond County Marriage Register, Vol. 1. (Unless otherwise noted all participants were single and born in Nansemond County. Pts. donotes parents.)

p. 7.)   Dec. 18, 1867
Thomas N(athaniel) Beamon, 23 yrs.; widowed; Pts. Richard H(enry) and Rebecca J(ane Applewhite) Beamon, AND Lucy S(wepson) Bernard, 29 yrs.) Pts. Allen R(odney) and Lucy (Swepson) Bernard.

p. 2)   Feb. 26, 1868
Joseph Boothe, 35 yrs.; Pts. Nathaniel and Mary (E. Griffin) Boothe AND Mary E. Brinkley, 27 yrs.; Pts. Admiral and Margaret Jane (Saunders) Brinkley.

p. 16)   Feb. 23, 1870
Lazarus P(arke) Brinkley, 24 yrs.; Pts. Jackson and Martha A(manda Parker) Brinkley, AND Sarah E. Rogers, 23 yrs.; Pts. Jonathan Rogers and Mary Eliza, his wife.

p. 5)   April 3, 1867, in Suffolk
Exum B(ritton) Britt, 36 yrs.; widowed; born in Isle of Wight Co.; Pts. Exum O. Britt and Miranda, his wife, AND Ellen C(ustine) Riddick, 22 yrs.; Pts. Benjamin and Eliza J(erusha Porter) Riddick.

p. 5)   Feb. 21, 1867
Daniel Brothers, 36 yrs.; Pts. Riddick and Thamer (Copeland) Brothers, AND Cornelia Brinkley, 24 yrs.; Pts. Admiral and Margaret Jane (Saunders) Brinkley.

p. 43)   Feb. 18, 1875
W(illiam) R(iddick) Brothers, 27yrs.; Pts. E(dward) Brothers and P(eggy) A(nn), his wife, AND Vandalia Jones, 22 yrs.; Pts. D(empsey) and (Mary) E(lizabeth Holland) Jones.

p. 8)   Feb. 4, 1868
Caleb R. Busby, 23 yrs.; born in Gates Co., N.C.; Pts. James Busby and Mary Ann, his wife, AND Emily A. Lassiter, 23 yrs.; Pts. James and Elizabeth (Meredith) Lassiter.

****

p. 10)   Oct. 28, 1868
George H(enry) Crump, 50 yrs.; widowed; born in Surry Co.; Pts. Genl
John C(rafford) Crump and Mary B., his wife, AND Louie (i. e. Louisiana)
Finney, 24 yrs.; Pts. Dr. Crawley and Margaret (Ann Whitfield) Finney.

p. 4)   Feb. 7, 1867
Dempsey L(angston) Darden, 24 yrs.; Pts. William W(right) Darden and
Nancy, his wife, AND Alice N. Skinner, 18 yrs.; Pts. Henry (M.) and
Maria (Riddick) Skinner.

p. 16)   Feb. 10, 1870
William E(dward) Darden, 25 yrs.; Pts. William W(right) and Nancy
(Langston) Darden, AND Judith A(nn) Parker, 28 yrs.; Pts. Joseph and
Susan (Dorlon) Parker.

p. 19)   Nov. 24, 1870
Edward D(enby) Hargroves, 24 yrs.; Pts. James Hargroves and U. Eliza,
his wife, AND Fannie Day Eley, 24 yrs.; Pts. William and Lydia E(ley
Day) Eley.

p. 13)   July 29, 1869
Ezekiel P(owell) Kelly, 30 yrs.; widowed; Pts. Jacob H(olland) and
Susan (Powell) Kelly, AND Mary Connally Williamson, 20 yrs.; born
in Dinwiddie Co.; Pts. P. E. Williamson and Martha, his wife.

p. 14)   Nov. 17, 1869
Abel Upshur Kilby, 25 yrs.; Pts. Thomas J(efferson) and Anne U(pshur)
Smith) Kilby, AND Eudora Lydia Ballard Eley, 21 yrs.; Pts. William and
Lydia E(ley Day) Eley.

p. 5)   April 17, 1867
Virginius S(mith) Kilby, 24 yrs.; born in Suffolk, Va ; Pts. Thomas
J(efferson) and Ann Upshur (Smith) Kilby, AND (Diana) Ophelia E(ppes)
Saunders, 19 yrs.; Pts. James R(iddick) and Diana O(phelia Eppes)
Saunders.

p. 13)   May 25, 1869
Willis J(ohn) Lee, 23 yrs.; Pts. Patrick H(enry) and Joanna (Rawles) Lee,
AND Mary J(ennet) Jones, 18 yrs.; Pts. William H(enry) and Emma (Copeland)
Jones.

p. 10)   Aug. 13, 1868
James Murray, 34 yrs.; widowed; minister of gospel; born in Southampton
Co.; Pts. Robert and Elmira W(ilkinson Godwin) Murray, AND Lucy France
Allen, 24 yrs.; Pts. Archibald and Mary (Swepson) Allen.

p. 16)   March 3, 1870
William Walker Murray, 24 yrs.; born in Southampton Co.; Pts. Dr. Robert
and Elmira W(ilkinson Godwin) Murray, AND Susan Smith Kilby, 24 yrs.;
Pts. John R(ichardson) and Martha J(ane Louisa Smith) Kilby.

p. 30)   Nov. 18, 1872
James B. Norfleet, 60 yrs.; widowed; Pts. Abram Elizabeth
(Ashburn) Norfleet, AND Fannie D. Smith, 43 yrs.; widowed; Pts.
Thomas R(idley) and Edith Day.

p. 32)   Jan. 12, 1873
Wilson Norfleet, Jr., 22 yrs.; Pts. N(athaniel Cowper) and S(ophia) A(nn
Riddick) Norfleet, AND Clara S(usan) Hunter, 22 yrs.; Pts. L(emuel)
R(iddick) and J(ulia Parker) Hunter.

p. 18)   Sept. 27, 1870
Nathan B. Prichard, 22 yrs.; born in Petersburg, Va. AND Marian B(lount)
Riddick; born in Suffolk, Va.; Pts. Washington L(afayette) and Frances
M(arion Blount) Riddick.

p. 6)   July 10, 1867
Albert K(elly) Rawls, 52 yrs.; widowed; Pts. Willis and Ann (Kelly) Rawls,
AND Martha Susan Eley, 40 yrs.; Pts. Jacob H. and Celia (Cross) Eley.

p. 17)   April 28, 1870
Robert E(dward) Riddick, M.D. 24 yrs.; Pts. Edward C(unningham) AND
Eunice C(atherine Pierce) Riddick, AND Alice O(phelia) Brinkley, 23 yrs.;
Pts. Daniel Brinkley, Sr., and Eliza, his wife.

p. 20)   Feb. 28, 1871
Richard T(aylor) Riddick, 33 yrs.; widowed; residence in Chuckatuck; Pts.
Josiah and Elizabeth (Wright) Riddick, AND Marietta C(osby) Tynes, 25 yrs.
residence in Chuckatuck; Pts. Henry L(exington) and Caroline (Powell) Tyne

p. 5)   1867
    Edwin (E.) Smith, 67 yrs.; widowed; minister and farmer; Pts. Richard R.
    and Mary (Cross) Smith, AND Sophia Ann Norfleet, 55 yrs.; widowed; Pts.
    Robert and Mary(Smith) Riddick.

p. 1)   Feb. 15, 1866
    Henning E(zekiel) Smith, 26 yrs.; Pts. Robert R(iddick) and Sarah J(ackson
    Powell) Smith, AND Virginia Wilson Norfleet, 21 yrs.; Pts. Wilson and
    Caroline V(irginia McGuire) Norfleet.

p. 1)   March 20, 1866, in Suffolk
    Robert R(iddick) Smith, 20 yrs.; Pts. Robert R(iddick) and Sarah J(ackson
    Powell) Smith, AND Laura B(oswell) Daughtrey, 19 yrs.; Pts. Mills
    C(opeland) Daughtrey and Margaret P(atience Beale) Daughtrey.

p. 18)   March 27, 1870, in Suffolk
    Thomas W(ashington) Smith, 37 yrs.; Pts. Washington and Mary (Powell)
    Smith, AND Harriott G(odwin Borland) Borland, 32 yrs.; widowed; born in
    Murfreesboro, N. C.; Pts. Roscius C(icero) and Tempe(rance Ramsay)
    Borland.

p. 35)   May 8, 1873
    C(laude) W(illis) Wright, 23 yrs.; Pts. W(illiam) J(oseph) and M(ary) A(nn)
    Keeling) Wright, AND Margaret E(lizabeth) Riddick, 19 yrs.; Pts. Willis
    S(mith) and M(ary) A(nn Riddick) Riddick.

Marriage Bonds of Gates County,
North Carolina. (Bondsmen are
designated (B). The witnesses
have been deleted.)

Nov. 5, 1839
Daniel Brinkley & Mary Eliza Eppes, Wm. T. Parker (B).

March 11, 1811
John Brinkley & Christian Skinner. Humphrey Parker (B).

March 1, 1812
Riddick Brothers & Tamar Franklin. Daniel Franklin and Benjamin Sumner (B).

Nov. 10, 1812
Samuel Browne & Elizabeth Minton. Thomas E. Gary (B).

Oct. 7, 1818

Hamlin L(ee) Eppes & Christian Brinkley. Robert Riddick (B).

July 11, 1813

John Granbery & Elizabeth Cowper. James Granbery (B).

Feb. 12, 1846

Dixon H. Holland & Mary Eliza Sumner. Thomas B. Langston (B).

July 1, 1826

Edward R(iddick) Hunter & Ann Dorlon. Wm. M. Harvey (B).

Nov. 23, 1824

John O(mega) Hunter & Eliza Ann Pugh. James W. Riddick (B).

July 17, 1818

Wm. P. Jamerson & Margaret Copeland. John M. Skinner (B).

Dec. 10, 1821

Wiley W. Jenkins & Mary Riddick (ward of Josiah Parker). Kedar Parker (B).

Dec. 17, 1791

John Riddick (of Nansemond Co.) & Mourning Smith. William Cleaves (B).

Aug. 22, 1829

Richard Riddick & Margaret (Copeland) Jamerson. Miles Lassiter (B).

Nov. 10, 1803

Robert Riddick (son of Solomon Riddick of Nansemond Co., Va.) & Polly Riddick. Richard Austin (B).

Sept. 7, 1847

Willis F(olk) Riddick & Sarah Ann Hunter (niece of I. R. Hunter). Wm. H. Harrell (B).

Dec. 18, 1798

Washington Smith (of Nansemond Co.) & Nansy Cunningham. John Cross, Jr. and Wm. Goodman, Jr. (B).

****

Abstracts from Norfolk City
Marriage Bonds. (George Holbrook
Tucker, 1934)

p. 91)   Jan. 31, 1822
Colonel Josiah Riddick and Miss Mary Louisa Riddick. Jonathan Cowdrey (B).
Note: The above couple were married the same day by the Rev. Enoch Lowe,
Rector of Christ P. E. Church.

p. 123)   March 2, 1831
Thomas S. Shepherd and Miss Eliza Brown(e). William Shepherd (B).
Note: Miss Ann Eliza Brown(e) was the ward of John C(owper) Cohoon
of Nansemond Co.

****

Marriages of Isle of Wight County,
Virginia, 1628-1800 (Blanche Adams-
Chapman, 1933)

p. 59)   1795
Edward Allen & Mrs. Elizabeth (Reid) Driver, R(elict) of John Driver.
O. B. 1795-97, p. 214.

p. 3)   1786
(Benjamin) Blake Baker & Catherine Bridger, dau. of Joseph Bridger.
Isle of Wight Land Tax Bk. 1786.

p. 90)   Nov. 1, 1785
Frederick Hall and Peggy Jordan. (Under: "Marriages solemnized by the
Rev. Wm. Hubbard in the Parish of Newport, Isle of Wight Co. ")

p. 95)   Oct. 10, 1791
Robert Jordan and Elizabeth Copeland. (Under: "Marriages solemnized by
people called Quakers").

p. 41)   1800
Dixon Pinner and Nancy Driver, dau. of Robert Driver. W. B. II, p. 485.

****

Southampton County Marriage Register,
1750-1853. (VSL)

p. 16)   July 2, 1771
Cordall Norfleet and Mary Wilkinson, daughter of John Wilkinson.

Northampton Co., N. C. Marriage Bonds

August 29, 1827
Nathaniel Norfleet and Joannah Darden. Hugh H. Kelly (B).

Webb-Prentis Papers

Saml Carr's (Marriage) License Bond

Know all men by these Presents, that we Samuel Carr & Willis Riddick are held, firmly bound and indebted to our Sovereign Lord George the Third by the Grace of God, of Great Britain, France & Ireland, King Defender of the Faith &c in the sum of Fifty Pounds currt: money to be paid to our sd Lord the King, his heirs and successors to which payment will and truly to be made, we bind ourselves, our heirs, Exrs: & adminrs: jointly and severally, firmly by these presents -
Sealed with our Seals & dated this 18th day of January 1768.

The Conditon of the above obligation is such that whereas there is a marriage suddenly intended to be had and solemnized between the above bound Samuel Carr and Eliza Riddick, spinster: Now if there is no lawfull cause to obstruct the sd intended marriage, then, the above obligation to be void, else to remain in full force, power & virtue.

Signed, sealed and	Saml: Carr (Seal)
delivered in presence of	Willis Riddick (Seal)
William Pugh	

I Joseph Prentis clerk of the county Court of Nansemond in the State of Virginia do hereby certify that the foregoing is a copy of the original Marriage License Bond which is filed in the office of the said Court.
Certified under my hand this 10th day of December 1849.

Joseph Prentis, Clerk.

***** ***

(Suffolk Herald, Vol. VIII, No. 11, March 17, 1880)

Married. Mr. Joseph P(atton) Hall, Jr., of Suffolk, and Miss Anna J(ones) Copeland, of St. Catherine's Hall, Jackson, N. C., were united in marriage on Thursday last, March 11th.

(Ibid), Vol. VII, No. 24, June 11, 1879)

Married.

Our friends Capt. J(ethro) Bal(lentine) Riddick and Miss M(ary) Kattie (Catharine) Copeland were married yesterday afternoon, at the ... residence of Col. John R. Copeland, Rev. E. W. Beale, officiating.

****

(Ibid, Vol. VII, No. 8, Feb. 25, 1880)

Married.

At the residence of the bride's father, Maj. James R(iddick) Saunders,
February 18, by Rev. W. T. Walker, Mr. Hersey Woodward, and Miss
Augusta E(ppes) Saunders.

****

3.

Nansemond County Wills

(Listed parenthetically are: 1. birth and death dates;
2. date of will and year of probate.)

Vol. I, pp. 47-48)

John C(owper) Cohoon, Jr. (b. 1789-d. 1863. June 17, 1850; Mar. 12,
1866). Three sons: Willis, Thomas, John P. C. Wife: unnamed.

Ibid, pp. 92-97)

Hardy Cross (b. 1777-d. 1858. Jan. 20, 1856; April 16, 1866). Wife:
Martha N(icholson) Cross. Daughters: Sarah Jane Cross, and Mary Louisa
Cross. Son: Thomas Hardy Cross. Granddaughter: Sarah Frances Councill, wife
of Henry B. Councill. Sister: Prudence (Cross) Williams. Nephews: Lemuel R.
Hunter, William B. Daughtrey, William H(ardy) Cross, Samuel E. Smith,
Patrick H(enry) Daughtrey. Nieces: Mary Ann Brownley, wife of John Brownley;
Sarah Rawls; Martha Smith; Margaret Cross; Martha Ann (Cross) Ealey (sic);
Mary Cross, wife of Edwin Cross; Nancy Rawls, wife of Henry Rawls; Elizabeth
Smith, wife of John Smith; Sally Ann Cross; Susannah Pratt. To Mary Effa
Smith and Margaret Maria Smith, daughters of Edwin Smith. "My father, the
late Hardy Cross."

Ibid, pp. 168-169)

Sarah J(ackson Powell) Elliott (b. 1812-d. 1866. Aug. 3, 1866; Oct. 8,
1866). To "My relative Patsie Powell." "To Emma Susan Smith (an orphan child
now living with me, the daughter of Thos. P. Smith". Relative Pence King, wife
of James R. King. Sons H(enning) E(zekiel) Smith, Robert R(iddick) Smith.

Ibid, p. 155)

Sarah K(incheon Godwin)Wrenn (widow of 1. Thomas Godwin, and 2. of
Charles Wrenn. Feb. 6, 1873; Feb. 13, 1874). Nephew: James E. Godwin and
wife Addaline. Grand-nieces: Julia Agnes Godwin, Zulien Hunter Godwin, Rosa
Mills Godwin, and Lillian Jordan Godwin.

192

Ibid, pp. 218-219)
    Edith (Eley Ballard) Holladay (widow of 1. Thomas R. Day, and 2. Joseph Holladay, Dec. 10, 1857; April 8, 1867). Niece: Virginia D. Eley. Daughters: Lucy (Edith Ballard) Holladay, and Frances Smith, wife of Benjamin D(evania) Smith. Deceased daughter: Lydia Eley Holladay.

Ibid, pp. 334-335)
    Francis David Holladay (b. 1817-d. 1868. June 29, 1868; July 13, 1868). Sisters: Elizabeth Brown, Mrs. Mary Ann Harris.

Vol. 2, p. 430)
    Isaac Lee (b. 1788-d. 1869. May 31, 1866; Feb. 20, 1869), of Nansemond Co. Daughter-in-law: Mary Eliza Lee, widow of Richard H(enry) Lee, decd, and her children. Daughter: Margaret A(nn) Norfleet, wife of John Norfleet, Jr.

Ibid, pp. 270-271)
    William D(eans) McClenny (b. 1798. July 4, 1873; Oct. 13, 1874). Son: Adolphus M. McClenny, now living in Missouri. Daughter: Martha A., wife of Menalcus Lankford, of Franklin Co., N. C. Brother: James M(adison) McClenny.

Vol. I, pp. 89-90)
    James Riddick (son of Jethro Riddick. Oct. 21, 1822; May 10, 1824; rerecorded, April 9, 1866), "of the Upper Parish, Nansemond County." Wife: Katharine (Goodman) Riddick (b. 1793-d. 1861). Son: Edward (Cunningham) Riddick. Daughters: Nancy Riddick, Mary Ann Riddick, Mariah Riddick.

Ibid, pp. 158-160)
    Col. Josiah Riddick (b. 1772-d. 1838. Sept. 16, 1838; Nov. 12, 1838; rerecorded, Feb. 7, 1866), of "Soldier's Hope, Nansemond Co." Son: Josiah Henry Riddick, and his wife who was Lavinia Mathews. Brother: Mills Riddick. Friend: Dr. William S(umner) Riddick. Nephews: Richard H. Riddick (son of Mills Riddick), and Josiah Riddick, Jr.

Vol. 2, pp. 2-3)
    Mary A(llen Riddick) Webb (b. 1809-d. 1873. Oct. 25, 1866; Feb. 10, 1873), "of the Town of Suffolk." Daughter: Mary D(iana Webb) Upshaw, wife of Thomas E(dmund) Upshaw.

Ibid, pp. 386--387)
    Mary (Taylor)Riddick (b. 1788-d. 1875. Dec. 31, 1872; Aug. 14, 1875).

Vol. I, pp. 283-285)
    Mills Riddick (b. 1780-d. 1844. Feb. 28, 1844; Oct. 14, 1844; rerecorded Feb. 7, 1866), "of the Town of Suffolk." Wife: Mary (Taylor) Riddick. To son Mills Edward Riddick the plantation on the White Marsh called "the

Old Place." To my son Josiah Riddick, rights to the plantation with the mill attached, called "Soldier's Hope," late property of my deceased brother Col. Josiah Riddick. Sons: Washington Lafayette Riddick, Richard H(enry) Riddick, Senr, Nathaniel Riddick. Daughters: Mary A(llen) Webb, Julianna Wood, Cornelia Hatton, Diana Disosway, Maria T. McGuire.

Vol. 2, pp. 432-434)
Willis S(mith) Riddick (b. 1818-d. 1875. July 26, 1875; Dec. 18, 1875) "of the Town of Suffolk." My five children. Sons: John B(allentine) Riddick, Willis S(mith) Riddick, Jr. Daughters: Maggie (Elizabeth Riddick) Wright, Rosa May Riddick, Lucy C(aroline) Riddick. Son-in-law: Claude W(illis) Wright.

Vol. I, pp. 25-27)
Arthur Smith (b. 1779-d. 1849. Aug. 25, 1838; Oct. 8, 1849), "of the Town of Suffolk." Wife: Susan (Richardson) Smith. Daughter: Martha Jane Louisa Smith. Son: Doctor Arthur R(ichardson) Smith. Son-in-law: the Revd James Morrison.

Vol. 2, pp. 263-264)
James C. Smith (b. 1796-d. 1837, son of Thomas and Ann Smith. No date; Sept. 11, 1837). Wife: Elizabeth (Odom) Smith. Sons: William (Jackson) Smith, Richard Smith, James Thomas Smith. Daughters: Lucy Frances and Diana. Brother: Washington Smith.

Vol. I, pp. 23-24)
Washington C. Smith (d. 1865, son of Robert Riddick Smith. Sept. 6, 1864; Feb. 27, 1866). My brothers: H(enning) E(zekiel) Smith, and R(obert) R(iddick)Smith.

Wills. Settlement of Estates.

Vol. I, p. 245)   Feb. 12, 1866
Estate of Joseph B(ridger) Dorlan, John R. Copeland, administrator. Richard H(enry) Baker, a brother of the half-blood, Judith A(nn) Parker, daughter of Elizabeth (Susan Dorlon) Parker, deceased, a sister of Joseph B(ridger) Dorlon, of the whole blood. Edward B(everly) Hunter, son of Catharine H(annah Dorlon) Hunter, deceased, a sister of the whole blood of Joseph B(ridger) Dorlon, deceased. John R. Copeland in right of his wife, Judith A(nn Hunter), a daughter of said Catharine H(annah Dorlon) Hunter.

****

194

Abstracts of Copies of Nansemond
County Wills That Were Recorded
and Then Destroyed by Fire.

Edward Allen (b. June 23, 1753-d. Jan 7, 1815. May 11, 1814; Feb.
12, 1816), of Nansemond Co. Son: Henry John Allen ("land that lies back of
Jericho, which is in three separate tracts..., known by the names of
Blanchards patent, the Planters Delight, & Danl Pugh's patent of 144 acres."
Four sons: Henry John Allen, Archibald Allen, Cornelius Edward Allen,
and Thomas William Gilbert Allen. Executors: sons Henry John Allen, Archibald
Allen. No witnesses. Proof of handwriting made by Matthias Jones, James Evans
and Harrison Minton. (Copy of will in Military Land Warrants, VSL.)

Robert H. Fisher (b. 1765-d. May 26, 1815. May 1, 1813-no date of probate
"physician, of the town of Suffolk." Wife: Charlotte Fisher (real or personal
property to the value of $10,000 in fee simple). The "four orphan
children of my deceased half-brother Daniel Webb, that is to say Robert,
Richard, Mary Ann and Tembte Webb" (remainder of estate at death of widow).
"I desire...that my carcass be interred in as plain and little expensive a
manner as shall be consistent with decency, and that there be no preaching
over it." Executors: wife Charlotte Fisher, and Joseph Prentis. (Webb-
Prentis Papers).

Job Holland, Senr (Dec. 11, 1826; Jan. 12, 1829). Daughters: Elizabeth
Barnes (tract of land purchased of Henry Norfleet) and Mary Lee. Grandchildren
Eliza Ann, Robert, Zachery Everett, and Dixon Holland, children of son Zachar
Holland, deceased. Executors: Isaac Lee and James Barnes. Witnesses: Jos.
G. Holland, Seth Everett, John H. Lee. (Printed in The Hollands and Their Kin
by Lee Pretlow Holland.)

John Rawls, Sr. (Feb. 21, 1835; date of probate not given), of Nansemond
Co. Wife: Mary Ann (Norfleet). use of the plantation on east side of Somerton
Swamp, including the plantation "Providence." Abram Porter, William Porter,
Richard Porter, Elizabeth Porter and Lydia Porter. Nephews: John Norfleet,
Justin Norfleet, sons of John Norfleet (home plantation after death of wife
and mill and land purchased from Isaac Porter's Estate.) Nephew: Joseph
Porter ("the Quarter on the east side of Wainoke Road"). Nephews: Willis
Parker, John Parker. Two nieces: Polly Russell and Margaret Langston (the
James Rawls tract). Nephew and nieces: John Freeman, Patsey and Harriet
Freeman (land I purchased from my brother, David Rawls, and Marmaduke
Jones). Nephew: Albert K. Rawls and nieces Mary Ann Rogers, Joanna Rawls
and Stella M. Rawls, children of my brother Willis Rawls (the "Pocoson Land").
Executors: John Norfleet, John Hare, Sr. Witnesses: Wm. M. Jones, Andrew
Rawls, Richard Porter, John G. King, Jr. (From the manuscript collection of
Mrs. Marion Kelly Kendrick.)

Edward Riddick (b. 1765-d. Oct. 10, 1849. Feb. 2, 1849; Nov. 1849.
Endorsed: "Edward Riddick, Sr.'s will / A copy for Solomon J. Holland.")
Wife: Nancy (J. Goodman). Daughter: Mary Holland, wife of Solomon J.
Holland. Grandson: William T(homas) Riddick. Son: Jethro Riddick. Two
grandsons: Joseph R(iddick) Duke and David W(ashington) Duke. Granddaughter:
Margaret J(ane) Brinkley. Grandson: James R(iddick) Saunders. Witnesses:
James Goodman, Philip Rogers, Edward C. Riddick.

Robert Moore Riddick (d. Dec. 4, 1804. Dec. 1, 1804; Jan. 14, 1805),
"of Jerico." Daughters: Polly Jones and Nancy Swepson. Wife: Mary.
Daughter: Susan (Caroline). Son: Richard (W.). "Child that my wife is now
enseint with." Executors: Son-in-law Thomas Swepson, and wife Mary.
Witnesses: Sarah Yarborough, Eliz Williams, Ri Yarborough. (Included in
the "Account Book of Joseph Prentis, II," microfilm in the Alderman Library,
University of Virginia.)

Willis Riddick (1725-1782, April 10, 1781; April 8, 1782). "Whereas I
have reason to judge that the General Assembly of this State will think it
just that a proper allowance should be made me for the damage I have
sustained in the burning and destroying of my houses by the British forces,
in such case I give whatever the said allowance may be (if any) unto my
son Willis, and his heirs forever." (A single clause preserved from Willis
Riddick's will quoted in a report of the Committee on Revolutionary Claims,
April 17, 1834. Kilby Papers.)

Washington Smith (b. 1772-d. 1835. April 13, 1835; May 11, 1835),
"of Somerton." My present wife: Mary (land purchased of Robert R. Smith,
James C. Smith, and Henning T. Smith). Son: James Edward Smith. Son:
Benjamin Devany Smith. Daughter: Margaret Ann Smith ("all my right and
interest in the dower of Susan Smith in the land of her late husband Riddick
Hunter, deceased.") Daughter: Mary Jane Harrison. Son: Robert Riddick Smith.
Daughter: Sophia Emeline Hart ("land I purchased of Thos. P. Smith").
Daughter: Anne Cunningham Smith ("land I purchased of Josiah W. Parker and
Henry C. Parker"). Daughter: Elizabeth Frances Smith. Daughter: Martha
Cornelia Smith. Son: Thomas W(ashington) Smith ("land I purchased of Jacob
Daughtrey and wife, also land on the Suffolk road adjoining land of Jethro
Hamilton, Josiah Parker and the dower lands of Susan Smith late Susan Hunter
it being the right of land I purchased of George Reed and wife, John S(treeter)
Hunter and Ann B(arron) Hunter, heirs of Riddick Hunter, deceased." Son:
Robert R(iddick) Smith ("land I purchased of Lemuel B. Cunningham in 1812
for which no deed was ever obtained or recorded.") Executor: son Robert R.
Smith. Witnesses: E. Smith, W. B. Cary, Thos. B. Riddick. (The Mss. was
formerly in the possession of Marmaduke E. Woodward.)

Henning Tembte (b. c. 1700-d. 1771). See Note under Lemuel Riddick Bible.

4.

Obituaries.

Death notices in The Norfolk Gazette and Public Ledger,
1804-1816.

Allen, William, at his father's house in Suffolk	Dec. 4, 1809
Allmand, Mrs. wife of Harrison Allmand	Nov. 6, 1811
Calvert, Mrs. Margaret, relict of John Calvert, at Suffolk	Oct. 8, 1814
Cowper, Mrs. Rebecca, wife of William Cowper, at Murfreesboro, N. C.	Feb. 26, 1808
Cowper, Capt. Robert, at his residence in the county of Nansemond	Mar. 23, 1812
Fisher, Dr. Robert (H.), at Suffolk	Mar. 29, 1815
Godwin, Dr. Burgh, at his residence in Nansemond	Apr. 9, 1810
Godwin, Mrs. Clotilda, in Nansemond	Jan. 23, 1810
Granbery, George, son of John Granbery, lost at sea	Sept. 5, 1816
Granbery, John, lost at sea	Sept. 5, 1816
Holliday, John, in Nansemond, at "Mt. Pickney"	Apr. 23, 1814
Hunter, Mrs. Sally, wife of Dr. Edward R. Hunter, at "Piney Pleasant," Nansemond County	Jan. 28, 1811
Jordan, Robert, in Nansemond	Feb. 26, 1810
Parker, Mrs. Eliza, wife of Copeland Parker	Feb. 27, 1807
Pitt, Edmond, in Chuckatuck, in the County of Nansemond	Oct. 12, 1815
Riddick, Lemuel, at Suffolk, one of the representatives to General Assembly for the county of Nansemond	Feb. 22, 1811
Stowe, Willis R., of Bermuda, only brother of Mrs. (Susanna Butterfield) Granbery, lost at sea	Sept. 5, 1816
Webb, Kedar, in Nansemond County	Oct. 8, 1814
Wilkinson, William, at his seat in Nansemond	Oct. 5, 1807.

(Va. Mag., Vol. 63, pp. 332-348)

****

Index to Obituary Notices / in the / Richmond Enquirer
from May 9, 1804 / through 1828, / and the / Richmond
Whig from January, 1824, / through 1838.

Allmand, Col. Albert, Richmond, Whig, April 25, 1831, (page) 3.
Cohoon, Mrs. Ann (Willis), Suffolk, Enquirer, July 15, 1823, 3.

Cohoon, Gen. John C., Norfolk, Enquirer, Oct. 24, 1823, 3.
Copeland, Elisha, Nansemond, Whig, Aug. 19, 1839, 3.
Dorlon, Capt. John, Nansemond, Enquirer, May 14, 1824, 3.
Hall, Frederick, Suffolk, Enquirer, Oct. 24, 1823, 3.
Hunter, Mrs. Antoinette (Stith), near Wythe Court House, Whig,
    May 22, 1835, 3.
Jordan, Robert, Suffolk, Enquirer, Jan. 27, 1824, 3.
Kilby, John Thompson, Nansemond, Whig, June 19, 1834, 4.
Minton, Col. John, Nansemond, Whig, April 17, 1830, 3.
Murdaugh, Dr. John, Nansemond, Whig, Jan. 18, 1830, 3.
Riddick, Mrs. Anna Maria (Syme), Rocky Mills, (Hanover Co.), Enquirer,
    Aug. 29, 1804, 3.
Riddick, Lemuel, Hanover, Whig, Oct. 3, 1826, 3.
Webb, Col. Richard D., Suffolk, Whig, Jan. 28, 1825, 3.
Whitlock, Charles, Richmond, Enquirer, Aug. 25, 1820, 3.
Whitlock, Mrs. Charles (Peninnah Copeland), Enquirer, April 2, 1811, 3.
Wrenn, Maj. Charles, Isle of Wight, Whig, April 21, 1837, 2.
(Bulletin of the Virginia State Library, Vol. XIV, No. 4, Oct. 1921,
pp. 156-237).

****

Obituaries from Newspapers

(Unless identified, the source is unknown.)

Death of Dr. Jas. S(amuel) Browne
    Suffolk, Va., May 1, 1874. Dr. James S. Browne, an old and prominent
citizen, died here to-day of pneumonia. ... He was faithfully nursed in his
last hours by his nephew, Captain Joe Sam Browne, his son-in-law, J. M.
Binford, and Dr. Maupin, of Portsmouth, as well as by Drs. Kilby, Cropper
and Eley, of Suffolk. His body will be conveyed to the Masonic Lodge, of
which he was a Past Master..., where it will lie in state until Sunday
afternoon, when it will be buried from the Methodist Church. ...

(Suffolk Herald, Vol. XIII, No. 25, June 25, 1880)
Died
    Mrs. Judith A(nn Hunter) Copeland, wife of Col. Jno. R. Copeland, died
at her home in Suffolk, June 18th, aged 61 years. She was married in 1836,
and leaves two children, Mrs. A. F. Holladay and Mrs. J. B. Riddick.

(Christian Sun, May 16, 1879)
Death of Dr. Copeland.
    We regret to learn from the Northampton Reporter, that Dr. W(infield)
S(cott) Copeland died of paralysis at his home in Jackson, N. C., on Sunday,
the 4th inst. Dr. Copeland was born in Nansemond County, Va., in November,
1817. For several years he pursued the study of medicine under Dr. Webb,
of Suffolk. In 1840 he removed to Northampton Co. ... He leaves a son and
two daughters to mourn his death.

198

(Probably the Christian Sun, January, 1874)
Obituary.
Died suddenly of apoplexy, at his residence near Cypress Chapel, in
Nansemond County, on the morning of the 17th inst., Capt. Jethro Riddick,
in the 71st year of his age.
The death of this excellent citizen, has brought deep grief to a large
family of children, grandchildren, relatives and friends...but more than
any his bosom companion, who had lived with him nearly fifty years, feels
her loss. He had been for twenty-five years a prominent member of the
Christian Church at Cypress Chapel. ...

(A clipping; probably the Christian Sun, 1880)

Death of Mrs. Elizabeth Riddick

We regret to announce the death of Mrs. Elizabeth Riddick, which...
event occurred on Sunday morning last at her residence near Cypress
Chapel. ...
Sister Riddick was born in the year 1806 and in the year 1825 was
united in the bonds of matrimony to Captain Jethro Riddick, who preceded
her to the grave several years since. The deceased professed religion
and joined the Baptist Church in 1827, ... She was the mother of eight
children, five of whom are still living; ... During her long illness,
she was most tenderly nursed by her younger daughter...
The funeral took place at the late residence of the deceased on
Monday morning last, the services being conducted by the Rev. Mr.
Walker, of the Christian Church at Suffolk. At the conclusion of the ...
service the remains were deposited in the old family burying ground. ...

(A clipping; source unknown)

OBITUARY. - Died at her residence in Suffolk, Va., August 8th, 1875,
at five o'clock, A.M. Mrs. Mary (Taylor) Riddick, aged 87 years, 4 months
and 18 days.
Her father, Capt. Richard Taylor, lived on the Peninsula, at Williamsburg. He served as an officer in the Revolutionary war, in command of an
armed frigate belonging to the Virginia navy, and died before she was born.
Her mother, whose maiden name was Diana Allen, afterwards married again.
Mary Taylor, the subject of this sketch, was the only child. She was born at
Williamsburg, Va., March 20th, 1782, and came to this county in the month
of May, 1803, at the age of 15 to visit her uncle, Edward Allen. Here she
met her late husband, Mills Riddick, to whom she was married on the 27th
October of the same year, being only 15 years, 7 months and 7 days old.
She never returned to her home, and often said that she had made a long
visit.

Capt. Riddick died Sept. 13th, 1844, leaving his widow in her own right more than a competency of worldly goods, which, during her widowhood of nearly thirty-one years, she distributed largely to her children in works of benevolence.

She was an exemplary member of the Methodist Church in Suffolk for more than 50 years... She was the mother of 13 children, 10 of whom, 5 sons and five daughters, lived to be married... Six of the ten children are now living. ...

When the evacuation of Suffolk took place during the late war, she went South and spent most of her time in North Carolina as a refugee. After the war she returned to her home to be stricken in the month of October, 1865, for the first time with rheumatism. ...

Her funeral was preached at the Methodist church at ten o'clock, Monday morning, by Rev. Mr. Booker....; from thence her remains were conveyed to the old family burying-ground about four miles from town, and deposited in the place reserved for them. ...

(Richmond Examiner, Oct. 24, 1800)

Obituary

Died on the 12th instant very suddenly at his seat near Suffolk Willis Riddick, Esq. He long represented the County of Nansemond in the Virginia Assembly with honour to himself and utility to his constituents. He was unswervingly and zealously attached to republican principles and the Consitution of his Country. This was sufficiently evidenced by the undeviating tenor of his public conduct; by his votes during the memorable sessions of 1778-1779.

But as a private character Mr. Riddick was truly estimable. He was an affectionate husband and so amiable was he in the intercourse of social and domestic life that he possessed the esteem and friendship of all who knew him.

(A clipping; source unknown; year 1845)

Died in Suffolk, on the 29th January last (1845), Mrs. Susan Smith, wife of Arthur Smith, of that place.

Sister Smith was the daughter of Archibald and Christian Richardson, who were residents of Suffolk, in the memorial year of 1780. In that year (sic), while her father was absent with the American army, the British army succeeded in burning the town of Suffolk. Mr. Richardson's family fled for safety to the adjoining State of North Carolina, where his daughter Susan was born. As soon as her father could re-build his house, he returned with his family to Suffolk, where Sister Smith resided to the time of her death. She lived a stranger to the converting grace of God, seeking her happiness in the pleasures of the world, until the revival of religion, which commenced in Suffolk the latter part of the year 1822. ... On the 27th of May, 1826, she attached herself to the M. E. Church, in Suffolk, of which she continued an acceptable member to the time of her death. ... The Wednesday before her death she met with the Sewing society of Suffolk, of which she was a member, and appeared to be in usual health, but so uncertain is life, the next Wednesday her funeral was preached in the same room! ...

Sister Smith has left an affectionate husband, a son and two daughters to lament their loss. ...

A. E. S.

****

50.
Miscellaneous

(John Thompson Kilby Papers)

Retreat Farm / Abstract of Title.

(110 acres Campbell's, No. 1) was purchased by Col. Josiah Riddick by deed on 26 Sept. 1817 of Jno. Meredith & Fanny his wife...which Fanny was a daughter of David Campbell & obtained same by his will & who heired it of Jno. Campbell who patented 15 Aug. 1764.

(No. 2, 353 acres) was purchased by Col. Josiah Riddick of Leml Hoops Riddick by Deed dated 19th May 1821, called 540 acres which he heired from his father Willis Riddick (II) who got the same by will of Col. Willis Riddick (I) about 1783 who patented it on 15th Aug. 1764.

(Note. The will of Col. Willis Riddick, I, was dated April 10, 1781, and proved April 8, 1782. Willis Riddick, II, died Oct. 12, 1800.

On Aug. 15, 1764, Willis Riddick, I, patented 353 acres in Nansemond County "At a place called the White Marsh, Beg. in the great swamp adj. land o John Camble, to Wright's line, to a corner tree of the land on Ezekias Riddick, 145 acres part of a patent for 2,250 acres formerly granted to William Wright, March 18, 1662, 1208 acres never before granted." Patent Book No. 36, p. 591, VSL.)

(Inscriptions on two memorial shafts in St. Luke's (Old Brick) Church, Isle of Wight County.)

Thomas Smith / and his wife Christiana / of Suffolk. / Their children / Anne Maria, Virginia, Josiah / and Evelina Belmont Smith. / George Purdie / and his wife Evelina B. Smith / and their children / Anne Maria, Nannie Moore / and Mary Robinson Purdie.

In memory of / My Mother / Evelina Belmont / Purdie, / Daughter of / Thomas & Christiana / Riddick Smith / Born Apr. 26, 1818 / was married in this church April 26, 1836 / and died / Mar. 21, 1888.

Bibliography with Abbreviations.

Clement, Mary Dean, Henning Tembte, the Virginia Magazine of History and
Biography, Vol. 65, 88-108. Henning Tembte.

Kilby, Clinton Maury, Genealogy, Kilby, Tynes, Riddick, Smith,
Glazebrook, &c., Lynchburg, Va., 1924. Kilby.

Norfleet, Fillmore, Census of 1850, being Volume II of "Nansemond
County, Virginia," 1949, 93 pp., mimeographed.

Norfleet, Fillmore, Elisha Norfleet (1800-1869): His Family and
Documents, being volume II of "Nansemond County, Virginia."
1959, 55 pp., photo-offset, Elisha Norfleet.

Norfleet, Fillmore, Suffolk in 1843. Letters from Archibald Allen,
of "Rose Hill," Nansemond County, to William G. Driver. The
Virginia Magazine of History and Biography, Vol. 64, pp. 78-102.
Suffolk.

The Vestry Book of the Upper Parish, Nansemond County, Virginia,
1743-1793. Richmond, 1949

The Virginia Magazine of History and Biography. Va. Mag.

Manuscript Sources.

The John Richardson Kilby Papers (1755-1919, 33,262 items, Suffolk,
Va. Flowers Collection, Duke University Library.) Kilby Papers.

The Webb-Prentis Papers (1700-1908, ca. 10,000 items. Correspondence,
accounts of the Prentis family and numerous other Virginians chiefly
in the eastern section of the state. 41-36. Jan. 1953. Deposit, Mrs.
R. H. Webb. Alderman Library, the University of Virginia.) Webb-
Prentis Papers.

The Virginia State Library, Archives Division. VSL.

****

INDEX TO BIBLE RECORDS

Listed are the names of people not bearing the
surname of those to whom ownership of the Bibles
is attributed.

Edward Allen Bible.

Bernard, Rev. Allen R(odney).
(Calvert), Maria W(alke).
Crowder, Rev. Thomas.
Driver, Capt. John; John Reid.
Hope, Rev. R. B.
(Reid), Elizabeth.
Riddick, Mary; Col. Robert Moore.
(Swepson), Mary.
Tabb, Mary.

Allmand (Notes)

Archer, Caroline.
Campbell, Lucy.
Frith, Susannah.
Harrison, Ann.
O'Grady, Capt. (John); Margaret.
Parker, Copeland; Elizabeth Sinclair; Col. Josiah; Mary Ann .
Roberts, Capt. Thomas.
Tabb, P. E.
Walker, Elizabeth; Mary Thomas; Thomas.
Washington, Gen.

Walter Wood Ballard Bible.

Custis, Leah.
Duke, Aunt Katie (Goodman);David W(ashington); Virginia L(ouisa Parker).
Holland, Polly (Riddick).
Norfleet, Annie Riddick; Elisha; Sarah (Elizabeth Riddick).
Parker, Mary Louisa; Virginia; Wiley, Jr.
Smith, George; John; Mary Louisa; Otis.

Boothe Bible.

Griffin, Elizabeth; Mary; Nathaniel.
Walker, Mrs. James Vincent Knott.

Boothe (Notes)

Walker, Mrs. James Vincent Knott.

Admiral Brinkley Bible.

Boothe, Joseph.
Brothers, Daniel.
Daughtrey, Frances Fern; Catherine Susan.

Griffin, Apsley.
Harrison, Keely.
Land, Annie.
Roundtree, Mary Eliza.
Saunders, Job (Rawles); Margaret Jane.
Warren, Laura O.
Welton, Charles Reuben.

Jackson Brinkley Bible.

Barr, Sarah.
Bentley, Louise Gayle.
Byrd, C. E.
Corbin, Elizabeth Tayloe; Gawinae; Gawin Lane; Luther Carroll; Maria;
    Marion Xerxes; Philip Syng Physic.
Darden, Mary Alice.
Eppes, Francis; Hamlin; Josephine; Louisa J.
Norfleet, James Jacob; Seth.
Parker, Amanda; David; Jeanette; Martha.
Rogers, Mary Louisa; Richard Henry; Robert Frank; Sallie E.
Skinner, Christian.
Williams, May Thirza.

John Preston Brothers Bible
Norfleet, Elisha; Sarah Elizabeth (Riddick).
Parker, Allie Francis.
Riddick, Sarah Elizabeth.

Browne Bible.
Blamire, Catherine Bruce; Elvington Knott; E. T.; Edward Bruce; Edward G.;
    James Alexander; James Edward; John Elvington; John H.; John N.;
    Mary Ann E.
Bruce, Ann; Catharine; Edward; James M.; Jno.; Mary; Mary A.; William.
Dawson, Laura McGuire.
Hudnal, John.
Keeling, Rev. Jacob.
Knott, Ann; Elvington; Mary.
McGuire, James; Joseph.
Minton, Eliza; Mills, Senr.
Shepherd, Ann Mallory; Mary; Thomas.
Sumner, Col.

James Samuel Browne Bible.
Binford, Col. James.
Green, James G.; Mary F(rances).
(Hancock), Ann T. R.

204

Causey Bible.

Colvin, Mary.

Charles Henry Causey Bible.

Barton, George Lloyd.
Crump, Marguerite Whitfield.
Miller, Thos. Spindle.
Phillips, Eliza Wrenn Causey; Dr. John Edwin.

Charlton Bible.

Flynn, Mary Ann.
Harvey, James.
Holladay, Col. Joseph.
Stone, Elizabeth.
Woolford, Dr. Arthur; Ann Elizabeth.

John Cowper Cohoon Bible.

Beamon, Sallie L(ouise).
Everit, Louisa.
Flynn, Emily E.; Emily J.; Owen R(iddick).
Gamble, Francis B.
Muren, Frances W. C.
Reed, Margaret.
Smith, Rev. Aristidas.
Wilkinson, Alexander; Martha; Willis.

Benjamin Copeland Bible.

Arnold, Rev. Isaac M.
Christian, Mary Augustine; W(alter) S(cott).
Clarke, Rev. Meade.
Cunningham, Grace Beale.
Curtis, Thos. C.
Fitzgerald, Rev. Frederick.
Grigg, S. E.
Hall, Anna J(ones Copeland); Catherine Randolph; Joseph P(atton), Jr.
Hill, Sarah.
Jones, Ann; Dorcas; Sophia; Whitmel.
Lacy, Lane.
Laird, Rev. William H.
Mullen, Judge (Joseph P.).
Norfleet, Mary Abigail Fillmore; Robert Fillmore; Robert Fillmore, Jr.
Osburn, Detta Beverley; Herbert S.
Randolph, Bryan; Catherine E(lizabeth); Martha.

Scott, Rev. John G(arlick); William H(enry).
Wheelwright, Rev. W. E.

Elisha Copeland - Whitlock Bible.
(Deleted are the Copeland and Whitlock names.)

Bogart, William S.
Cotton (Cotten), Alexander; Ann; Emma; Salley; Samuel; Sellia.
Daughtrey, Albert Gray; Charles; Derren; Nancy (Copeland); Mills.
Ellyson, Orinia; Samuel.
Evans, James.
Everett, Elisha; John; Mary; Mary Ann; Seth; William.
Finney, Dr. Crawley; Evelina Maria.
Grice, Mary Eliza.
Griffin, Mary.
Hall, Fred(erick).
Harwood, George D.
Jones, Allen; Andrew; Brittain; David; John; Nansey; Sophia; Zelpha (Zehpa).
Jordan, David; Elizabeth; Florence G(rice); Mary Eliza; Richard David;
    Robert; Robert W.; Susanna; William Robert.
Pedin, James W.
Porter, Ann; Benjamin; Elizabeth; John; Joseph; Lydia; Mary; Peninah; Sarah;
    William.
Swepson, Eliza Ann.

Henry Copeland Bible.

Beavers, Mamie.
Hunter, Dr. Henry Holmes.
Jamerson, William P.
Odom, Dempsey; Elizabeth Brownley; Mary Shepard; Patty Borland;
Parker, Surry.
Riddick, Jas. R.; Mary; Mary S.; Martha L. B. (Pattie); Robb; Sarah S.;
    Thomas; Thomas B.; William A.
Smith, Ann; Arthur; Sarah.

Thomas Copeland Account Book

Everett, E.
Faulk, Betsey.
Hare, Jas.; Jesse.
Holland, Job.
Jones, Whitty.
Shepherd, Ann; John.

Samuel Cross (Notes)

Copeland, Elizabeth.
Daughtrey, Alice; Charles; Rebecca (Haynes).
Eason, Jesse.

Crump - Godwin Bible

Everite, Ann; Elizabeth; Etheldred.
Finney, Lulie.
Godwin, Allen G.; Ann Cowper; Bernadotte; Jennett M(cRae) J(ack); John;
    Joseph H.; Mary; Susanna Holladay; Susanna J(ennette) M(cRae) J(ack).
Keeling, Rev. Jacob.
Meador, Jas. C.; Susanna.
Rochelle, Ann; Clement; Elizabeth Judith.
Whitfield, Frances N.; Henry Holladay G(odwin); Margaret Ann.

Algernon Sidney Darden Bible.

Allen, Mary; Mary Swepson.
Bernard, Rev. A. R.
Murray, Rev. James.
Prentis, Mary Allen; Janet Whitehead; Mary Allen; Robert Riddick.
Webb, Robert Henning; Joseph Prentis; Annie; Blanche Farrington.

Abram Daughtrey Bible.

Brinkley, Admiral, Jr.; Hugh Griffin, Jr.
Brownley, John; Mary Ann E.
Cleaves, Lemuel.
Copeland, Elizabeth.
Cross, Hardy; James Augustus Hardy; Mary Elizabeth; Samuel; Sarah Ann;
    William Charles; William H.
Dicson, Fannie.
Haynes, Elizabeth; Erasmus D.; George Thomas; John L.; Martha Sarah;
    Mary A.; Mary Elizabeth; Rebecca; Rebecca Frances; Sarah; Patrick
    Henry.
Moodey, Elizabeth Hervey.
Simmons, Sarah.

William Eley Bible.

Day, Edith; Thos. R.
Duke, E(dith) Wortley (Eley).
Hargrove, Fannie Day.
Riddick, John; Sarah; Sarah Caroline.

Crawley Finney Bible.

Bernard, Rev. Allen R.
Cox, Rev. Robert.
Crump, Lulie F(inney).

Dance, Rev. M(atthew) M.
French, Dr. John.
Jordan, Robert; Susanna.
Kilby, John R(ichardson); Wilbur John.
McGee, Rev. W.
Percival, Rebecca.
Phillips, Drury; Eliza; Eliza W.; Mary Drury.
Whitfield, Fanny A.; Henry Holladay Godwin; Rev. J. C.; Margaret A.
Woodward, Eliza; James.

Allen G. Godwin Bible.
Keeling, Rev. Jacob.

Mills Godwin Bible.
Blount, Sarah.
Burgess, Rev. Henry John.
Holladay, Joseph.

Samuel Godwin Bible.
Jossey, Col. James.
Wallis, (Rev.) Sam'l.

Granbery (see "The Journal of Abigail Langley")

Joseph Patton Hall Bible.
Copeland, Anna Jones.
Craighill, Rev. James B.
Higg, Rev. Gilbert.
Jordan, Louis Walton, Virginia Hall.
Keeling, Rev. Jacob.
Murdaugh, Jerusha Walke; Laura Ann.

Amos Harrell Bible.
Rabey, Abram; Christian; Nancey.
Williamson, Annie.

Reubin Harrel, "A Book of Ages."
Warren, Drusilla; Elizabeth; Jesse.

Thomas and Isabel Harrell Bible.
Brinkley, Admiral; Apsley; Jacob.
Norfleet, Basheba; Elisha; Martha.
Rogers, Emily; James; James E.; James G.; Mary F.; Nancy; Philip L.;
    Richard T.; Robert U. I.; Sarah E.
Stallings, Charity; James; Peninah; Robert; Virginia.

Hatton Bible.

Daggett, Rev. D. J.
Methaner, Sarah Eliza.
Woodward, Isabella.

Holladay (Notes)

Baker, Sallie.
Copeland, John; John R.; Judith Ann; Judith Beverly Hunter; Mary
    Catherine.
Dorlon, Ann P(arker); Joseph Bridger.
Hodges, Catherine H(annah); William Dorlon.
Hunter, Benjamin Blake Baker; Catharine Hannah; E. Beverly; Edward
    Beverly; Edward Riddick; Judith Ann; Judith Beverly.
Riddick, J(ethro) B(allentine).
Sinclair, Catherine M.
Saunders, Mary.
Stith, Antoinette.

Joseph Holladay Bible.

Charlton, Elizabeth; Elizabeth E(ellener) S(tone).
Pinner, Dixon; Emily; Emily Susan.

Augustus H. Holland Bible.

Cross, Abram; Eliza; Sarah Catharine Abra.
Luke, Isaac V.; James M. C.
Winborn, Ann.

Lemuel Carr Holland Bible.

Bernard, Rev. A(llen) R(odney)
Boardman, Rev. George.
Brewer, Annie Woodley; Elfrida Alice Bruce; Elfrida C(harlotte); Jesse B(ruce);
    Sarah.
Crowder, Catherine Seymour Lewis.
Hall, Nettie.
Keeling, Rev. Jacob.
Lewis, Clifford; Catharine Seymour; Elfrida C(harlotte); George Holland;
    George W.; Lemuel; Mary Augusta.
Martin, Rev. Mr.
Pinner, Monimia.
White, Fred B.; Jesse B.; W. Harrison; W. W.
Wingfield, Rev. (John Henry).
Woodley, Catharine B(ryant); Rev. Robert D(oyne).

Howell Bible.

Freeman, Harriett; John; Joseph; Nanse; Patsey; Polly.
Rawles, Christine.

Edward Riddick Hunter Bible.

Baker, Antoinette (Stith); Benj(amin) B(lake); Sally.
Bridger, Judith.
Copeland, John R.; Judith Beverly Hunter.
Dorlon, Ann P(arker); Catharine H(annah); John.
(Hodges), Catharine H(annah) Dorlon (widow of).
Hodges, William D.
Sinclair, Catharine M.

Isaac Hunter Bible.

Burwell, Spotswood.
Capehart, A. B.
Currier, Adeline Burr.
Gordon, Benjamin; Barsha; Jacob; Mary; Tamar Copeland.
Hodges, Rev. Mr.
McCampbell, E. J. H.; Mary Elizabeth.
Parker, Leah.
Pugh, Elizabeth Ann.
Riddick, Elizabeth; Emily Maria; Mary Elizabeth; Micajah; Sophia; Willis
   F(aulk or Folk).
Smith, Orren Randolph.
Williams, John.

John Streeter Hunter Bible.

Jackson, Joab; Mary.
Nixon, Nancy Barron (Hunter).

Matthias Jones Bible.
(See Robert Moore - Riddick - Matthias Jones Bible)

Hugh Kelly Record.

Holland, Margaret.
King, Ann.

Jacob Eley Kelly Bible.

Brothers, Mamie.
Goodrich, Carroll Kelly; Ernest E.; Elizabeth Holladay Kelly.
Holladay, Lucie Edith Ballard.
Rives, Hattie B.

Solomon King Bible.

Hare, Mary.
Hiry (?), Elizabeth.
Lee, John.
Porter, Bathsheba.

"The Journal of Abigail Langley".
(Deleted are the Granbery names.)

Cowper, Elizabeth, Gilby; John; Old Aunt (Elizabeth Granbery); Robert,
  William; Wills.
Doeber, Widow (Frederick).
Gibson, James.
Hargroves, Abigail; Abigail Langley; Hillary; Margaret; Robert; William.
Harvey, Mary; Col. Thos.
Hastings, Jonas.
Jenkins, Bety.
Jones, Mr. (Nicholas)
Langley, Abigail.
Parrin, Page.
Riddick, Lemuel.
Stowe, Susanna B(utterfield).

Isaac Lee Bible.

Barnes, Nancy.
Holland, Job; Marcelon Ann; Mary.
Norfleet, John; Mary E.; R. C.
Rogers, Emily; Mamie V.; Richard H.; Richard T.
Savage, Almira; Herman.

McClenny Bible.

Bradshaw, Lucy Ann; Willis.
Clayton, Amelia; Eliza Carolina; James.
Deans, Daniel; Judith; Mary.

Mills Ross Minton Bible (Excerpts)

Campbell, Sarah Jane; William.
Jones, Eliza.

Thomas Minton Bible.

Browne, Edward; Elizabeth; Dr. Elvington Knott; Dr. Samuel.
Knott, Anne.
Shepherd, Elizabeth.

John Murdaugh Bible.

Hall, Jos. P(atton); Olive; William.
Jordan, Ann; Elizabeth; Robert.
Sumner, Ann (Jordan); Wm.

Cordall Norfleet Bible.

Blunt, Ann Gilliam; Elizabeth (Norfleet);Elizabeth N.; Eliza Norfleet; John
    Norfleet; Louisa Rebecceh; Martha Priscilla; Mary Wilkerson; Sarah
    Norfleet; William Cordall; William, Jr.; William N.; William, Sr.
Gee, James; James Henry; Lovinia N(orfleet); Mary; William Henry.
Johnston, Elizabeth (Blunt).
Jones, Sarah (Norfleet).
Ridley, Thomas.
Wilkerson, Ann G.; John; Nathaniel, Jun.; Nathaniel, Sr.

Elisha Norfleet Bible.

Beamon, Alida; Clifford V(irginius); George (Vanderslice); Ivy; John Richard;
    Mary Virginia (Vanderslice); S(arah) Katie; William S(impson); William
    Simpson, Jr.
Ballard, Annie Riddick (Norfleet);Virginia Norfleet; Walter W(ood).
Brothers, Ethel Preston; Minnie Olivia; Preston; S(arah) Katharine; Sarah
    Lucille.
Brosius, William K.
Buff, Amelia L(ouise); Dr. A(ugust).
Copeland, Elizabeth Randolph.
Fillmore, Lottie N(orfleet).
Lassiter, Elizabeth; Jason; Sallie A(nn).
Parker, Allie F(rancis); Ethel Frances.
Stephens, Carlotta Douglass.
Riddick, Elizabeth; Jethro; Sallie E(lizabeth).
Vanderslice, Mary Virginia.
West, Joshua Cottingham; Joshua Cottingham, III; Katherine Beamon; Sarah
    Elizabeth; S(arah) Katharine; Virginia Reed.
Wirkler, John E.; John E., Jr.; Richard Ballard; Sarah Elizabeth; Virginia
    B(allard).

John and Elizabeth
Riddick Norfleet Bible.

Baker, John.
Ellis, John.
Gordon, Jacob.
Lewis, Sarah.
Riddick, Abraham; Elizabeth; Pleasant.
Twine, John.
Winburn, John

Joseph Norfleet Bible.

Darden, Matilda Jane.
Ethridge, Samuel.
Lee, Margaret.
Rawls, John; Mary; Polly; Robt.
Sumner, Jethro.

Nathaniel Norfleet (I) Record.

Barksdale, Randolph.
Berman, Ann.
McNeile, Ursula.
Milner, Jacobina; Priscilla.
Read, Elizabeth.
Roan, Mary C.
Ver(r)ell, Susan (M.).
Willson, John G.

Nathaniel Norfleet (II) Bible.

Allen, Andrew J.; Ann; Edward N.; Edward T.; James W.; Stella M.
Benn, Mary Ann.
Darden, Elijah: Joanna; Margaret Ann.
Dumville, Benjamin B.; Elbridge G. B.; Sarah.
Hunter, Jackson: Julia A.; Lemuel R(iddick); Lucy J.; Clara Susan; Walter
  Scott.
Jordan, Belson; Jane.
Kirby, Julia Riddick; Lewis Kemper.
Mizzell, Jane.
Parker, Julia.
Riddick, Sophia Ann.
Smith, Mark W.
Yates, Joseph Henry.

Thomas Norfleet Bible.

Bisbee, Horace V.
Camp, Rev. C(harles) W.; Guy William Arthur, Jr.; Millard Fillmore; Vaille
  Louise.
Dawson, Anne (Rawline); Hugh; Susanna.
Duke, Lottie.
Copeland, Elizabeth Randolph.
Fillmore, Charles DeWitt; Edward Valentine; George Millard; George Thomas;
  Ina Laurelle; Lottie (Alice) Norfleet; Millard Norfleet; Susie Juliette.
Green, Julia Etta.
Griffin, Ina.
Rawline, Anne.
Robinson, Flora May; John Kunkle; John Norfleet; Margaret Jane; Myron Ainger
  Walter Bennett.
Williams, John Hugh Dawson; Susanna (Dawson); Thomas.

Wilson Norfleet Bible.

Bernard, Rev. Allen R.
McGuire, Caroline Virginia; Emily; James.
Norfleet, Rev. William J.
Peterson, Rev. E. W.
Riddick, Rev. James A(ndrew).
Waller, Dr.

David Parker Bible.

Brinkley, Jackson.
Carter, Jennett.
Costen, Mrs. Julia C.; Mrs. Lazeretta.
Doughtie, Mrs. Margaret Parker.
Freeman, Felicia.
Geoffroy, Mary Eliza; Victor.
Wright, David P(arker).

Wiley Parker Bible.

(Brinkley), Ann P(leasant).

Dixon Pinner Bible.

Applewheat, H. W.; Sally.
Bernard, Rev. Allen R.
Eley, Dr. Adolphus White; Ida Pinner.
Ellis, Margaret F. Pinner; William R.
Everitt, Emily; Martha; Thomas.
Green, Mrs. Ann T. R. (Hancock).
Holladay, Alto F(rancis); Francis D(avid); Col. Joseph; Joseph Francis;
    Martha Ann; Sarah Eliza Emily; Susan.
Jordan, John G.; Joseph G.; Sarah B.
Keeling, Rev. Jacob.
Parker, Eliza; Josiah; Josiah C(owper).
Riddick, Archibald A(llen); Ellen Eudora; Maud S(umner).
Sumner, Elizabeth.
Tynes, Carrie; Henry L(exington).
Walker, Clara P(auline).

James H. Pinner Prayer Book.

Godwin, James H(unter).
Webb, Rosa V(irginia).

Joseph Prentis Bible.

Causey, Capt. Charles Henry.
Jones, Matthias.
Keeling, Rev. Jacob.
Kilby, Capt. John T(hompson).
Riddick, Joseph Prentis; Richard H(enry), Jr.; Col. Robert M(oore); Susan Caroline; Walter Prentis.
Webb, Joseph Prentis; Dr. Robert H(enning); Margaret Susan; Mary Henning; Robert Fisher.
Whitehead, Margaret A.
Wrenn, Eliza.

Joseph Prentis Record.

Bowdoin, M(argaret).
Jones, Matthias.
Jones, Rev. W. G. H.
Keeling, Rev. Jacob.
Kemp, Bishop.
Moore, Bishop.
Riddick, Elizabeth (Riddick); Robert Moore; Susan Caroline.

Benjamin Bridger Riddick Bible.

Bridger, Priscilla.
Britt, Exum (Britton).
Eley, Howard; Richard Seth.
Pinner, Maud Sumner.
Porter, Eliza D(igges); Eliza J(erusha); Timothy.

Edward Riddick Bible.

Holland, Solomon J.
Saunders, Job Rawles.

Euphane Fiveash Riddick Bible.

Carr, Eliza Minor.
Honey, Euphan(e) T.; John William; William.
Riddick, Jason; Thomas Fiveash.
Von Steuben, Baron.

James Edward Riddick Bible.

Brothers, Ellen, Katharine (Riddick).
Butler, (Rev.) W. H.
Eley, Nancy J(ane Riddick).
Forsyth, Rev. R. W.

Funston, Rev. J. B.
Holland, Mary (Riddick).
Jones, Dempsey.
King, Edward Riddick; John Walter; John Walter, Jr.; Martha E.; W(oodville)
    A(lbinus).
Pearce, Mary Edna.
Rabey, Harriet D(eborah).
Thorpe, Mrs. Jennie H.
Wingfield, Emily S(wepson).

Jethro Riddick Bible.

Ames, James E(dwin).
Brinkley, Sallie Ophelia; Margaret F.
Butler, Rev. H. H.
Crage, Rev.
Duke, Catherine (Riddick).
Eley, Nancy J(ane Riddick).
Goodman, Barnes; James; Nancy.
Hardcastle, Rev. H. S.
King, Dora (Riddick);Edward Riddick; John G.; John Walter, Jr.; John Walter,
    Sr.; Martha A.; Martha E.
Norfleet, Elisha; Sarah E(lizabeth Riddick).
Rabey, Harriet D(eborah).
Skinner, Henry; Margaret.
Wingfield, Emily S(wepson).
Wellons, Rev. W(illiam) B(rock).

John Robert Riddick Bible.

Allen, Mrs. Julia D(rew).
Bernard, Rev. Allen R.
Freeney, Eliza.
Minnegerode, Rev. Dr.
Roberts, Margaret; William Drew.

Josiah Henry Riddick Bible.

Riddick, Lavinia (Matthews).
Wright, James; Martha Ann.

Lemuel Riddick Bible.

Baker, Mildred; Col. Will(iam).
Boone, Susan.
Borland, Harriett G(odwin).
Cunningham, Ann; David; Edward Riddick; Henning Tembte; Lemuel Riddick;
    Margaret Riddick; Samuel B(arron); William White.

Daughtrey, Laura Boswell; Mills C(opeland).
Dinkins, James.
Elliott, Sarah J(ackson <u>Powell</u>).
Harrison, Dr. James.
Hart, Anne Cunningham; James E.; John; Capt. John Drew; John W.; Lynn
    Dinkins; Lynn Hamilton; Mary S.;Myriam Cynthia; Robert H.; Sarah Jane;
    Sophia Emeline; Susan Emeline.
Jones, Frank T.
Parham, Ann Cunningham; Elizabeth; Thomas; Dr. William Lewis.
Pipkin, Martha G.
Powell, Ezekiel; Jackson; Rachel; Sarah J(ackson); ____illy.
Pugh, Esther (<u>Robins</u>); Theophilus.
Robbins (Robins), John; Katherine.
Robinson, C. G.
Smith, Anne; Anne Cunningham; Henning E(zekiel); Henning Tembte; Jennie
    Wilson; Jennie W(ilson<u>Norfleet</u>);Laura Boswell`(<u>Daughtrey</u>); Margaret Anne;
    Mary Jane; Robert Riddick; Sallie Jackson; Sophia Emmeline;Thomas;
    Washington; Washington C.; Willie Anna; Virginia Wilson.
Tembte, Capt. Henning.
White, Elizabeth.
Wright, Stephen.
Wurdeman, Frank G.

Mills and Mary (Taylor) Riddick Bible.

Ayres, Daniel.
Blount, Frances Marion.
Disosway, Diana Tabb (<u>Riddick</u>); Gabriel P(oillon).
Eason, Amelia Ann; Elizabeth; Henry.
Hatton, Cornelia (<u>Riddick</u>); Daniel H(erring).
Jordan, Martha M.
Judkins, Clara Ann.
Kilby, Missouri Ann Jones.
McGuire, Maria Taylor (<u>Riddick</u>); William Henry.
Taylor, Diana; Mary; Richard.
Webb, Mary Allen (<u>Riddick</u>); Richard D(aniel).
Withers, Nathaniel Riddick.
Wood, Rev. David; Juliana (<u>Riddick</u>); Wm. David Riddick.
Wright, Elizabeth.

Mills Edward Riddick Bible.

Bensten, Jeannette.
Bernard, Rev. Allen R.
Brittain, James.
Corbitt, Margaret.
Elliott, Arthur.

Judkins, Clara Ann; Content (Whitehead); Jarrett; Rev. Wm. E.
Owen, Rev. A. E.
Peterson, Rev. E.
Pruden, John Brooke.
Williams, Ursula.

Nathaniel Riddick Bible.

Darden, W(illiam) H(erbert).
Etheredge, Christopher Melville; Frank Hunter; Frances Marion; Laura
    Fraser; Leoline Catharine; Mary Rosa; Mary Washington.
Kilby, Ann Newton; John Thompson; Missouri Ann Jones.
Jones, Phoebe; Sarah Virginia; William H.
Taylor, Mary; Capt. Richard.
Withers, Anna Chinn; Austin Chinn; John Thornton; Jennett (Janet) Alexander;
    Missouri Kilby, Missouri Taylor; Nathaniel Riddick; Robert W(alter);
    Susan D.
Woolford, Annie P.; Arthur; Arthur G.; Missouri Kilby (Withers).

Robert Moore Riddick - Matthias Jones Bible.
(Deleted are the Jones names)

Baker, Joseph B(lake).
Carr, Samuel.
Darden, David.
Godwin, Jeremiah.
Kilby, John Thompson; Missouri Ann Jones.
Lewis, Sarah.
Prentis, Joseph.
Riddick, Eliza G.; Elizabeth; Euphane Fiveash; Mary; Mills; Nathaniel; Polly;
    Richard W.; Robert Moore; Susan Caroline; Theresa; Thomas Fiveash;
    Willis.
Swepson, Thomas.
Webb, Robert H(enning).

Solomon Riddick Bible.

Bracy, Annie Smith; Virginius S.
Copeland Margaret.
Jamerson, Willie.
Smith, Ann; Thomas.

Willis Riddick (1), Record A.

Carr, Capt. Samuel.
Faulk, Mary
Richardson, Archibald.

Willis Riddick (I), Record B.

Allen, Edward Archibald; Mary (Swepson); Robert Riddick.

Ayres, Amelia.
Baker, Mamie (Mary Claudia).
Cowper, Mrs. Virginia (Smith).
Darden, Mary Swepson (Allen)
Disosway, Diana T(abb Riddick).
Eason, Henry.
Godwin, Elizabeth.
Hatton, Cornelia (Riddick).
McGuire, Maria T(aylor Riddick).
Murray, Lucy (Frances Allen).
Phillips, Mrs. Dr. Ned.
Prentis, John B.; Peter B.; Robert Riddick; Susan (Caroline Riddick).
Purdy (Purdie), Mrs. Evelina (Belmont Smith).
Richardson, Archibald.
Simms (Syme), Anna Maria.
Smith, Mrs. Dr. Arthur; Thomas P(arker); Thomas P., Jr.
Swepson, Ann (Riddick).
Walters, Caroline.
Webb, Margaret S(usan Prentis); Mary Allen (Riddick).
Wood, Julianna (Riddick).

Rogers Bible.
Riddick, Edward (Cunningham); Emeline; Eunice (Catherine Pierce).

Thomas Swepson Shepherd Bible.
Allen, Maria F(rances); Thomas William Gilbert.
Swepson, Fanny.
Summer, Emmeline.

Simons Bible.
Ashburn, Robert Walter.
Darden, Annie J.; Leonard S.
Daughtrey, Jacob; Margaret Ann.
King, Lizzie; Margaret Emeline.
Nelms, Clarence.
Phillips, Lottie Hunt.
Pierce, Parthenia.
Powell, Paul J.; William.
Rogers, Maggie (Simons).

Benjamin Devania Smith Bible.
Bernard, Rev. A(llen) R.
Brewer, Elizabeth Frances (Smith): Jesse Bruce.

Day, Fanny R.
Norfleet, James B.

Arthur Smith - Susan Richardson Bible.

Herbert, Jane E.
Keeling, Arthur Smith; Robert; Virginia.
Kilby, Annette Maria; Arthur Turpin; John Richardson; Leroy Richardson;
    Livingston Clay; Martha J(ane)L(ouise Smith); Susan; Wallace; Walter
    Glazebrook, Wilbur John.
Morrison, Almira; Anna Maria; Amirella; Edwin Smith; Rev. James; James
    Arthur; Joseph Smith; Sarah Caroline; Susan Fletcher; William Francis.

Thomas Smith Bible.

Odom, Elizabeth.
Riddick, Mary L.

Sumner Bible.

Lawrence, Elizabeth Mary.

Webb Record.

Anderson, William Lewis.
Gardner, Mary Darden.
Gunn, Martha Caroline Miles; Miles; Tembte F(isher).
Jones, Mary Prentis.
Prentis, Joseph; Margaret Susan.
Scott, Martha C. M.; S. H.
Tembte, Henning; Mary.
Watkins, Ballard; Tembte F(isher).

Williams - Gwinn - Cherry Bible.
(Deleted are the Cherry names)

Gwinn, Eldora Gertrude; Louisa (Williams); William; William H(enry).
Hines, Jemina.
Saunders, Peggy M.
Williams, Louisa; Jemina (Hines); Moses.

Whitlock Bible.
(See Elisha Copeland - Whitlock Bible)

Swepson Whitehead Bible.

Boyd, Alexander.
Brooks, Dr. Anson.
Cornick, Capt. James.
Hoggard, Margaret; Mary; Nathaniel.
Riddick, Claudius James.
Swepson, Elizabeth.

Wingfield, Emily Swepson; Rev. J(ohn) H(enry).

Woodward Bible.
(Baker?), Jamymay.

Wright Bible.
Duke, Christian; Hardy; Margaret Ann.
Gray, Josiah; Mary; Marina D.
King, Cephas.
Owens, R. R.
Parker, Elizabeth; Ida.
Richardson, Amanda Anne.
Savage, Cornelius F.
Wellons, Rev. Wm. B(rock).

————————

COMMUNITY PRESS
Culpeper, Va.
1962

www.ingramcontent.com/pod-product-compliance
Lightning Source LLC
Chambersburg PA
CBHW070414270326
41926CB00014B/2808